Sandlapper®

Coo

Rose T. Wilkins, Editor

Illustrations and Covers by Laura Dickson

Photographs by Patrick D. Wright and Raymond Muzika

Sandlapper Society, Inc.
Lexington, South Carolina

The proceeds from the sale of this cookbook will be used by Sandlapper Society, Inc. to further its mission of promoting the positive aspects of South Carolina.

PREFACE

In 1973 Sandlapper Press, Inc. published The Sandlapper Cookbook dedicated to the loyal readers of Sandlapper magazine. Now twenty-five years later and on the anniversary of Sandlapper's thirtieth year, we bring you another cookbook dedicated to our loyal readers.

In no way is this cookbook intended to take the place of the original Sandlapper Cookbook but is intended to be an additional culinary treasure of the rich heritage of the state. We have added recipes from readers, bed and breakfast owners, chefs from restaurants around the state, and recipes reviewed from some of our finest home grown cookbooks. Also included are recipes which we have printed in the magazine through the years.

No cookbook takes place without the help of many and this one is no exception. To the Sandlapper Society staff, Associate Editor Aida Rogers and retired Executive Director, Dolly Patton, bless you. To faithful board members for their support and recipes; with a special thanks to Peggy and Jim Waller who helped me get organized and fed me a delicious lunch and Wiggie and Martin Jones who helped carry copy from typesetter to proofer and furnished the proofer. To the proofer, Betsi Jo Baker; to Amy Quait and Celia Truesdale who responded to my cries of help for the last proofing; to Wilkins family members who responded to my pleas for recipes; to Laura Dickson for her illustrations and cover; to Patrick Wright and Raymond Muzika for their photographs; to the bed and breakfast owners who responded to our call for recipes; to the restaurants who also parted with some of their signature recipes and to all our readers who submitted their favorites, thank you! We greatly appreciate our friend Jeannette Durlach's permission to use her wonderful poem, "Mañana" on page viii. Also thanks to Barbara Anderson for her poem on page 312.

And to Jan Pollack, our skilled typesetter, who went far beyond the call of duty to make sure that style was right and words spelled correctly.

My eternal thanks to my husband and partner in life, Bob Wilkins, for his encouragement and expertise in computers and design and for his ability to get this cookbook published.

Rose T. Wilkins
Lexington, SC

August 1, 1998

List of Photographs

Photographs by Patrick D. Wright

Church, Edisto Island, SC 1; Cow, Clinton, SC 49; Hagood Mill, Pickens, SC 61, Statue in park, Aiken, SC 77; Barn, Oconee County, SC 129; Table Rock, Pickens County, SC 171; Trees and railroad track, Winnsboro, SC 213; Oconee Station Cove Falls, Oconee County, SC 285.

Photographs by Raymond Muzika

Eagles Nest Golf Course 27; Dunes, North Myrtle Beach, SC 101.

Sandlapper Society, Inc.

"What is a Sandlapper?" That's the most often asked question we hear. Well, in order to give the quickest answer we usually say: "It's an affectionate nickname for someone living in South Carolina."

Sandlapper, the Magazine of South Carolina has been telling the South Carolina story since 1968 and is now published by Sandlapper Society, Inc., a nonprofit 501(c)(3) educational organization. As a quarterly magazine, we tell people what it is to be a Sandlapper and the great things our state has to offer. We cover South Carolina: our people, places, history and culture. Our goal is to promote the positive aspects of the Palmetto State through interesting articles and beautiful photographs.

How is *Sandlapper* used? Many of our patrons give *Sandlapper* as special thanks to clients or use it as a recruiting tool to attract new employees. Several patrons participate in our "*Sandlapper* Goes to School" program. They give magazines to third and eighth grade teachers in local school districts. Other supporters simply enjoy giving *Sandlapper* to favorite friends.

Sandlapper Cooks is another product of Sandlapper Society, Inc. Through it, we hope to show the wonderful recipes submitted by our readers for the enjoyment of everyone.

Sandlapper Society, Inc. is a nonprofit 501(c)(3) educational organization dedicated to promoting a positive perspective of the Palmetto State. We accomplish this through *Sandlapper, The Magazine of South Carolina* and our accompanying Internet site (http://www.sandlapper.org (established 1996) and publications like *Sandlapper Cooks*.

Sandlapper, the magazine, is written about, for and by people who love South Carolina. *Sandlapper* encompasses all good things about our state--people, places, culture and history. Since 1968, *Sandlapper* has been telling the South Carolina story through in-depth educational articles and beautiful photography, presenting the essence of our Palmetto State.

Membership in Sandlapper Society allows us to continue educating the public about South Carolina. All Sandlapper Society members receive special discounts for our products and receive a subscription to *Sandlapper* magazine, issued quarterly in March, June, September and December.

Members will receive a membership card with discounts to South Carolina attractions such as Riverbanks Zoo. Members will also receive discounts on special publications including the Sandlapper Festival & Events Calendar (planned for the year 2000), this *Sandlapper Cooks* and other Sandlapper products.

Many people enjoy giving *Sandlapper* to friends. Others participate in our "*Sandlapper* Goes to School" program, giving magazines to South Carolina history teachers. Businesses give memberships to thank clients and recruit new employees.

Valuable support and direction is provided by Sandlapper Society members and their donations. We urge you to add your support to promoting South Carolina at its finest. Join Sandlapper Society, Inc. The amounts shown below are in effect as of August 1, 1998 and are subject to change.

PLATINUM PATRONS $10,000
  Receive 240 magazines each issue for one year
  Full-page, four-color display ad for one year
  Listing on the Patrons Page
GOLD PATRONS $5,000
  Receive 80 magazines each issue for one year
  Half-page color or black and white display ad for one year
  Listing on the Patrons Page
SILVER PATRONS $3,000
  Receive 40 magazines each issue for one year
  Quarter-page black and white display ad for one year
  Listing on the Patrons Page
BRONZE PATRONS $1,000 or more
  Receive 50 magazines or more each issue for one year
  Listing on the Patrons Page
PATRONS $200 or more
  Receive 10 magazines or more each issue for one year
  Listing on the Patrons Page
INDIVIDUAL/GIFT MEMBER $20
  Receive or give 1 magazine each issue for one year

Write: P. O. Box 1108, Lexington, SC 29071 or call at (803) 359-9954.

Table of Contents

MAÑANA

I must resume my diet this week,
My avoirdupois has scaled a new peak.
This time, I vow to be far more abstemious
Than during the course of my efforts previous.

I shall eat broccoli sans hollandaise,
Tuna fish minus mayonnaise.
I'll just say no to buttered maize
And expect for my discipline no lavish praise.

I might even begin this very day,
Permitting myself no further delay,
Were it not that I feel a deep sense of duty
To finish first, the larder's booty.

The quiche lorraine, the charlotte russe,
the lobster from Maine, the mocha mousse;
The veal parmigiana; the torte siciliana.
Oh elusive nirvana! I'll start mañana.

Jeannette V. Durlach
West Columbia, SC

Appetizers and Beverages

Appetizers

Appetizer Spread

2-3	hard boiled eggs, cooled, peeled and grated
1/2	cup ham finely minced
1	cup cheddar cheese, grated
1	small sweet pickle, finely minced
1/2	cup fat free mayonnaise
1	tablespoon mustard (I use Dijon type.)
	pinch of salt and pepper

Mix all of the ingredients well and chill in refrigerator overnight. I take washed lettuce and pita bread rounds and fill them with this spread when we have a picnic. It is also great served with crackers as an appetizer. *Yield: 2 cups (4 sandwiches)*

Ursula Monika Lain
Lexington, SC

Zesty Artichoke Appetizer

1	(14-ounce) can artichoke hearts, drained and chopped
1	cup grated Parmesan cheese
1	cup mayonnaise
	dash garlic salt
	dash Worcestershire sauce
	dash hot sauce

Combine ingredients, stirring well. Spoon into a lightly greased 1-quart casserole or soufflé dish. Bate at 350° for 20 minutes. Serve with toast points, melba rounds or oval Town House crackers. Best served warm. *Yield: 3 cups.*

Dudley Williams
Columbia, SC

Bowknots

1	loaf sandwich bread, thinly sliced
1	can condensed cream of mushroom soup, undiluted
12	bacon strips (uncooked), cut in half
24	toothpicks

Trim crust off bread. Spread soup on 1 side of bread slices, being careful to cover edges. Roll each slice from one corner to opposite corner. Wrap bacon strip around middle of each roll and secure with toothpick. Place on cookie sheet and bake at 250° for 1 hour. The Bowknots will be dry, crisp and delicious. *Yield: 2 dozen.*

Southern Tailgating: Game Day Recipes and Traditions
Reviewed Autumn 1996
Sandlapper

Annie's Hot Broccoli Dip

2	(10-ounce) packages frozen, chopped broccoli, cooked and drained
1	pound Mexican Velveeta, cut in chunks
1	pound jalapeño Monterey Jack cheese, cut in chunks
1	(16-ounce) jar mushrooms
4	celery stalks, cut in bite size pieces
1	large onion, cut in bite size pieces
1	can cream of mushroom soup (If mixture is too thick, may add 1 more can soup.)

In large stock pot, sauté onion, celery and undrained mushrooms in ½ stick margarine until onions are transparent. Slowly add both cheeses on medium heat, stirring constantly. When mixture is smooth, add broccoli and soup. Serve hot in chafing dish with Escort crackers. This is a crowd pleaser with a "bite". *Yield: Serves a crowd.*

Anne Wilkins Brooks
Lexington, SC

Broccoli-Cheese Squares

3	tablespoons margarine
2	(10-ounce) packages frozen chopped broccoli
3	eggs
1	cup all-purpose flour
1	cup milk
1	teaspoon salt
1	teaspoon baking powder
1	pound mild cheddar cheese, grated (6 cups)
2	tablespoons finely chopped onion

Preheat oven to 350°. Melt margarine in 9x13-inch baking dish. Cook broccoli until partially cooked, about 5 minutes. Transfer to food processor and chop finely. Beat eggs well in large bowl. Add flour, salt, milk and baking powder. Mix thoroughly. Stir in cheese, broccoli and onion. Spoon into prepared dish, spreading evenly. Sprinkle top with seasoned salt, if desired. Bake until set (about 30-35 minutes). Let stand 5 minutes before cutting into bite-sized pieces.

Debra C. Allen
St. Matthews, SC

Cheese Dreams

8	ounces sharp cheddar cheese, grated
1	egg white
2	sticks soft oleo
1	tablespoon evaporated milk

Place all ingredients in mixer and beat until consistency of whipped cream. Take a loaf of salt-rising bread. Trim off all crusts and cut each piece into 4 pieces. Smear mixture all over top and sides of each. Brown under broiler. Serve hot. May be made ahead and frozen. Pop right into oven.

Agnes Ivey
Lexington, KY

Cream Cheese and Caviar

8	ounces cream cheese
1/4	cup sour cream
1	tablespoon grated onion
4	ounces red caviar
	melba toast (or rounds)

Soften cream cheese. Add sour cream and onion (mix well) and add caviar. Reserve one spoonful of the caviar as a garnish for the top. Chill. Serve in a bowl with melba toast.

Ann Warshaw
Walterboro, SC

Cheese Ball

2	(8-ounce) packages cream cheese
1	small onion, finely chopped
2	tablespoons Worcestershire sauce
2-3	small dill pickles, finely chopped
	dried beef or ham
	assorted crackers

Mix together and form into a ball. Cover with dried beef or ham. Serve with assorted crackers.

Janice Gurley Shoemaker
Georgetown, SC

Chicken Ball

2	cans chicken
2	(8-ounce) packages cream cheese
1	tablespoon lemon juice
1	tablespoon onion salt or 1 small onion chopped fine

Mix together. Roll in chopped pecans. Serve with crackers.

Betty Dean
Anderson, SC

Date Nut Cheese Ball

2   **(8-ounce) Neufchatel cream cheese**
8   **ounces chopped dates**
1   **teaspoon vanilla extract**
1/2 **cup chopped pecans or walnuts**

Let cream cheese get to room temperature. Mix cream cheese, dates and vanilla together. Form a ball and roll in nuts. Serve with water crackers or another bland cracker.

Donna Rone
West Columbia, SC

Crab Biscuits

1   **(10-ounce) can flaky biscuits**
1   **(6-ounce) can crab meat, drained**
1   **bell pepper, chopped**
1   **(6-ounce) can water chestnuts, chopped**
1   **cup Swiss cheese, grated mayonnaise (enough to blend)**
     salt to taste

Divide each biscuit into three thinner biscuits. Mix next 4 ingredients with mayonnaise. Spoon haystack-style on top of each biscuit. Bake at 350° until slightly brown. You may use shrimp with crab meat or just shrimp. Good to freeze.

Doris Cattail
Gates, Gaits, and Golden Plates
Camden Junior Welfare League
Reviewed Summer 1997
Sandlapper

Crab Muffins

1	pound crab meat
1	stick butter, softened
6	English muffins
	Worcestershire sauce to taste
1	jar cheese (Kraft Old English, sharp)
	seasoning salt and cayenne pepper to taste

Mix together butter and cheese. Add crab meat. Season with Worcestershire, seasoning salt and cayenne pepper. Mix well. Spread on English muffin halves. Heat 15 minutes at 350°. May be cut into finger-size appetizers or served as a light lunch with a salad and fresh fruit.

Sylvia Kirby
Rock Hill
1995 First Lady Cookbook
American Cancer Society
Reviewed Summer 1995
Sandlapper

Chaucer's Roasted Garleek

1	garlic bulb for each guest
	virgin olive oil to cover
	Greek olives
	fresh dill
4	large pieces of French bread for each garlic bulb

Cut off pointed end of garlic bulbs and place cut end up in Pyrex dish. Sprinkle 2 tablespoons of bits and sprigs of dill and 6 Greek olives for each garlic bulb in bottom of pan. Drizzle garlic with virgin oil until all is covered. Cover and bake at 425° for 45 minutes. Serve with French bread. Guests will fork the garlic pulp from the peeling and spread on bread.

Nancy Rhyne
Myrtle Beach, SC

Diane's Divine Dip

2	cups mayonnaise
4	tablespoons tarragon vinegar
1	teaspoon salt
1/2	teaspoon thyme
1/2	teaspoon curry powder
4	tablespoons chili sauce

Mix well and serve with fresh vegetables for dipping.

Diane DeVaughn Stokes
Myrtle Beach, SC

Harbor Dip

1	(14-ounce) can artichoke hearts, drained
1	(6-ounce) jar marinated artichoke hearts, drained
8	ounces fresh mushrooms, sautéed
1	(4-ounce) can black olives, drained
1/3	cup (or more) chopped jalapeños
1	cup mayonnaise
1	cup shredded fresh Parmesan cheese
1	(8-ounce) jar salsa

Combine the artichokes, mushrooms, olives and jalapeños in a food processor. Process until finely chopped. Combine the chopped vegetables, mayonnaise, Parmesan cheese and salsa in a bowl and mix well. Pour into an oven proof serving dish. Bake at 350° until heated through. Serve with corn chips. May substitute one 6-ounce can mushrooms for the fresh mushrooms. *Yield: serves 20.*

Tested by Time
Porter Gaud School Parents Guild
Charleston, SC
Reviewed Summer 1998
Sandlapper

Vidalia Onion Dip

1	cup chopped Vidalia onion or other sweet onion (like Wadmalaw)
1	cup shredded cheddar cheese
1/2	cup mayonnaise
4	drops hot pepper sauce

Combine the onion, cheese, mayonnaise and hot pepper sauce in a bowl and mix well. Spoon into a shallow 6x9-inch baking dish. Bake at 350° for 30-40 minutes or until the edges are brown. Serve hot with corn chips or crackers. *Yield: 8 servings.*

Tested by Time
Porter Gaud School Parents Guild
Charleston, SC
Reviewed Summer 1998
Sandlapper

Mushroom Delight

8	slices bacon
2	chopped onions
1	chopped bell pepper
16	ounces chopped mushrooms
1	teaspoon salt
1	teaspoon pepper
1	teaspoon minced garlic
2	tablespoons flour
8	ounces cream cheese
1	cup sour cream
2	teaspoons soy sauce
2	teaspoons Worcestershire sauce

Sauté bacon until crisp. Reserve bacon. Sauté onion, peppers, mushrooms in bacon drippings. Add all other ingredients. Serve hot or cold with crackers. A favorite with men!

Nancy Welch
Greer, SC

Juxa's Hot Cheese Dip

8	ounces extra sharp cheddar cheese, grated
1	cup mayonnaise
1	medium onion, shredded
1	tablespoon horseradish

Slightly butter an 8-inch round baking dish. Bake at 375° for 25 minutes until bubbly and brown around the edges. Serve hot with Triscuit crackers. *Yield: 6-8 servings.*

Jay Uhrig
Juxa Plantation
Union, SC

Lobster Dip Eleganté

1	(8-ounce) package cream cheese
1/4	cup mayonnaise
1	clove garlic
1	teaspoon grated onion
1	teaspoon sugar
	dash seasoned salt
1	cup lobster, flaked
3	tablespoons cooking sautérne
1	teaspoon prepared mustard

Melt cream cheese over low heat, stirring constantly. Blend in mayonnaise, garlic, onion, mustard, sugar and salt. Stir in lobster and cooking sautérne. Heat through. Makes 1 3/4 cups. Serve hot in chaffing dish with melba toast rounds. *Yield: 6 servings.*

Marguerite Garrett
Beaufort, SC

Hot Reuben Dip

8	ounces cream cheese, softened
1/2	cup sour cream
1	cup drained sauerkraut
1/2	pound pastrami or corned beef, chopped fine
2	teaspoons chopped onion
1	tablespoon ketchup
2	teaspoons brown mustard
1	cup grated Swiss cheese
	Rye or Triscuit crackers

Combine all ingredients. Bake at 350° for 30 minutes. Serve with crackers. *Yield: 12-20 servings.*

Innkeeper Kyle Segars
Missouri Inn B&B
Hartsville, SC

Black Bean Salsa Dip

2	cans Progresso black beans, drained and rinsed
1	small can yellow corn
1	jar salsa
1	red bell pepper, chopped
1	green bell pepper, chopped
1	bunch green onions, chopped
1/2	tablespoon ground cumin
1	tablespoon fresh cilanto (optional)

Drain black beans and corn in colander. Combine all ingredients in large bowl. Serve with tortilla chips. *Yield: at least 20 servings.*

Trish DuBose
Columbia, SC

11

Fiesta Salsa

1 (7-ounce) can shoe peg corn, drained
1 (15-ounce) can black beans, drained
garlic salt and cumin to taste
1 (16-ounce) jar medium salsa
1/4 cup green bell peppers, chopped

Combine the corn, black beans, salsa, green pepper and seasonings in a bowl and mix well. Chill covered until serving time. Serve with tortilla chips. *Yield: 20 servings.*

Tested by Time
Porter Gaud School Parents Guide
Charleston, SC
Reviewed Summer 1998
Sandlapper

Salsa Dip

1 (15-ounce) can pinto beans
1 (15-ounce) can whole kernel corn
1 (4-ounce) jar pimentos
1 (4 1/2 ounce) can black olives, sliced
2 (16-ounce) jars salsa, thick and chunky
1 bell pepper, chopped
1 bunch spring onions, chopped
2 bags tortilla chips

Wash and drain beans and corn. Drain pimentos and olives. Mix first 7 ingredients together in large serving dish or bowl. Chill for several hours. Serve with chips. *Yield: 40 servings.*

Catherine deLoach
Gates, Gaits, and Golden Plates
Camden Junior Welfare League
Reviewed Summer 1997
Sandlapper

Spinach Dip

1 package frozen chopped spinach, defrost and squeeze dry, but do not mash
1 whole green onion (top and bottom), chopped finely
1 cup mayonnaise
few drops lemon juice
melba rounds

Mix all together. Spoon into serving dish. Serve with melba rounds. *Yield: 6-8 servings.*

Dudley Williams
Columbia, SC

Party Snack

1	box oyster crackers
1	package (dry) Hidden Valley Ranch dressing
1/2	cup oil (more, if needed)
2	teaspoons dill weed

Stir, stir and stir!

Jan Bozard
Lexington, SC

Nacho Nachos

1	bell pepper, chopped
1	medium onion, chopped
1	cup water
1	(16-ounce) can baked beans, mashed
1	pound ground meat
1	jar chunky salsa (medium or hot, whichever is preferred)
2	cups shredded extra sharp cheese
1/2	cup jalapeño peppers, sliced thin (if desired)
1	medium bag tortilla chips

Fry ground meat with onion and bell pepper. Drain excess grease. Add water, mashed beans and salsa and heat thoroughly. Arrange chips on platter, pour mixture over chips, top with cheese and peppers.

Kathy Cagle
North Myrtle Beach, SC

Onion Hors d'oeuvres

Onion
Hellman's mayonnaise
Parmesan cheese
white bread

Cut rounds from bread about the size of a half dollar and toast lightly. Spread rounds with mayonnaise. Next place very thin slice of onion on round and cover with mayonnaise. Sprinkle with Parmesan cheese. Broil until light brown.

Evelyn Williams
Columbia, SC

13

Smoked Oyster Roll

16	ounces cream cheese, room temperature
2	tablespoons mayonnaise
2	teaspoons Worcestershire sauce
	dash of Tabasco
1	tablespoon grated onion
1/4	teaspoon garlic salt
	salt and freshly ground pepper to taste
2	cans (3 3/4 ounces each) smoked oysters
	minced fresh parsley

Place cream cheese, mayonnaise, Worcestershire sauce, Tabasco, onion and garlic salt in food processor bowl and process until smooth. Add salt and pepper to taste. Drain oysters, rinse away excess oil and pat dry. Place in shallow bowl and mash with fork. Spread cheese mixture into a rectangle on piece of plastic wrap. Spread oysters on top of cheese, leaving 1/2 inch cheese uncovered on all sides. Roll up, jelly-roll fashion, and sprinkle top of roll with minced parsley. Refrigerate 3 or 4 hours before serving. *Yield: 8-10 servings.*

Kitty Spence
Lexington, SC

Ham Loaf Paté

1	pound ground ham
1	pound ground pork
1 1/4	cup graham cracker crumbs
2	eggs
3/4	cup evaporated milk

Mix together and place in loaf pan. Cover with foil and place a brick on top. Bake 30 minutes at 400°. Pour off fat.

Sauce:

1	can tomato bits
1	cup brown sugar
1/2	cup vinegar
1/2	cup water

Put sauce on loaf and bake for additional 45 minutes at 350°. Serve with crackers. Excellent hot or cold. *Yield: 10-12 servings.*

Walnut Lane B&B
Lyman, SC

Buddy's Original Roasted Portabello Mushroom Paté

6 ounces portabello mushrooms, sliced
6 cloves garlic, peeled and crushed
4 scallions, chopped
2 tablespoons extra virgin olive oil
 pinch of kosher salt
 fresh ground pepper
1 1/2 pounds cream cheese

Toss all ingredients (except cream cheese) in shallow baking dish. Roast (uncovered) in 400° oven until mushrooms are dark and tender. Cool completely. In food processor, blend mixture into cream cheese just until mixed. Serve with bagel chips or your favorite crackers. Makes a delicious bagel spread *Yield: 6-8 servings.*

Libby Wiersema
Buddy's Bagelry
Florence, SC

Boiled Peanuts

Boiled peanuts are best when made of peanuts fresh from the ground, or what is called "green peanuts." Boiling peanuts is not the same as boiling water. Some people say there is a gift to making good boiled peanuts. Not everyone can do it. Some boiled peanuts are too mushy, others too salty, but if you are from the southeastern coast, it's a pretty good bet that you can boil peanuts.

1 bushel peanuts
1 pound salt
 water to cover

Add all ingredients to pot and heat slowly. Don't let the water come to a rolling boil. Cook until peanuts swell and yield without a fight when opened.

Nancy Rhyne
Myrtle Beach, SC

Tortilla Roll-ups

8	ounces cream cheese, softened
1	cup sour cream
1/2	envelope taco seasoning mix
1/8	teaspoon garlic powder
1	(4-ounce) can chopped green chilies
1	(4-ounce) can chopped black olives
1	cup finely shredded sharp cheddar cheese
1/2	cup chopped green onions, optional
1/4	teaspoon chili powder, or to taste
5	(10-inch) flour tortillas

Combine the cream cheese, sour cream, taco seasoning mix, garlic powder and chili powder in a bowl and mix well. Add the green chilies, olives, cheddar cheese and onions and mix well. Spread a thin layer of the mixture over each tortilla. Roll to enclose the mixture. Wrap each roll in plastic wrap. Store in the refrigerator for at least 1 hour. Cut into 1-inch slices, discarding the end pieces. Place on a lettuce lined serving plate. May substitute low-fat cream cheese and low-fat sour cream in this recipe. Yield: 40 servings.

Tested by Time
Porter Gaud Parents Guild
Charleston, SC
Reviewed Summer 1998
Sandlapper

Cocktail Sausage Balls

1	pound bulk sausage (hot)
3 1/2	cups biscuit mix
1	(10-ounce) package shredded cheese

Combine all ingredients with hands. Shape loosely into small balls and bake at 350° for 15-20 minutes. *Yield: 100 cocktail size balls.*

Linda Easlic
Greenville, SC

Cooper River Pickled Shrimp

1	medium onion, sliced
1	medium bell pepper, cut into strips
2	large carrots, julienned
2	teaspoons celery seeds
3-4	bay leaves
2	bottles zesty Italian dressing salt and pepper to taste
3	pounds shrimp, cooked, peeled and deveined

Separate the onion slices into rings. Combine the onion, bell pepper, carrots, celery seeds, bay leaves, Italian dressing, salt and pepper in a glass bowl and mix well. Stir in the shrimp. Chill covered in the refrigerator for at least 24 hours before serving. *Yield: 20 servings.*

Tested by Time
Porter Gaud School Parents Guild
Charleston, SC
Reviewed Summer 1998
Sandlapper

Shrimp Mold

8	ounces cream cheese
4	teaspoons lemon juice
1	package unflavored gelatin
2	packages Good Seasons Italian dressing mix
2	cups sour cream
1/2	cup water
1	cup shrimp

Mix water with gelatin and let stand for a few minutes. Add lemon juice and heat until gelatin dissolves. Add all other ingredients. Mix and pour into greased mold. Refrigerate and serve with crackers. *Yield: 12-14 servings.*

Nancy Welch
Greer, SC

Holiday Shrimp Mold

1	envelope unflavored gelatin
1	(10-ounce) can cream of shrimp soup
1	cup celery, chopped
4	green onions, chopped
1	tablespoon lemon juice
2	tablespoons milk
6	ounces cream cheese
1	(4 1/2-ounce) can shrimp, drained
1	cup mayonnaise
1/4	teaspoon curry powder

Soften gelatin in milk. Heat undiluted soup and cream cheese over low heat until cheese is melted. Stir in softened gelatin. Add remaining ingredients. Pour into lightly greased mold (fish-shaped, if available). Chill for several hours. Serve with crackers. *Yield: 12-14 servings.*

Becky Hipp
Lexington, SC
Reprinted from Winter 1995-96
Sandlapper

Party Sandwiches

3	(5-ounce) green olives, drained
1	cup pecans
1	small onion
2	eggs, hard boiled
	loaf of bread
	mayonnaise

Chop olives, eggs, pecans and onion. Mix with a small amount of mayonnaise. Can use regular loaf of bread or party bread. *Yield: 12 sandwiches.*

Paula F. Paul
Orangeburg, SC

Bourbon Wieners

1	cup ketchup
1	cup brown sugar
1	cup bourbon
3	pounds wieners

Mix ketchup, sugar and bourbon. Cut wieners into bite-size pieces. Simmer in sauce for several hours. Serve hot in chafing dish. Better when made about 6 hours before serving. *Yield: 30 servings.*

Evelyn Williams
Columbia, SC

Salmon Mousse

2	envelopes unflavored gelatin
1/2	cup cold water
1	cup Hellman's mayonnaise
1/3	cup lemon juice
1	(16-ounce) can salmon
	salt and pepper to taste
1	cup celery, chopped
1	bell pepper, chopped
1	teaspoon onion, chopped
2	eggs
1/2	cup heavy cream, more if desired

Combine gelatin with water and let stand 1 minute and then stir over medium heat until gelatin is dissolved. Cool mixture. Mix mayonnaise with lemon juice until smooth. Slowly blend gelatin with mayonnaise-lemon mixture. Chill until mixture begins to jell slightly. Fold in salmon which has been drained and flaked. Remove bones while flaking. Chop vegetables in food processor and add to salmon mixture. Separate eggs, folding in yolks to salmon mixture. Beat egg whites until stiff and add to salmon. Then beat the cream until whipped and fold into mixture. Pour into a 1 quart fish mold and chill overnight. Unmold for serving. *Yield: 10 servings for lunch or 40 at a cocktail party.*

Sauce:

	several bunches fresh dill
1	cup plain yogurt
1	cup mayonnaise
1	cup sour cream

Chop dill up and mix with yogurt, mayonnaise and sour cream. Chill overnight.

Serving Suggestions: At a cocktail party, use Triscuits. Decorate unmolded salmon with vegetables and flowers. The decorated salmon mousse makes a dramatic presentation.

John H. Bennett, Jr.
Charleston, SC

Beverages

Banana Slush Punch

6	cups water
3 1/2	cups sugar
2	cups orange juice
3	cups pineapple juice
3-4	bananas, mashed

Combine ingredients and freeze. Remove 2 hours before use and mix with ginger ale or 7-Up; or while still frozen, scoop into an ice cream glass, cover with ginger ale or 7-Up and eat like an ice cream float.

Cathy Anderson
Charlotte, NC

Champagne Punch

8	quarts champagne, chilled
2	(6-ounce) cans frozen orange juice, undiluted
1	(6-ounce) can frozen limeade, undiluted
2	quarts club soda, chilled
2	quarts 7-Up, chilled
1	pint apricot brandy, chilled

Blend all ingredients together. Float ice mold in punch bowl. *Yield: 100 4-ounce servings.*

Kathleen Bischoff
Darlington, SC

Coffee Punch

An early morning eye-opener and unfortunately very rich, very caloric. Oh come on, just one glass! Great for a coffee, even those who are not coffee lovers will try a glass.

1	cup hot coffee
1 1/2	cups sugar
1	gallon very strong coffee, chilled
1	quart milk
1 1/2	tablespoons vanilla
1	quart vanilla ice cream, softened
1	quart chocolate ice cream, softened
2	cups whipping cream, whipped

Dissolve sugar in hot coffee; add to chilled coffee. Chill until ready to serve. At serving time, add milk and vanilla to chilled coffee. Stir in softened ice creams; keep extra punch well chilled. Immediately before serving, fold in whipped cream. *Yield: 2+ gallons.*

Jim any Peggy Waller
The Inn at Merridun
Union, SC

Crimson Cider

1	gallon apple cider
1	quart water
8	ounces of cinnamon candies
1	cup sugar (vary to desired sweetness)
1	teaspoon cinnamon

Heat water to boiling. Then on moderate heat, add cinnamon candies. Stir until candies melt, making sure they don't stick to bottom of pan. Add cider and sugar. Stir until sugar is dissolved. Add cinnamon. Continue to heat until mixture comes to boil. Remove immediately and serve or put in thermos to serve later. Makes 20 servings.

Southern Tailgating: Game Day
Recipes and Traditions
Reviewed Autumn 1996
Sandlapper

Mulled Cider

2	quarts apple cider
1/2	cup sugar
12	sticks cinnamon (one small container)
12	whole allspice
12	whole cloves

Put all ingredients together and bring to a tumbling boil. Reduce heat and simmer for 15 minutes. Strain out spices. Place in jars or containers with loose lids and allow to stand for 12 hours. Reheat and serve hot. Whole spices must be used as ground spices leave a scum-like residue. Cinnamon sticks may be reused. If kept in the refrigerator, mulled cider will keep for several weeks. Not good cold.

Lexington County Museum
Lexington Landmark Recipes
Lexington Woman's Club
Reviewed Winter 1997/98
Sandlapper

Citrus Bloody Mary

1	cans tomato juice (1 quart 14 ounces each)
2 2/3	cups orange juice
2/3	cup lemon juice
2 1/2	teaspoons Tabasco sauce
2	tablespoons Worcestershire
2	cups vodka

Mix and chill.

Candice Kirven
Anderson, SC

Tea Techniques: 6 Options for the Perfect Cup

■ Always start with fresh, cold water. Never use hot water from the hot water tap.
■ Bring the water to a good rolling boil, but don't let it boil too long or you'll boil all the oxygen out. Just as soon as it's a rolling boil, immediately pour the water on the tea. Never put the tea in the hot water. If you do, the tea leaf doesn't open fully, and it needs that burst of hot water for it to unfurl. If you drop the tea bag in, it will float and not get a chance to fully open as the water cools.
■ Brew it long enough to get the strength you want, perhaps 3-5 minutes.

For iced tea by the glass, follow the same directions and pour over ice.

For a larger quantity of iced tea, use 7 tea bags for one gallon of tea. Bring one quart of fresh, cold water to a rolling boil and pour it over the tea bags. Squeeze and remove the tea bags. Add three quarts of fresh, cold water. Sweeten to taste and allow to cool. Pour over ice or refrigerate.

For Sun Tea, put 7 tea bags in a gallon glass container filled with fresh, cold water. Cap loosely and place in the sunshine, away from combustible material, for 3-4 hours. Squeeze and remove the tea bags. Sweeten to taste. Pour over ice or refrigerate.

If you're trying to cut down on caffeine, sample Moon Tea, which reduces caffeine by 75-80%. Put 7 tea bags in a gallon container filled with fresh, cold water. Cap loosely and let them stand at room temperature for 6 hours or overnight. Squeeze and remove the tea bags. Sweeten to taste. Pour over ice or refrigerate.

To microwave tea, put one quart of fresh, cold water in a microwave-safe container. Add 7 tea bags and heat on high for five minutes. Steep for an additional 5 minutes, or to desired strength.

Squeeze and remove the tea bags. Add 3 quarts of fresh, cold water to make one gallon. Sweeten to taste. Allow to cool. Pour over ice or refrigerate.

Charleston Tea Plantation
Mac Fleming and
William Barclay Hall
Charleston, SC
Reprinted from Autumn 1993
Sandlapper

Opening Kickoff Iced Tea

3   **quarts medium strength tea**
1   **(12-ounce) can frozen lemonade**
1/2   **cup sugar**
1   **quart ginger ale**

Mix first 3 ingredients and chill. Pour in ginger ale at last minute and serve over crushed ice. *Yield: 15-20 servings.*

Southern Tailgating: Game Day Recipes and Traditions
Reviewed Autumn 1996
Sandlapper

Merridun's Plantation Iced Tea

This is Merridun's official iced tea and was created soon after we opened. It makes a nice refreshing beverage for any occasion.

4   **family-size Lipton tea bags**
1/2   **cup packed mint leaves, crushed**
6   **ounces lemonade concentrate, thawed**
2   **cups sugar, or to taste**

Pour 1 quart hot water over tea bags and crushed mint; let steep for 4-5 minutes. Strain and pour into a gallon container containing the sugar and lemonade concentrate; stir well to dissolve sugar. Repeat steeping with another quart of hot water. Pour into container. Add 1 quart of cold water to tea bags and steep; repeat with another quart of cold water. Chill, well covered. Tea only keeps well 1-2 days; make new--tea is inexpensive. *Yield: 1 gallon.*

Jim and Peggy Waller
The Inn at Merridun
Union, SC

Roslyn Drive Mint Tea

2	cups boiling water
5	family-size decaffeinated tea bags
24	sprigs of mint
2	cups sugar
2	cups boiling water
1	cup lemon juice
12	cups cold water

Pour 2 cups boiling water over the tea bags and mint in a heatproof pitcher. Steep for 20 minutes. Combine the sugar, other 2 cups boiling water and lemon juice in a 1-gallon heatproof container, stirring until the sugar dissolves. Strain the tea and add to the sugar mixture. Add the cold water and mix well. Chill, covered, until serving time. Pour over ice in glasses. May substitute 4 family-size caffeinated tea bags for 5 decaffeinated bags. *Yield: 16 8-ounce glasses.*

Down By the Water
Junior League of Columbia, Inc.
Reviewed Spring 1998
Sandlapper

Hot Spiced Tea

1st pot:

2	cups sugar
8	cups water
2-4	large cinnamon sticks
22	whole cloves

2nd pot:

8	tea bags
8	cups water, simmer

Add ingredients together in first pot and boil 10 minutes. To first pot add 1 large can pineapple juice, 1 12-ounce can frozen juice. Strain to remove spices. Pour 2 pots together.

Mrs. T.B. Fersner, Jr.
Orangeburg, SC

Lemon Cooler

3	(6-ounce) cans lemonade concentrate, thawed
3	cups unsweetened pineapple juice
1	(2-liter) ginger ale
1	small bottle white wine

Chill liquids; mix together. Pour into glass. Add a slice of fruit or a cherry. Delightful brunch or luncheon drink. *Yield: 20 5 1/2-ounce flutes.*

Dianne H. Cohen
Orangeburg, SC

Homemade Kahlua

4	cups water
4	ounces of instant coffee granules
6	cups sugar
1	750 ml bottle of plain brandy
2	vanilla beans, split and cut into small pieces

Bring water to a boil, add coffee granules, then sugar. Cool. Add brandy and vanilla beans. Set aside in a cool place for 30 days. Open, strain and enjoy. *Yield: about 2 quarts.*

Crème de Cocoa: Substitute unsweetened cocoa for coffee granules.

Tia Maria: Substitute vodka for brandy.

Peggy Waller
The Inn at Merridun
Union, SC

Tozi's Tonic

Fresh cherries with stems
vodka
cinnamon sticks
10-12 cloves
orange peel
1-1 1/2 cups sugar
large jar (If using quart, cut
    sugar to 1 cup.)

Fill jar with cherries, cinnamon, orange peel and cloves. Fill jar with vodka, add sugar. Mix by shaking. Small gift jars can be made for holiday gifts. One a day will add bounce to your step!

Janice S. Creasy
Palmyra, VA

Breads

Breads

Angel Biscuits

5	cups flour
3	teaspoons baking powder
2	cups buttermilk
1	teaspoon soda
1	cup Crisco
1/4	cup sugar
1	package yeast, dissolved in 2 tablespoons warm water
1	teaspoon salt

Sift dry ingredients, cut in shortening. Add yeast and buttermilk. Knead. Cut in rounds. Bake 15 minutes at 400°.

Maro Rogers
Lexington, SC

Best Quick Biscuits

1	box buttermilk biscuit mix (Jiffy)
2/3	cup milk
1	cup grated cheese

Remove from oven and toss each one into:

1	stick melted, hot butter
2	teaspoons garlic
2	teaspoons parsley

Mix all. Grease cookie sheet and drop by tablespoons. Bake at 400° for 10 minutes.

Mary Shaw
The Shaw House B&B
Georgetown, SC

Cheese Biscuits

2	cups Bisquick Baking Mix
2/3	cup milk (plus 1 tablespoon)
1	cup shredded cheddar cheese
1	tablespoon sour cream pinch of baking powder
1/4	cup margarine or butter, melted
1/4	teaspoon garlic powder (or other garlic/herb seasoning)

Mix baking mix, milk, cheese, sour cream and baking powder until a soft dough forms; beat vigorously 30 seconds. Drop by spoonfuls onto ungreased cookie sheet. Heat oven to 400°. Bake 8-10 minutes or until golden brown. Mix margarine and garlic seasoning; brush over warm biscuits before removing from cookie sheet. Serve warm. Hint: Smaller biscuits are better than big ones. *Yield: 15-25, depending on size.*

Debra C. Allen
St. Matthews, SC

Garlic Biscuits

1	teaspoon garlic spread
1	tablespoon butter flavored Crisco
1	cup sifted self-rising flour
1/4	cup milk or 1/2 cup buttermilk

Mix all ingredients and knead on floured board. Separate into biscuits and bake 12 minutes at 450°. Brush with melted 1/2 teaspoon butter and garlic spread.

Kathy Miller Johnson
North Myrtle Beach, SC

Sour Cream Biscuits

2	cups Bisquick
1	stick margarine, melted
1	(8-ounce) carton sour cream

Mix Bisquick and sour cream. Add melted margarine and mix well. Bake in a miniature size muffin pan at 425° until light brown. Serve hot. Yummy! *Yield: 4 servings.*

Joan Todd
Walhalla, SC

29

Banana Bread

4	bananas
2	eggs
1/2	teaspoon vanilla
2	cups sugar
2	cups self-rising flour
1/2	teaspoon salt
1	cup chopped nuts (pecans, walnuts or English walnuts)

Mash bananas well and add other ingredients. Bake in a tube pan, bundt pan or 2 loaf pans. Bake at 350° for about 45 minutes.

Joan Todd
Walhalla, SC

JuJu's Banana Bread

1 1/2	cup sugar
1/3	cup shortening
2	eggs
3 1/4	cups plain flour
1 1/4	teaspoons baking powder
1/2	teaspoon soda
3/4	teaspoon salt
1	cup black walnuts
2-3	bananas, mashed

Cream together sugar, shortening and eggs. Mix together dry ingredients, then add to above mixture. Add mashed bananas and walnuts. Bake in greased loaf pan at 350° for 55 minutes.

Paula F. Paul
Orangeburg, SC

Cheddar and Zucchini Bread

1 medium onion, chopped finely
3 tablespoons butter or margarine
2 1/2 cups baking mix (Bisquick or Pioneer)
1 small zucchini, washed, shredded and drained
2 large or 3 small eggs
1/2 cup milk
1 cup shredded cheddar cheese
1 tablespoon each fresh basil, thyme, parsley and tarragon *or* 1/2 teaspoon each dried herbs (Can use other herbs if you like.)

Preheat oven to 400°. Grease and flour a 9-inch round pan well. Sauté onion in butter or margarine and set aside to cool. Beat eggs in milk and add herbs (if using dry). In large bowl, measure baking mix. Add zucchini, egg/milk and onion. Mix well and add cheese and herbs. Mix with hands or large spoon. Pour into pan and bake 35-40 minutes until lightly browned. This is one of my favorite breads to take on a picnic or just to serve with a hearty tomato soup.

Ursula Monika Lain
Lexington, SC

Bread Machine Real Sourdough Bread

1/2 cup active sourdough starter
3/4 cup water at room temperature
1 tablespoon honey
1 teaspoon salt
2 1/2 cups bread flour
1/2 teaspoon soda
1 tablespoon red star active dry yeast for bread machines (Other brands may be used, but do not work as well for me.)

Place ingredients in bread machine in order listed. Set to regular cycle, delayed timer also works well. Real sourdough bread made in a bread machine is both a challenge and rewarding. This recipe works fine for me every time. An important tip to remember is to measure all ingredients *precisely*. My favorite starter is Pioneer Hop Starter from Nichols Nursery, 1190 N. Pacific Hwy., Albany, Oregon 97321. *Yield: 1 loaf.*

E. Guy Shealy, Jr.
Batesburg-Leesville, SC

31

Cranberry Bread

1/2	cup cranberries
2	tablespoons melted shortening
1	egg, beaten
1/2	cup orange juice
1/3	cup lemon juice
2 1/2	cups flour (plain)
2	teaspoons baking powder
1/2	teaspoon soda
1/2	teaspoon salt
1 1/4	cups sugar
1/2	cup nuts

Blend together cranberries, shortening, egg, orange and lemon juice. Set aside. Mix together the dry ingredients then add to above. Mix in nuts. Fill one loaf pan 1/2 to 2/3 full. Bake 350° for 1 1/4 hours. Cool 20 minutes. Turn out on rack. Cool completely. Wrap and let stand overnight to improve flavor and allow easier cutting.

Paula F. Paul
Orangeburg, SC

Strawberry Bread

2	(10-ounce) packages frozen strawberries
4	eggs
1 1/4	cups oil
3	cups flour
2	cups sugar
1	teaspoon baking soda
1	teaspoon salt
3	teaspoons cinnamon
1	cup nuts, chopped

Stir thawed strawberries, eggs and oil together. Mix dry ingredients and add to the strawberry mixture. Stir until blended. Add nuts and mix well. Pour into 2 greased and floured loaf pans. Bake at 350° for 1 hour.

Sally Lightsey-Jones
Greenwood, SC

Unbelievably Delicious Coffeecake

2 1/2 cups all-purpose flour
3/4 cup sugar
1 cup brown sugar
1/8 teaspoon nutmeg
1 teaspoon cinnamon
3/4 cup vegetable oil
2/3 cup crushed pecans
1 egg
1/2 teaspoon salt
2 teaspoons soda
1 cup buttermilk (May substitute 1 tablespoon lemon juice or vinegar plus whole milk to make 1 cup. Let stand 5 minutes before adding to batter.)

Optional garnish: Cool Whip or whipped cream, cinnamon sugar, fresh fruit slices: strawberry, kiwi, peach

Preheat oven to 350°. Combine first 6 ingredients until crumbs are formed. Remove 1/3 crumbs. In a separate bowl, mix 2/3 cup crushed pecans and crumbs. Set aside for topping. Add remaining ingredients and mix well. Pour into a greased 8x11.5-inch 2-quart or 9.5x13.5-inch 3-quart glass baking dish. Sprinkle topping over batter. Bake for 30 minutes or until seems firm on top. It's fine when appears collapsed in center as long as sides have lifted slightly from baking dish. Serve warm. Just before serving, place a dollop of Cool Whip or whipped cream on each piece. Sprinkle cinnamon sugar and top with fresh fruit slice. *Yield: 2-quart serves 6; 3-quart serves 8.*

Wesley and Bonnie Park
The Breeden Inn & Carriage House
Bennettsville, SC

Wake-Up Coffee Cake

1	box yellow or white cake mix
1	cup low fat sour cream
4	eggs (or egg beaters)
1/2	cup sugar
1/2	cup oil
1	tablespoon cinnamon
1	teaspoon vanilla
1	banana, mashed
1/2	cup grated apples
1/4	cup light brown sugar
1	teaspoon cinnamon

In large bowl blend cake mix, sour cream and eggs until fluffy. Add 1/2 cup sugar and oil. Blend 3 minutes. Add cinnamon, vanilla, mashed banana and apples. Stir with wooden spoon until well mixed. Use bundt pan. Spray with Pam, then sprinkle with nuts. Pour 1/2 mixture. Add brown sugar and cinnamon. Add remaining mixture. Bake 350° for 1 hour. *Yield: 12-15 servings.*

Naomi S. Perryman
Richland Street B&B
Columbia, SC

Rich Corn Bread A La Jocelyn

1	cup corn meal
1	cup flour (all-purpose)
4	tablespoons sugar
1	teaspoon salt
2 1/2	teaspoons baking powder
1	tablespoon butter (or maybe a little more), melted
1	tablespoon bacon grease (May omit and add a little more butter.)
2	eggs, well beaten
3/4	cup half and half
1/4	cup milk (I use 2% fat. You may need a little more, depending on batter thinness.)

Preheat oven to 425°. Pour 1 tablespoon of bacon grease (or butter, if substituting) into a 9x9x2-inch pan and place in cold oven to heat up with oven. In the meantime, mix dry ingredients together in large mixing bowl. Quickly add half and half, milk, eggs and melted butter and stir to mix. Do not over beat. Check pan in oven. When smoking hot, pour in batter and bake for about 20 minutes. When top is light golden brown and springs back when touched, take out of oven. Cool and cut into squares and serve immediately with butter and molasses or honey. *Yield: 6-8 servings.*

Jocelyn Turner Ferber
Charlotte, NC

Fancy Corn Bread

1	cup self-rising corn meal
1	cup buttermilk
1	cup sour cream
1	cup cream style corn
1	egg, well beaten
1/2	cup canola oil

Mix all ingredients together. Pour into 8x8-inch pan. Bake in oven at 425° until browned (35-40 minutes). Great with a meal or as a snack! *Yield: 9-12 pieces.*

Debra C. Allen
St. Matthews, SC

Southwestern Corn Bread

1	cup yellow corn meal
2	teaspoons cream of tartar
1	teaspoon baking soda
1/2	teaspoon salt
2	egg whites or 1/4 cup egg substitutes
1/2	cup canola oil
1	(8-ounce) container low fat plain yogurt
1	(7-ounce) can corn niblets, drained
3/4	cup shredded Monterrey Jack cheese with Jalapeños

Combine corn meal, cream of tartar, baking soda and salt. Add eggs, oil and yogurt. Blend thoroughly and fold in cheese and corn. Pour into a 9-inch round cake pan that has been sprayed with Pam. Bake at 375° for 25-30 minutes. Cut into wedges to serve.

Donna Rone
West Columbia, SC

Tapp's Fountain Room Corn Sticks

6	quarts of plain corn meal
4	quarts of plain flour
1	cup of baking powder
1	cup salt
3	cups sugar
15	eggs
1	gallon milk
3	cups shortening
2	cups water

Mix ingredients well. Cook at 350° until nice and brown (about 15 minutes). Yield: 448 corn sticks.

Cheryse Tapp
Irmo, SC

To make 48 corn sticks or 24 corn muffins:

3	cups plain corn meal
2	cups all-purpose flour
2	tablespoons baking powder
2	tablespoons salt (or less)
6	tablespoons sugar
2	eggs
2	cups milk
6	tablespoons shortening
1/4	cup water

Stir all ingredients until just well blended. Spoon into greased corn stick pans or muffin cups. Bake at 350° until nice and brown (about 15 minutes) for corn sticks. Bake at 375° for muffins.

Smaller version adapted by:
Jim and Peggy Waller
The Inn at Merridun
Union, SC

Corn Mullins
(Mullins, SC)

1/2	cups cream style corn
1 1/2	cups Bisquick
1	stick butter

Mix corn and Bisquick together. Melt butter on cookie sheet with sides and drop mixture by spoonful into butter. Tilt pan and spoon butter over top. Bake at 400° for 20 minutes. *Yield: 10 cocktails; about 6 dinner.*

Betty Sutton
Greensboro, NC

Mexican Corn Bread

1 1/2 cups yellow corn meal
2   eggs
2/3   cup Wesson oil
1   cup cream corn
3   chopped jalapeño peppers
3   teaspoons baking powder
1   teaspoon salt
1   cup grated cheddar cheese
1   cup sour milk (May be made
      by adding 1 tablespoon
      vinegar to sweet milk.)

Mix all ingredients but cheese. Pour half batter into greased hot baking dish. Sprinkle half of the cheese over it. Pour in rest of batter and sprinkle with the remaining cheese. Bake in oven at 425° for 45 minutes. You can use a black frying pan which has been greased and heated. *Yield: 8 servings.*

Mary B. Marsh
Florence, SC

Hush Puppies

2   cups yellow corn meal
1   cup buttermilk
1   cup self-rising flour
4   eggs
1/2   cup sugar
1/2   teaspoon baking powder
2   teaspoons salt
      whole milk, if needed
      oil for frying

Combine all ingredients except milk and oil in large mixing bowl. Mixture should be firm but not dry. If dry, add small amount of whole milk. Heat oil in deep fryer until very hot (375°). Drop teaspoons of batter into hot oil; cook only a few at a time, turning once. Fry 3-5 minutes or until golden. Drain on paper towels. *Yield: 48 hush puppies.*

Uptown Down South
Junior League of Greenville
Reviewed Spring 1996
Sandlapper

Southern Hush Puppies

2	cups yellow corn meal
1	cup all purpose flour
3	tablespoons sugar
2	teaspoons baking powder
2	teaspoons salt
3/4	cup milk
2	large eggs, well beaten
1 1/2	teaspoons plus 1/4 cup vegetable oil
2	medium onions, finely chopped
1	green bell pepper, cored, seeded and finely chopped

Combine the corn meal, flour, sugar, baking powder and salt in a bowl and stir until thoroughly blended. Make a well in the center of the dry ingredients and add the milk, eggs and 1 1/2 teaspoons of the oil. Stir the dry ingredients into the wet ingredients until just moistened. Add the onions and green peppers and stir until just blended. Pour the remaining 1/4 cup of vegetable oil into a large skillet over medium heat. Using a tablespoon, form the batter into half-dollar-size cakes and fry, turning once, until golden brown on both sides; about 5 minutes. Drain on paper towels. *Yield: about 20 hush puppies.*

From *Sylvia's Soul Food*
Copyright 1992 by Sylvia Woods
William Morrow & Co. Used with
permission from Autumn 1997
Sandlapper

Cranberry Poppy Seed Muffins

1 3/4 cups Bisquick baking mix
(reduced fat type)
1/2 cup sugar
1/2 cup skim milk
1/4 cup plain nonfat yogurt
2 egg whites or 1/4 cup
cholesterol-free egg product
1 tablespoon poppy seeds
1 teaspoon grated lemon peel
1/2 cup cranberries (fresh or
frozen, that have been
thawed)

Heat oven to 400°. Line 12 muffin cups with paper baking cups or grease the bottoms of 12 muffin cups. Use muffin pans with medium sized cups (2 1/2x1 1/4-inch). Stir all ingredients *except cranberries* until the mixture is moist. Stir cranberries into mixture. Fill each muffin cup 3/4 full with mixture. Bake 18-20 minutes or until golden brown. Remove muffins from pan immediately. *Yield: 12 muffins.*

Glaze (optional):
1 tablespoon lemon juice
1/4 cup confectioners sugar

Mix ingredients. Drizzle onto cool muffins. I rarely have time to cool the muffins, and they do just as well warm.

Jackie Morrison
Laurel Hill Plantation B&B
McClellanville, SC

Mayonnaise Muffins

1 cup self-rising flour
2 tablespoons mayonnaise
1/2 cup milk

Combine all ingredients. Stir until smooth. Spoon batter into greased muffin pans. Fill 2/3 full. Bake at 425° for 10-12 minutes. *Yield: 1 dozen small muffins or 1/2 dozen large.*

Ann M. Huntley
Taylors, SC

Pumpkin Chip Muffins

4	eggs
2	cups sugar
1	(16-ounce) can pumpkin
1 1/2	cups vegetable oil
3	cups all-purpose flour
2	teaspoons baking powder
2	teaspoons baking soda
1	teaspoon cinnamon
1	teaspoon salt
1	(12-ounce) package butterscotch morsels

Preheat oven to 400°. In large mixing bowl, combine first 4 ingredients. Beat until smooth. In another bowl, sift together dry ingredients. Slowly add flour mixture to pumpkin mixture, stirring well. Stir in butterscotch morsels. Fill greased or paper lined muffin cups 3/4 full of batter. Bake 16-20 minutes or until center of muffin springs back when touched. Cool in pan 10 minutes; remove to wire rack. *Yield: 48 regular or 72 miniature muffins.*

Virginia Buckley
Easley, SC

Pumpkin Pancakes

2	cups biscuit mix
2	tablespoons packed brown sugar
1	teaspoon vanilla extract
2	teaspoons ground cinnamon
1 1/2	cups (12-ounce can) undiluted evaporated milk
1	teaspoon ground allspice
1/2	cup solid pack pumpkin
2	tablespoons oil
2	eggs

In large mixer bowl combine biscuit mix, sugar, cinnamon and allspice. Add milk, pumpkin, oil, eggs and vanilla. Beat until smooth. Pour 1/4 to 1/2 cup batter on heated greased griddle. Cook until bubbly, turn and cook until golden. Serve with maple syrup or with cranberry maple syrup made by heating 1/2 cup syrup and 1/2 cup cranberries in small saucepan, covered for about 5 minutes or until berries burst. *Yield: 4 servings.*

Emmagene Rhodes
Bed & Breakfast in Summerville
Summerville, SC

Rolled French Pancakes

1/2 cup all-purpose flour
1/8 teaspoon salt
1 egg, beaten
1/2 cup milk
    salad oil for frying
    jelly
    powdered sugar

Make pancakes using normal crepe techniques. Spread each pancake with jelly; roll up jellyroll fashion. Place on baking sheet and sprinkle with powdered sugar. Place under broiler just until glazed. *Yield: 4 servings.*

Dudley Williams
Columbia, SC

Easy Refrigerator Rolls

2 cups luke warm water
1/2 cup sugar
1 teaspoon salt
1 package yeast
1 egg
1/2 cup soft shortening
6 1/2-7 cups all-purpose flour

Mix together first four ingredients. Stir in egg and shortening. Add flour. Knead until smooth. Place in greased bowl. Grease top of dough and cover with damp cloth. Place in refrigerator. About 2 hours before baking, shape into rolls. Cover and let rise. Bake at 350° for 12-15 minutes.

Joan Todd
Walhalla, SC

Butterscotch Scones

4   **cups all-purpose flour**
1   **well rounded tablespoon**
       baking powder
       dash salt
2 1/2 **sticks unsalted margarine or**
       butter, softened
1   **egg**
1   **cup milk**
2   **cups butterscotch chips**

In a large bowl, mix dry ingredients. Add softened butter and incorporate well. Add egg and milk and stir to a slightly lumpy consistency. Add butterscotch chips. Place scone size globs of dough on Teflon or greased cooking sheet (they should hold form) and bake at 350° for 10-14 minutes or until golden brown touches appear on top. Serve with fresh whipped cream. *Yield: 10.*

Jay Shreve
Courtyard Coffeehouse
West Columbia, SC

Chocolate Chip Scones

2	cups self-rising flour
3	tablespoons sugar
1/2	cup vegetable shortening
1	teaspoon vanilla
1	large egg
1/2	cup milk or half and half
1/2	cup semi-sweet chocolate chips
1/4	cup walnuts or pecans (optional)

Chocolate butter: creamed butter and Nestles Quick; preserves of choice.

Chocolate butter: With fork, combine 1/2 cup creamed butter with 2 tablespoons Nestles Quick.

Preheat oven to 425°. Combine flour and sugar. Cut in shortening with pastry blender until crumbs are formed. In separate bowl, combine egg, vanilla and milk with a wire whisk. Add to dry ingredients, with chocolate chips and nuts. Mix with pastry blender until soft dough is formed. Dust hands in flour and gently knead 5 or 6 times on lightly floured surface. Dust rolling pin with flour and roll dough into an 8-inch round. Using a serrated knife, cut into 8 wedges. Wipe knife clean before each slicing. Place 1 inch apart on greased cookie sheet. Pierce tops with fork. Bake 15-20 minutes or until slightly browned. Serve warm with creamed butter, chocolate butter or preserves and jellies of choice. *Yield: 8 servings.*

Wesley and Bonnie Park
The Breeden Inn and Carriage House
Bennettsville, SC

Spoon Bread

1	cup corn meal
2	cups cold water
2	teaspoons salt
1	cup milk
2	eggs
2	tablespoons Crisco

Put small amount of oil in 2-quart baking dish. Preheat in 375° oven. In meantime, mix corn meal, water and salt. Boil 5 minutes, stirring constantly. Add milk, well beaten eggs and Crisco. Mix well. Pour into hot baking dish. Bake 50 minutes at 375°. Serve from container. Best made with stone ground corn meal.

Wiggie Jones
Columbia, SC

Almond French Toast

1/4	cup butter, melted (can be reduced if desired)
1/4	cup sugar, divided
1/2	teaspoon ground cinnamon, divided
3	eggs
1/2	cup milk
1/2	cup whipping cream
1/2	teaspoon salt
1/2	teaspoon vanilla extract
1	teaspoon almond extract
8	slices firm French bread strawberries, sliced

Combine butter, 1/8 cup sugar and 1/4 teaspoon cinnamon; spoon evenly in 15x10x1-inch pan, set aside. Combine eggs, milk, cream, flavorings and remaining 1/8 cup sugar and 1/4 cinnamon; mix well. Dip bread into egg mixture; place in single layer in pan. Pour any remaining egg mixture over bread. Bake at 400° 20 minutes, turning bread slices half through. Serve with sliced strawberries and dust with powdered sugar. *Yield: 4 servings.*

Sharon W. Bickett
Chester, SC

Apple-Cinnamon French Toast

10-12	slices day-old bread (crust removed)
1	package low-fat cream cheese (8 ounces)
1 1/2	cups grated apples
1	carton egg beaters
2	cups 2% milk
1/3	cup honey
2	teaspoons cinnamon
2	teaspoons vanilla

Cut bread into cubes. Place 1/2 (approximately 6 slices) in greased 13x9-inch baking dish. Sprinkle cinnamon, add 1/2 of the apples. Add remainder cubed bread. Place in blender the eggs, milk, cream cheese, vanilla and honey. Blend 2 minutes. Pour over cubes. Top with remainder of the grated apples. Bake at 350° 45 minutes. Serve with warm syrup, sausage and fruit. *Yield: 6-8 servings.*

Naomi S. Perryman
Richland Street Bed and Breakfast
Columbia, SC

Baked French Toast

1	**loaf French bread, cut into 1-inch slices**
1	**cup brown sugar**
1	**stick butter or margarine**
1	**tablespoon white corn syrup**
5	**eggs**
2	**cups milk**
1	**teaspoon vanilla**

Combine brown sugar, softened butter and corn syrup. Press into the bottom of a 9x13-inch baking dish. Place French bread slices on top of the brown sugar mixture. Beat eggs with milk and vanilla. Pour over bread. Cover and refrigerate overnight. Bake at 350° for 20-30 minutes until light golden brown. (If not brown enough, run briefly under broiler). This dish creates its own sauce while baking and also freezes well.

Patty Griffey
Abingdon Manor B&B
Latta, SC

Comfort French Toast

1/4   cup butter, room temperature
1/3   cup sugar
3/4   teaspoon cinnamon, ground
1/3   cup Southern Comfort, 80 proof
1   loaf French bread, 26-30" long
6   large eggs
2   cups half and half cream
1/4   teaspoon salt
2   tablespoons butter
2   tablespoons vegetable oil

Comfort Syrup:
In medium saucepan combine 1/2 cup water, 2 cups firmly packed brown sugar and 1/2 cup butter. Bring to a boil and boil 3 minutes. Remove at once from heat and stir in 1 cup Southern Comfort. Serve warm. Makes about 2 1/2 cups. (Syrup may be made ahead and reheated over low heat for a few minutes just before serving.)

Cream butter until fluffy. Beat in sugar, cinnamon and Southern Comfort. Slice bread lengthwise and spread thickly with butter mixture. Replace top. Cut into 1 1/2-inch slices. Set slices, bottom crust down on a 13x9-inch pan or casserole. Beat eggs with half and half and salt, just until frothy; pour into pan, coating top crusts. Refrigerate at least 2 hours (or overnight). Turn slices occasionally for even absorption. Heat 1 tablespoon each butter and oil in heavy skillet. Over low heat, sauté the coated bread until golden brown and cooked through. Serve warm with Comfort Syrup. *Yield: 8 servings.*

Pat Clark
Anderson's River Inn
Anderson, SC

Orange Toasts

1   loaf thin sliced white sandwich bread
1   stick butter
1   cup granulated sugar grated rind from one medium orange

In food processor, mix the butter, sugar and orange rind. Spread some over each slice of bread. Cut each slice into thirds. Bake on ungreased cookie sheet at 225° for 45-55 minutes. Store in airtight container. Great for coffee/tea accompaniment or with fruit salads.

Janet Bruning
Greenville, SC

Overnight French Toast

1	loaf French bread (15-ounce or 1-pound size)
1 1/2	cups 1% milk
3	tablespoons sugar
6	eggs
1/2	teaspoon ground nutmeg
1 1/2	teaspoons vanilla extract
1-2	teaspoons margarine
12	sausage links (optional) Choice of maple syrup, preserves, confectioners sugar.

Slice bread diagonally into 18 1-inch thick pieces. Place into 2 well-greased 13x10-inch pans. Mix milk, sugar, eggs, nutmeg and vanilla in 4 cup mixing bowl. Pour over bread slices, let stand for a few minutes, then turn slices over to fully soak them. Place in freezer for about 30 minutes until slices are firm enough to place in freezer bags. Store in the freezer until needed. Six pieces in one bag is sufficient for two servings. Preheat oven to 450°. Place frozen slices on well-greased baking sheet. Dot with margarine. Bake in oven for 8 minutes then turn over and bake for 10 minutes or until golden brown. Meanwhile, cook sausage links (2 per serving). Present 3 slices with 2 links, powdered sugar, maple syrup or preserves. *Yield: 6 servings.*

Alan Kemp
Magnolia Inn B&B
Dillon, SC

47

Eggs and Cheese

Eggs and Cheese

Apple - Egg Casserole

1	(21-ounce) can apple filling
1/2	teaspoon cinnamon
1/2	teaspoon allspice
1/2	teaspoon nutmeg
2	cups cheese
1 1/2	cups biscuit mix
1 1/2	cups milk
4	eggs
1	pound sausage

Mix together milk, biscuit mix and beaten eggs. Mix apples with spices and spread in 13x9x2-inch baking dish. Sprinkle cheese over apples. Crumble sausage over cheese. Pour batter over all and bake at 375° for 35 minutes. *Yield: 10-12 servings.*

Mary Shaw
The Shaw House B&B
Georgetown, SC

Grits Casserole

| 6 | cups water with 1/2 teaspoon salt |
| 1 1/2 | cups quick grits |

Cook on top of stove 5-7 minutes, then add:

2	sticks butter, cut into pieces
2 1/2	cups cheddar cheese, grated (Save 1/2 for top.)
4	eggs, beaten
1/2	teaspoon garlic powder
	Parsley on top (optional)

Cook basic grits as described. Add butter, 1/2 of the cheese, beaten eggs and garlic powder. Pour into casserole. Add additional cheese on top and parsley, if desired. Bake at 325°-350° for 30 to 40 minutes until light brown. *Yield: 10-12 servings.*

Anna C. Painter
Bluffton, SC

Grits Breakfast Casserole

2   pounds bulk sausage (I use 1 pound of hot and 1 pound of regular Jimmy Dean sausage.)
1   cup raw grits, cooked
2   cups sharp cheddar cheese, grated
5   eggs
1 1/2 cups milk
1/2 stick butter or margarine
     salt and pepper to taste

Brown and drain sausage. Crumble the sausage into the bottom of a 9x13-inch greased casserole. Cook grits according to package directions. (Stiff is better than runny!) Add butter and cheese to cooked grits. Beat eggs, milk, salt and pepper together. Add egg mixture to slightly cooled grits mixture. Pour combined mixture over sausage in casserole. Bake at 350° for 1 hour. I do this ahead and freeze it. To freeze, do not bake. I thaw the casserole overnight and bake it the next morning. I often use the small Corning Ware "Grab-Its" and divide everything into 8 individual servings. This recipe can be halved for smaller groups. I make this for guests who swear they hate grits. Usually, they become grits lovers! *Yield: 8-10 servings.*

Jackie Morrison
Laurel Hill Plantation B&B
McClellanville, SC

Sausage-Cheese Grits Casserole

4 cups water
1 cup grits, wheat, quick cooking, uncooked
2 cups (8 ounces) sharp cheddar cheese, shredded
1/4 cup milk
2 tablespoons butter
2 teaspoons Worcestershire sauce
1 1/2 teaspoons garlic salt
6 drops Tabasco sauce
1 large egg, beaten
1 pound bulk pork sausage, cooked and drained
2 cups (8 ounces) sharp cheddar cheese, shredded for topping

Bring water to a boil in a large saucepan. Stir in grits. Return to a boil; cover, reduce heat and cook 5 minutes, stirring occasionally. Remove from heat and add 2 cups cheddar cheese, milk, butter, Worcestershire sauce, garlic salt and Tabasco, stirring until cheese melts. Stir a small amount of grits mix into beaten egg; add to remaining grits mix, stirring constantly. Spoon half of grits mix into a lightly greased 8-inch square baking dish; top with sausage. Spoon remaining grits mix over sausage. Cover and chill 8 hours. Great to make the night before. To bake, remove from refrigerator and let stand at room temperature 30 minutes. Bake uncovered at 350° for 30 minutes. Sprinkle with last 2 cups cheese and bake additional 10 minutes. *Yield: 8 servings.*

Pat Clark
Anderson's River Inn
Anderson, SC

Veggie-Ricotta Breakfast Casserole

1/2	cup mushrooms
1/4	cup pimento
1/2	cup green pepper, chopped
1/2	cup red pepper, chopped
1/2	cup onion, chopped
1	zucchini, chopped
6	eggs or 1 carton egg beaters
1	package ricotta
1/2	cup mild cheddar cheese
	dash salt, pepper, parsley, plus your favorite herbs

Sauté peppers, onion, zucchini in two tablespoons butter 5-6 minutes. Add 3 tablespoons flour. Continue cooking 3 extra minutes. Add salt, pepper, herbs of choice. In blender add ricotta and eggs until mixed. Use 1 1/2 quart casserole. Spray with Pam. Add mushrooms, pimento, sautéed peppers, onion, zucchini. Top with blended egg mixture. Add 1/2 cup cheddar cheese. Bake at 350° 45-50 minutes. *Yield: 4-6 servings.*

Naomi S. Perryman
Richland Street B&B
Columbia, SC

Sour Cream Scramblers

6	eggs
2	tablespoons sour cream
	sprinkle of Parmesan cheese
	dash of chives

Break 6 raw eggs into flat bottom microwavable casserole dish. Whisk 2 tablespoons sour cream into eggs. Blend well. Place dish in microwave oven. Set for one minute on high. At one minute intervals, check on progress. Mix with plastic or wood spatula. When eggs reach desired doneness, remove to serving plate. Top with Parmesan cheese and chives. Serve with bacon and English muffins. Hearty and delicious! *Yield: 2 servings.*

Craig Riley
195 East Main Bed & Breakfast
Pendleton, SC

Cheese Croissant Bake

Croissants: 8 small or 5
large, split in half
5-6 large eggs
1 cup milk
2 cups finely grated cheese
(cheddar, Gruyère, Jack,
etc.)
1/4 pound thinly sliced
mozzarella
1/2 cup Parmesan cheese,
grated
1/2 pound bacon, fried crisp
and crumbled

In a buttered 9x13-inch dish layer: bottom halves of croissants, then mix together the eggs and milk; pour half over croissant bottoms. Add most of the grated cheese, bacon crumbles, sliced mozzarella cheese and top with croissant tops, remaining grated cheese, Parmesan cheese, remaining eggs and milk mixture. Bake at 350° for 35-40 minutes. *Yield: 8 servings.*

Janet Bruning
Greenville, SC

German Baked Eggs

1 dozen eggs
1 pound Monterey Jack
cheese
2 cups cottage cheese
1/4 cup flour
1 teaspoon baking powder
1 stick margarine, melted

Mix above ingredients in a large bowl. Pour into a 13x9-inch pan. Bake at 350° for 35-40 minutes until eggs are set and top is light brown. *Yield: 6 servings.*

Spears Guest House
Cheraw, SC

Brunch Casserole

2   (6 1/2-ounce) jars marinated artichokes
1   bunch (5) green spring onions
    garlic powder
4   eggs, beaten
8   ounces grated sharp cheddar cheese
1/4 cup crushed Ritz crackers (about 6 crackers)

Cut artichokes into bite size pieces and reserve oil. Chop onions and sauté in reserved oil. Sprinkle with garlic powder. Combine all ingredients and stir. Spray pan with Pam and pour into the above. Bake at 350° for 40 minutes. You may prepare 1 day ahead and refrigerate or freeze. Thaw and reheat 15 minutes in 350° oven. Not necessary to keep hot. Delicious! *Yield: 6 servings.*

Dianne H. Cohen
Orangeburg, SC

Le Croissant Deux Soleil
(named by a TwoSuns guest)

6   medium or large croissants, sliced in half laterally
1 1/2 cups shaved turkey ham (approximately)
6   thin slices Swiss cheese
1   (6 1/2-ounce) jar marinated artichoke hearts, drained and chopped
4   large eggs (or egg beaters)
3/4 cup buttermilk or whole milk
    powdered sugar and raspberry preserves/jam

Spray 13x9-inch baking pan with Crisco or Pam. Mix eggs and buttermilk thoroughly. Quickly dunk bottom half of croissant in mixture, place in pan and add turkey ham and swiss cheese. Add drained, chopped artichoke hearts (optional) and dunked top half of croissants on top. Bake at 350° for 10-15 minutes and serve dusted with powdered sugar and a healthy dollop of preserves. Can be kept in warm oven covered for 10-15 minutes prior to serving. *Yield: 6 servings.*

Carrol and Ron Kay
TwoSuns Inn Bed and Breakfast
Beaufort, SC

Eggs Pettigru

5	hard-boiled eggs
1	tablespoon butter
2	tablespoons flour
1	cup milk
	Lawry's seasoned salt and pepper to taste
1/2	cup sour cream
1	tablespoon Dijon mustard
1	cup sliced fresh mushrooms, sautéed
1	cup sharp cheddar cheese, shredded
3	English muffins, split
6	tomato slices
6	turkey ham slices
	paprika and parsley for garnish

Shell eggs and dice whites. Mash yolks until crumbly. In medium saucepan, melt butter, gradually stir in flour to make paste. Add milk and seasonings, stir until smooth. Continue cooking, stirring frequently until thickened. Add sour cream, mustard and cheese, stirring until blended. Add mushrooms and egg whites, remove from heat and cover. Toast and butter muffins. Place tomato slice on each half, then top with slice of turkey ham or other breakfast meat. Warm in microwave, top with sauce and garnish with egg yolk, paprika and parsley. *Yield: 6 servings.*

Gloria Kiriakides
Pettigru Place B&B
Greenville, SC

Shirred Eggs

4	eggs
1/4	cup half and half
	dash of salt
	dash of pepper
	shredded sharp cheese
4	(6-ounce) Ramekins or custard cups.

Break 1 egg into each of the buttered cups. Sprinkle salt and pepper; add 1 tablespoon half and half. Set cups in a 9x9x1 3/4-inch baking pan or dish. Pour hot water into pan to a depth of 1 inch. Bake at 325° for 10-15 minutes or until eggs are firm. Remove from oven, top each egg with cheese, return to over and bake 5-10 minutes longer. *Yield: 4 servings.*

Dudley Williams
Columbia, SC

56

DuPre House Eggs Florentine

3	cups milk, scalded
1/4	cup flour
3	tablespoons butter
1	tablespoon bacon fat
3	tablespoons minced green onion
1/2	teaspoon crushed white pepper
1/2	teaspoon crushed black pepper
2	whole bay leaves
	pinch of nutmeg
1 1/2	cups frozen chopped spinach
6	English muffins
24	slices cooked bacon cut to top English muffins
12	poached eggs (use fresh eggs for poaching)
2	quarts simmering water, 1 tablespoon vinegar added fresh grated Parmesan cheese
2	chopped Roma tomatoes

Presentation: Place 2 toasted English muffins on a plate, topped with 4 bacon slices halved on each muffin. Place poached egg on bacon. Top each egg muffin with 1/4 cup spinach sauce. Grate fresh Parmesan cheese over sauce, followed by chopped Roma tomatoes. Garnish dish with fresh parsley.

In 1 1/2 quart saucepan, melt the butter and bacon fat, sauté the onion until soft, but not brown. Stir in the flour and cook the roux slowly, constantly stirring until it foams and turns golden brown. Stir in the scalded milk and bay leaves and cook, stirring until mixture comes to a boil and is thick and smooth. Season with white pepper, black pepper and nutmeg. Over low heat, simmer the sauce for 30 minutes or until reduced to 2/3 of the original quantity, slightly thickened. In the last few minutes of reducing the sauce, remove the bay leaves and add the spinach. Divide English muffins and toast.

To poach eggs, bring 2 quarts water to a simmer, not quite boiling, over medium heat. Add 1 tablespoon of vinegar, swirl water. Add raw eggs and cook for 3-4 minutes. When poaching eggs, it is better not to cook more than 6 at a time. Poached eggs may be cooked ahead and refrigerated overnight. DO NOT OVERCOOK.

Note: This sauce should be whisked during the simmering. This will eliminate the need to strain before adding the spinach. Long and slow cooking helps to remove any flour taste, as well as add to the flavor of the ingredients used. Yield: 6 servings (3 cups).

Marshall Wile
DuPre House Bed and Breakfast Inn
Georgetown, SC

Baked Egg Nests

1	tablespoon margarine
3	cups frozen hash brown potatoes
3/4	cup sharp shredded cheddar cheese
	diced ham
4	eggs

Melt margarine in skillet. Stir in potatoes, cook until slightly brown, add diced ham. Remove from heat and stir in cheese. Spoon mixture in 4 ungreased ramekins; make an indentation in center of potato mixture in each ramekin. Carefully break 1 egg into each indentation. Bake at 350° 20-30 minutes or until egg is set. Sprinkle cheese over egg last 5 minutes of baking. *Yield: 4 servings.*

Jo Ann Celaine
Candlelight Inn B&B
Camden, SC

Macaroni and Cheese

3	pounds dry elbow noodles (pasta)
1	pound shredded mild cheddar cheese
1	pound shredded American cheese
1	pound margarine
1 1/2	gallons milk

In an adequate size stock pot, place 1 gallon water. Place on stove (high heat), add 2 tablespoons salt, 2 ounces vegetable oil (Wesson or other). Bring to rolling boil and slowly add and stir pasta vigorously. Place lid on pot and bring back to boil, stirring intermittently. Pour in colander and run cold water over until cold. Place pasta in full size steam table pan, on top, spread cheese evenly. Pour on milk, stir it in. Add margarine to top after cutting into small pieces. Bake at 350° for about an hour. You may want to stir occasionally. We cook uncovered and stir. *Yield: 75 servings.*

Buck Surrett
Buck's Drive-in Restaurant
Easley, SC

Hearty Quiche

3	eggs
1	pound sausage
3/4	cup milk
1/2	cup mayonnaise
1 1/2	cups shredded cheese
1/2	teaspoon salt
1/2	teaspoon pepper
1	package (8) refrigerated biscuits

Sauté sausage and drain well. Beat eggs, milk, mayonnaise, salt and pepper. In a greased 10-inch quiche dish arrange 7 flattened biscuits around the edge of dish and place remaining biscuits in bottom of dish. Spread filling in crust. Bake at 375° for 25 minutes. *Yield: 6 servings.*

Mary Shaw
The Shaw House B&B
Georgetown, SC

Tasty Quiche

	Pastry for 9-inch pie
4	slices bacon
1	medium onion, chopped
1	(3 1/2-ounce) can sliced mushrooms, drained
1	cup (4 ounces) shredded Swiss cheese
4	eggs, beaten
2	cups half and half
1/4	cup grated Parmesan cheese
1/2	teaspoon salt
1/4	teaspoon ground nutmeg

Line a 9-inch quiche dish with pastry; trim excess pastry around edges. Prick bottom and sides of pastry with a fork. Bake at 400° for 3 minutes; remove from oven and gently prick with a fork. Bake 5 minutes longer. Cook bacon in a skillet until crisp; remove bacon, reserving 1 tablespoon drippings. Crumble bacon and set aside. Sauté onion in bacon drippings until tender. Sprinkle bacon, onion, mushrooms and Swiss cheese in pastry shell. Combine next 6 ingredients, mixing well. Pour into pastry shell. Bake at 350° for 45 minutes or until filling is set.

Margaret Ebener
Leesville, SC

Soups and Stews

Soups and Stews

Tex-Mex Black Bean Soup with Tortillas

1	tablespoon corn oil
8	slices smoked bacon, finely julienned
2	onions finely chopped
2	carrots finely chopped
2	stalks celery finely chopped
2	stalks celery finely chopped
2	garlic cloves minced
1	pound dried black beans, washed and soaked overnight
8	cups chicken stock
1	red, yellow and green bell pepper, cored, seeded and finely chopped
1/3	cup sherry vinegar or red wine vinegar
3	tablespoons Grand Marnier
3	tablespoons soy sauce
2	tablespoons honey
2	tablespoons molasses
1/2	cup chili peppers
1/4	cup cilantro, chopped
1/4	cup green onions
1	teaspoon oregano
1	teaspoon thyme
1	teaspoon cumin, ground
1	teaspoon Tabasco sauce
1/4	cup lemon juice
1/4	cup lime juice

Heat the oil in stock pot. Add the bacon and cook until crisp. Add onions, carrots, celery and garlic to bacon and cook until soft. Add black beans and stock and bring to boil. Lower heat and simmer for 2 hours or until beans are tender. Remove one third of the soup from the pot and pureé. Return pureé to the pot. Add all remaining ingredients to the soup and simmer for 1 more hour. Serve and garnish with sour cream and corn tortillas that have been deep fried.

Chef Jeff Carter
Cottage Cuisine
Greenville, SC

Red Beet Soup

3	(1 bunch) red beets
2	pounds extra lean beef (for stew)
3-4	potatoes
1/2	container cream cheese
	Salt and pepper to taste

Cut off green on beets and wash well. Cook beets in saltwater until tender. Take out and slide the skin off. If skin doesn't come off easily, they are not done. Cut into pieces and pureé very fine. Brown beef and simmer until tender in the red beet water until well done. While the beef is cooking, peel potatoes and cut into very small pieces. Cook until tender, pour off water. When beef is tender, add the potatoes and the red beet pureé and add cream cheese and allow to melt. Salt and pepper to your taste. If the soup is too thick, add milk.

Barbara Darden
Lexington, SC

Best Broccoli Soup

2	cups water
4	cups fresh broccoli, chopped
1	cup chopped celery
1	cup chopped carrots
1/2	cup (or more) chopped onion
6	tablespoons butter or margarine
5	tablespoons flour
3	cups chicken broth
2	cups milk (may use skim)
2	tablespoons minced parsley
1/2	teaspoon garlic powder
2	teaspoons onion salt
1/2	teaspoon salt

In large pan, boil 2 cups water with broccoli, celery and carrots. Boil 2-3 minutes, drain and set aside. In same pan sauté onions in butter until tender. Stir in flour to form smooth paste. Gradually add broth and milk, stirring constantly. Bring to a boil, stir 1 minute. Add vegetables and remaining ingredients. Reduce heat, cover and simmer 30-40 minutes until vegetables are tender. *Yield: 6-8 servings.*

Edith P. Pope
Winnsboro, SC

Broccoli Cheese Soup

1	cream of celery soup
1	cream of potato soup
1	package chopped broccoli (frozen)
1	package Velveeta or Cheese Whiz (small)
2	cans (soup cans) milk

Prepare broccoli according to directions. Combine soups and milk in pot. Add broccoli. Stir in cheese. When thoroughly heated, serve with crackers. *Yield: 4 servings.*

Norma Hines
Greenwood, SC

Cheddar Cheese Soup

1/2	cup margarine
1/2	cup chopped celery
1/2	cup chopped green pepper
1/2	cup chopped onion
1/2	cup chopped carrot
1/2	cup chopped cauliflower
2	cups water
1	tablespoon granulated chicken bouillon or 2 cubes
1/2	cup margarine
2/3	cup all-purpose flour
4	cups milk
1/2	pound cheddar cheese

Heat 1/2 cup margarine in a 4-quart saucepan over medium heat. Add vegetables and cook until tender. Add water and chicken bouillon; heat to boiling. Cover and cook over low heat for 10 minutes. Heat remaining margarine in a 2 quart saucepan. Stir in flour. Cook until bubbly. Remove from heat. With wire whisk, gradually stir in milk until blended in. Cook until thick, but do not boil. Stir in cheese until well blended. Stir cheese mixture into vegetables and chicken stock mixture until well blended. Serve while still hot. *Yield: 8-10 servings.*

Marian P. Wakefield
Iva, SC

Chick Pea Soup

3	center cut smoked pork chops (trim fat)
4-6	medium to large potatoes, diced
1	onion, chopped
1-2	large cans of chick peas (garbanzo beans)
1	pinch saffron, chopped

Note: 1 package of saffron yields about 10 pots of soup--use only a pinch.

Boil the pork chops for 20 minutes (40 minutes if uncooked pork chops used). Add diced potatoes and chopped onion; cook another 30-40 minutes. Add chick peas (drain one can; use liquid from the other) and saffron. Salt to taste and simmer until peas are done. (Saffron should add a rich yellow color to the soup and a classic flavor.) *Yield: 4-6 large servings.*

Cathy Anderson
Charlotte, NC

Chicken Soup

2-3	pound fryer, skinned and cut into pieces
2	ribs celery, cut into 1-inch pieces
2	carrots, cut into 1/2-inch rounds
2	large onions, quartered
1/2	lemon, seeded (squeeze juice into pot, then drop lemon in during cooking.)
1	teaspoon chopped garlic
1	quart water (approximately)
	salt and pepper to taste
1 1/2	cups medium flat egg noodles
1/2	cup fresh parsley

Boil all ingredients in large pot, except noodles. Debone chicken when tender, reserving broth in pot. Return broth to range. Add noodles, boil until tender. Add deboned chicken, parsley, remove lemon, adjust salt and pepper. Can be made ahead. Takes approximately 1 hour to prepare. (Can be done in pressure pot.) *Yield: 6-8 servings.*

Lynn B. Bagnal
Walterboro, SC

Chili

1	large bell pepper
1	large onion
1	stalk of celery
3	pounds ground meat
3	tablespoons chili powder
2	cans kidney beans
3/4	large bottle ketchup
	salt and pepper
3	cups water

In a large pot, let chopped pepper, onion and celery simmer in 3 cups water until the 3 pounds of ground meat browns in frying pan (seasoned with salt and pepper). Mix browned meat with pepper mixture. Add 3 tablespoons chili powder, two cans kidney beans and 3/4 bottle ketchup. Cook slowly about 1 1/2 hours. *Yield: Approximately 5 quarts.*

Emily Best
Bethune, SC

66

George's Chili

1 1/2	pounds ground beef
2	large onions, chopped
1	large green pepper, chopped
4	cloves garlic, minced
2	(16-ounce) cans chopped tomatoes, not drained
1	(15-ounce) can kidney beans, drained
1	(15-ounce) can black beans, drained
1 1/2	pounds fresh mushrooms, chopped
1	cup mild picanté sauce
3	tablespoons chili powder
3	teaspoons cumin
3	teaspoons salt
1 1/2	teaspoons oregano

Brown beef, onions, green pepper and garlic. Add remaining ingredients. Cook for 45 minutes. Serve topped with sour cream, diced avocado, green onions or cheddar cheese. You may pass hot picanté sauce.

George Boozer
Lexington, SC

Catfish Stew

5	pounds catfish
3/4	pound streak of lean meat
6	onions, chopped
6	medium potatoes, diced
2	cans tomatoes
1	can tomato soup
1	(8-ounce) can tomato sauce
3	quarts water
3/4	stick of butter
1/2	cup ketchup
3	tablespoons Worcestershire
	Salt, pepper and Tabasco sauce

Boil catfish for 30 minutes. Drain, remove bones. Save broth. Cut up lean meat in small strips and fry in skillet. Remove lean, add onions and potatoes. Cook until done. Pour off grease, place potatoes and onions in stew pot along with catfish and remaining ingredients. Season to taste. Simmer for 2 hours or more. *Yield: 12 or more servings.*

Louis L. Truesdale, Jr.
Lexington, SC

She Crab Soup

Roux:

1/4	pound butter	Melt butter. Add flour. Make roux.
1/4	pound flour	

Add:

1   cup heavy cream
3   cups milk
2   cups fish stock or water and fish base
1/4 pound crab roe
1   pound white crabmeat (special)
1   cup chopped celery, lightly sautéed with:
1/4 cup chopped carrots
1/4 cup chopped onion
1/4 cup chopped onion
1/4 cup sherry wine
1   tablespoon Tabasco sauce
1   tablespoon Worcestershire sauce

Add milk and cream, bring to boil. Add remaining ingredients, simmer for 20 minutes. Garnish with sherried whipped cream. *Yield: Makes 12 servings.*

Chef Kish
82 Queen
Charleston, SC

Cucumber Soup

1   (10 3/4 ounce) can cream of celery soup, undiluted
1   cup milk
1   large or 2 medium cucumbers, peeled and cut into pieces
1   small green pepper, cut into pieces
1/4 cup sliced pimento-stuffed olives
1   cup commercial sour cream
1   tablespoon lemon juice
     cucumber slices

Combine soup, milk, cucumber, green pepper, olives and hot sauce in container of electric blender; process 2 minutes. Add sour cream and lemon juice; stir well. Chill at least 4 hours. Garnish with cucumber slices. *Yield: 6 servings.*

Dudley Williams
Columbia, SC

Sarah's Corn Chowder Bisque

6	slices bacon
3	large onions, chopped
6	large potatoes, peeled and diced
1 1/2	quarts water
1	(28-ounce) can tomatoes, chopped
	salt and pepper to taste
1/2	teaspoon baking soda
2	tablespoons flour
1	large can evaporated milk
1	(15-ounce) can cream-style corn

In a large stock pot, fry bacon slowly until crisp; set aside to drain. Place onions in bacon drippings to cook slowly until clear. Add potatoes and water; simmer until potatoes are soft. Add tomatoes, salt and pepper. Bring to boil, then add baking soda. Mix flour with a little water until pasty. Pour flour paste, evaporated milk and corn into pot. Simmer slowly 25-30 minutes. Crumble bacon and add to chowder, cooking a final 10 minutes. Serve as is or with grated cheese and French bread. This recipe can be doubled and frozen.

Sarah Freestone
Gates, Gaits and Golden Plates
Camden Junior Welfare League
Reviewed Summer 1997
Sandlapper

Bloody Mary Gazpacho Rimmed with Shrimp

1	clove garlic
3	pounds tomatoes, peeled, chopped
2	unpeeled cucumbers, chopped
1/2	cup finely chopped onion
1/2	cup chopped green bell pepper
4	cups tomato juice
1/2	cup olive oil or vegetable oil
3	tablespoons red wine vinegar
1/4	teaspoon cayenne
	salt/black pepper to taste
	peppered vodka
	cooked, peeled, deveined shrimp

Rub a large bowl with the garlic. Add the tomatoes, cucumbers, onion and green pepper and mix well. Stir in a mixture of the tomato juice, olive oil, wine vinegar, cayenne, salt and black pepper. Add the desired amount of vodka and mix well. Chill, covered, thoroughly. Rim edge of bowl with shrimp just before serving. *Yield: 10-12 servings.*

Down By the Water
The Junior League of Columbia, Inc.
Reviewed Spring 1998
Sandlapper

Gazpacho

2	large tomatoes, peeled
1	large cucumber, peeled and halved
1	onion, peeled and halved
1	bell pepper, seeded and quartered
24	ounces tomato juice
1	clove garlic, split
1/4	cup chives
1/4	cup olive or salad oil
1/3	cup red wine vinegar
1/8	teaspoon Tabasco
1 1/2	teaspoons salt
1/4	teaspoon pepper
1/2	cup seasoned croutons

In a blender or food processor, pureé 1 tomato, 1/2 cucumber, 1/2 onion, 1/4 bell pepper and 1/2 cup tomato juice. Pour into a large bowl and add remaining tomato juice, oil, vinegar, Tabasco, salt and pepper. Cover and chill for at least 2 hours. Meanwhile, dice remaining vegetables and chill. Before serving, add garlic and vegetables. Mix well. Sprinkle soup with chives and serve cold with croutons as an accompaniment. *Yield: serves 6-8.*

Stir Crazy!
Junior Welfare League of Florence
Reviewed Summer 1996
Sandlapper

Hearty Soup

1   large can V-8 juice
2   cups grated carrots
1   cup chopped onion
1   can cream of celery soup
1   pound ground meat, cooked
     and drained
1   package cut frozen okra
     (10-16 ounces)

Put all ingredients except okra in pot. Bring to boil and add okra. Simmer 1 1/2 hours. (Note: cooks well in a crock pot, also.)

Donna Rone
West Columbia, SC

Jim's Cream of Fresh Mushroom Soup

1   stick butter or margarine
16   ounces mushrooms, sliced
3   small onions, sliced
1/2   cup flour
     salt and white pepper
3   cups beef stock
1   quart half and half
2   ounces dry sherry or to
     taste
8   dashes Angnostura bitters

Melt butter in heavy saucepan. Add mushrooms and onions. Cook over low heat until the mixture is soft, about 10 minutes. Stir in flour and add salt and pepper. When flour has been absorbed, sauté for about 2 minutes. Gradually add stock and half and half. Simmer over low heat for 10-15 minutes. Remove from heat and add sherry and bitters. Serve in warm soup bowls.

Jim Waller
The Inn at Merridun
Union, SC

71

Potato Soup

4	tablespoons margarine
2	large onions
12	cups potatoes, chopped or sliced
6	cans chicken broth
2	pints half and half milk

Sauté onion in margarine. Add potatoes and chicken broth. Cook until potatoes are tender. Pureé in blender or food processor. Put back in pot and add milk. Heat and season to taste. Serve with oyster crackers and toppings of shredded cheese and bacon pieces. *Yield: 10-12 servings.*

Wilma F. Gwinn
Laurens, SC

Irish Potato Chowder

4	stalks celery
2	medium onions
4	tablespoons margarine
12	large potatoes, cubed
4	carrots, sliced
6	cups water
10	chicken flavored bouillon cubes
1 1/2	teaspoons seasoned salt
1	teaspoon thyme leaves
1	teaspoon rosemary, crushed
1/4	teaspoon garlic powder
1/4	teaspoon pepper
4	cups milk
2	cups shredded cheddar cheese

Sauté celery and onions in butter. Add next 9 ingredients; cover and simmer about 20 minutes or until vegetables are tender. Remove from heat and mash vegetables with a potato masher. Add milk and cheese. Cook, stirring constantly until cheese is melted. *Yield: 20-25 servings.*

Tommy Condon's
Charleston, SC

Daddy's Chicken Stew

3-4	pound fryer chicken
2	cans tomato soup
1	large or 2 small potatoes
1	large or 2 small onions
2	tablespoons Worcestershire sauce
1	(16-ounce) can whole kernel corn
	salt and pepper to taste
1	stick margarine (optional)

Boil chicken in a gallon of water until done. Remove chicken and let cool. (I always remove the chicken fat from the broth.) Add the soup, potatoes, onions, Worcestershire sauce, corn, and salt and pepper to the broth. While the vegetables are cooking remove the chicken from the bone. Put the chicken in the pot with the broth and vegetables. Let it simmer 30-60 minutes. *Yield: 8 servings.*

Bobby Wilburn
Chester, SC

Peter Rabbit Stew

1	pound ground beef, browned
3/4	pound bacon
1	cup chopped onion
2	(15-ounce) cans pork and beans
1	(15-ounce) can kidney beans, drained
1	(15-ounce) can butter beans
1	cup ketchup
1/4	cup brown sugar
1	tablespoon Liquid Smoke
3	tablespoons white vinegar
1	teaspoon salt
	dash of pepper

Brown and drain ground beef. Put into crock pot. Brown bacon and onion and drain. Add bacon, onion and remaining ingredients to crock pot. Cover and cook on low 4-9 hours. When ready to leave for game, unplug crock pot, wrap in newspaper, paper bag, etc., to keep warm. Cold weather brings out this stew. *Yield: 10 servings.*

Southern Tailgating: Game Day Recipes and Traditions
Reviewed Autumn 1996
Sandlapper

Winter Squash Soup

In a large oven-proof roasting pan place the following:

1	**large butternut squash, cut in half and seeded**
1	**large acorn squash, cut in half and seeded**

Fill each cavity with:

1	**tablespoon butter and 2 tablespoons brown sugar**
2	**large onions sliced**
4	**carrots cut in 1-inch pieces**
2	**quarts reduced chicken stock**
1	**tablespoon kosher salt or 1 1/2 teaspoons regular salt**
1	**teaspoon freshly ground pepper**
1	**tablespoon leaf thyme**

Seal pan tightly with a layer of plastic wrap and a layer of foil. Cook overnight in a 225° oven. When cooled remove the squash from the skin and pureé all the ingredients in a food processor.

Add:

1	**pint heavy cream**
1	**teaspoon mace**
2	**tablespoons hot sauce - more or less, depending on taste**

Adjust salt and pepper. *Yield: 1 gallon.*

Virginia P. Huckabee
No. 10 Downing Street
Aiken, SC

Tomato Basil Soup

4	cups whole canned tomatoes, drained and crushed (save juice to thin, if necessary)
4	cups tomato juice, or part tomato juice and part chicken stock
12-14	fresh basil leaves, washed and patted dry
1	cup heavy cream
1	stick softened butter
1/4	teaspoon cracked black pepper
	salt to taste
	Parmesan to taste (up to 1/4 cup)

Combine tomatoes and tomato juice in large saucepan over medium heat and simmer for 30 minutes. Process in batches in food processor with basil leaves until smooth. Return to saucepan and reheat over low heat. Stir in heavy cream and butter; stir until melted. Add pepper and salt to taste. Add grated Parmesan cheese and stir to melt. Garnish with basil leaves. Yield: 8 servings.

For those who don't want it too tomatoey, dilute tomato juice with broth. Can be made day ahead.

B. Jean Wood
Edgefield, SC

Vichyssoise

2	fresh green onions
1	small onion, thinly sliced
2	tablespoons butter
3	medium raw potatoes, peeled and sliced thinly
2	pints chicken broth
1/2	teaspoon salt
	pinch cayenne pepper
1 1/2	cups light cream
	minced chives

Cut green onions into fine strips; add onion and sauté lightly in butter. Stir in potatoes, broth and seasoning. Cover and simmer gently for about 45 minutes. Put through blender or fine strainer, forcing as much vegetable pulp through as possible. Cool, stir in cream and correct seasonings. Chill thoroughly and garnish individual servings with chives. *Yield: 4 servings—easily doubled.*

Dudley Williams
Columbia, SC

Salads

Salads

Black Eyed Pea Salad

1-2	cans Luck's Black Eyed Peas, rinsed
1	cup chopped onion
1	cup chopped celery
1/2	cup chopped green bell pepper
2	teaspoons red wine vinegar
1	teaspoon olive oil
1	teaspoon salt
1/2	teaspoon pepper
1/2	teaspoon garlic salt

Mix all ingredients and chill well. Serve on crisp lettuce leaf. *Yield: 4-6 servings.*

Dianne H. Cohen
Orangeburg, SC

Broccoli Salad

2	heads broccoli, cut in small florets
1	cup raisins
1	cup sunflower seeds
1/4	cup purple onion, chopped
10	strips bacon, cooked and crumbled

Sauce:

1/2	cup light mayonnaise (or regular)
3	tablespoons sugar
1	tablespoon red wine vinegar

Mix first 5 ingredients.

Refrigerate broccoli mixture and sauce separately until ready to serve. Note: Can mix everything and let marinate. *Yield: 10 servings.*

Ethel Suber
Columbia, SC

Caesar Salad

2-3   **large garlic cloves, peeled**
2   **anchovy filets**
2   **dashes salt**
   juice of half a lemon
1   **tablespoon red wine vinegar**
2   **dashes Tabasco**
2   **dashes Worcestershire sauce**
1   **tablespoon Dijon mustard**
2   **egg yolks**
1   **cup extra virgin olive oil**
1-2   **large bunches romaine lettuce**
   croutons
2   **heaping tablespoons Parmesan cheese**

With a fork, press garlic, anchovies and salt into a paste in bottom of a bowl. Add next six ingredients, one at a time, beating after each. Add olive oil slowly while beating. Cut romaine into bite-size pieces. Add lettuce, croutons and cheese to dressing mixture and toss. Serve immediately.

Quick, reduced-fat variation - Follow above recipe omitting anchovies, eggs and reduce oil to 1/2 cup. Tastes just as delicious. Great as a meal with grilled chicken strips or sautéed shrimp. *Yield: 6 servings.*

Dawn B. Gates
Camden, SC

WARNING: *There have been warnings against consuming raw or lightly cooked eggs on the grounds that the egg may be contaminated with Salmonella, a bacteria responsible for a type of food poisoning.*

Calypso Salad

2/3	cup water
1/3	cup long grain rice
1/2	teaspoon salt
1	teaspoon olive oil
1/2	cup chopped onion
1/2	cup chopped green bell pepper
1	cup chopped seeded tomato
1/4	cup chopped fresh cilantro
1	(15-ounce) can black beans, rinsed and drained
1	tablespoon red wine vinegar
1	tablespoon lime juice
2	tablespoons olive oil
1	avocado, sliced

Bring water to boil in a saucepan. Stir in rice, salt and 1 teaspoon olive oil; reduce heat to low. Cook covered for 20 minutes or until rice is tender and water is absorbed. Rinse rice with cold water; drain. Combine rice, onion, green pepper, tomato, cilantro and black beans in a bowl; mix well. Stir in a mixture of the red wine vinegar, lime juice and 2 tablespoons olive oil. Chill, covered, for several hours. Top with avocado slices. *Yield: 6 servings.*

Kitty Spence
Lexington, SC

Chicken and Rice Salad

2	cups cooked chicken, diced
1	(6-ounce) package Uncle Ben's long grain and wild rice
1/4	cup chopped bell pepper
2	tablespoons chopped pimento
2	tablespoons Russian dressing
1	tablespoon lemon juice
	salt and pepper to taste
1	cup mayonnaise

Cook rice, cool. Add pepper and pimento. Mix mayonnaise, dressing and lemon juice. Chill. *Yield: 4 servings.*

Ella Calvert Bouknight
Lexington, SC

Beasley Chicken Salad

8	chicken breasts, cooked
4	eggs, hard boiled, chopped
1	cup sweet pickles, chopped
1	cup pecans, finely chopped
1	cup celery, finely chopped
1	cup mayonnaise
1/4	cup Durkee Sandwich Spread
	salt and pepper to taste
2	tablespoons pickle juice
3/4	pound butter, melted
6	tablespoons cider vinegar
4	tablespoons sugar
3	whole eggs

Cut the cooked chicken breasts into bite size pieces. Add chopped hard boiled eggs, sweet pickles, pecans and celery, toss lightly. Add mayonnaise, Durkee Sandwich Spread and season with salt and pepper. Add pickle juice and toss again. Place melted butter in a small heavy saucepan and whisk in the cider and sugar, stirring constantly until the mixture comes to a boil. Remove pan from the stove and whisk in the whole eggs one at a time, stirring constantly to blend thoroughly. Return to the stove top on a medium setting and cook until mixture thickens slightly. DO NOT BOIL. Add cooked dressing to the chicken salad and toss one last time. Refrigerate until ready to serve. *Yield: 12 portions.*

Governor and Mrs. David Beasley
Governor's Mansion
Columbia, SC

Chicken Salad

1	package boneless, skinless, chicken breasts (4-5)
1/2	cup celery, diced
1/2	cup red onion, diced
1/2	cup red or green apple, diced
1/2	cup pecans, chopped
3/4	cup mayonnaise, light or reduced fat may be used
	salt and pepper to taste

Boil chicken in salt water until done. Cube chicken and mix with other ingredients. Chill. Serve over greens, on crackers, or as sandwiches. *Yield: 6 servings.*

Dawn B. Gates
Camden, SC

81

Chicken Salad

several chicken breasts, boiled
sweet pickle relish
celery salt to taste
Miracle Whip salad dressing

Grind cooked chicken in a food processor. This works better if the chicken is slightly warm. Add pickle and celery salt to taste. Mix with Miracle Whip (I add enough Miracle Whip to make the salad very moist.)

Ella Sharpe
West Columbia, SC

Chicken - BLT Salad with Horseradish - Mayonnaise Dressing

1/2 cup mayonnaise
2 tablespoons prepared white horseradish
2 1/2 cups shredded, cooked chicken
2 cups coarsely chopped watercress
1 cup cherry tomato halves
6 loosely packed cups shredded (any kind) lettuce
4 slices crisp cooked bacon, drained and crumbled

Stir mayonnaise and horseradish in a large bowl until well blended. Add chicken, watercress and tomatoes. Toss gently to mix and coat. Put lettuce on serving plate. Mound chicken mixture on top and sprinkle with bacon. *Yield: 4 servings.*

Carol Coleman Yates
Seneca, SC

Judy's Chicken Salad

3/4 cup mayonnaise
2 teaspoons lime juice
2 cups cubed, cooked chicken
1 medium apple, diced
3/4 cup crasins
1/2 cup celery
1/4 cup pecans
2 tablespoons green onions

Mix all ingredients and chill. *Yield: 5 cups (4 servings).*

Janice S. Creasy
Palmyra, VA

Curried Chicken Salad

4	cups cooked chicken (cut up)
1	cup water chestnuts, sliced
1	pound green seedless grapes
1	cup chopped celery
1/4	cup sliced, toasted almonds
1	cup mayonnaise
1/2	teaspoon curry (optional)
1	teaspoon soy sauce
	juice of 1 lemon
1	large chopped apple

Combine and chill several hours. Put in large glass dish. *Yield: 12 generous portions.*

Mrs. Kelly Paul Joyner
Florence, SC

Mama's Chicken Salad

2	whole chickens
	salt, pepper and parsley
2	red apples
6	tender pieces of celery
2	tablespoons pickle relish
2	tablespoons mayonnaise
2	tablespoons salad dressing
	lemon juice
1	teaspoon sugar
	MSG (optional)

Cook chicken in Dutch oven with 2-3 cups water and salt, pepper and parsley until tender. Cool and remove chicken from the bone. Reserve stock for future use. Cut chicken into bite-size pieces. Cut apple, including peel, into small pieces; dip into lemon juice and sprinkle with sugar. Dice celery. Mix chicken, apple and celery with pickle relish, mayonnaise and salad dressing. Season with MSG, salt and pepper to taste. If needed, add equal parts mayonnaise and salad dressing to reach desired consistency. Chill for 2-3 hours before serving on a bed of lettuce with tomato wedges, boiled eggs and assorted crackers. *Yield: 4-5 servings.*

Lynn Nickles
Columbia, SC

Paul Newman's Chicken Salad

2   **cups diced, cooked chicken or turkey**
1   **(7-8-ounce) box thin spaghetti, cooked**
1   **bottle of Paul Newman's Italian Dressing**
      cherry tomatoes
1   **head of broccoli, steamed**
1   **cup chopped pecans**

Cook spaghetti. While still hot, pour dressing over the top. Toss with steamed broccoli, chicken and tomatoes. Chill. Just before serving, sprinkle with pecans. Toss in a plastic bag and carry to tailgate! Wonderful! *Yield: 6 servings.*

Nancy Welch
Greer, SC

Mike Calder's Cole Slaw

1	quart mayonnaise
1	cup mustard
3	tablespoons garlic powder
2	teaspoons Accent
3	teaspoons pepper
6	cabbages
3	bell peppers
6	carrots
1	onion

Wash all vegetables. Quarter cabbages; seed bell peppers; shred cabbage, peppers, carrots and onion. Mix these ingredients. Add mayonnaise, mustard, garlic, Accent and pepper. Mix well by hand. Ready to serve! *Yield: 25-30 servings.*

Mike Calder Bolchoz
Mike Calder's Pub
Charleston, SC

Cole Slaw and Dressing

1	cup mayonnaise (can substitute low fat)
2	tablespoons milk (can substitute low fat)
2	tablespoons vinegar
1	teaspoon sugar
3/4	teaspoon salt
1/4	teaspoon paprika
1/4	teaspoon pepper (black or white)
1	medium cabbage
2	medium carrots

Grate 1 medium head of cabbage and 2 medium carrots. Set aside. Mix dressing thoroughly with a whisk. Pour over cabbage and carrots, toss until completely coated with dressing. Refrigerate until ready to serve. *Yield: 12 servings.*

Janice Gurley Shoemaker
Georgetown, SC

Peanut Slaw

1 **cabbage, shredded**
  peanuts, crushed

My mother made cole slaw using only mayonnaise, salt and pepper. Special occasions called for Peanut Slaw. Using regular peanuts (not the ones with the red outer covering), she would use as many as she wanted (no measuring), placing them between two layers of waxed paper then crushing them with a rolling pin until they were small pieces. Add to cole slaw. Today we use a food processor or blender, making sure not to process too long or you may have peanut butter.

Janice Gurley Shoemaker
Georgetown, SC

Southern Slaw (Sweet/Sour and Marinated)

1 1/2 **cups sugar**
3/4 **cup vinegar**
1/4 **cup water**
1 **tablespoon salt**
1 **teaspoon mustard seed**
1/2 **teaspoon celery seed**

Heat together to dissolve sugar, but do not allow to boil. Pour this mixture over:

1 **large cabbage, finely**
  shredded
1 **large green pepper, cut up**
1 **small onion, minced**
1 **medium bottle pimento**
  pieces

When well mixed, place in a covered dish in refrigerator. It will keep for at least a week under refrigeration. *Yield: 6-8 servings.*

Sandra Taylor
Columbus, NC

24 Hour Slaw

Arrange in a large bowl as follows:
(DO NOT STIR)

2/3	quart chopped cabbage
2	large carrots, grated
1	chopped green pepper
1	medium onion, chopped

sprinkle 1 teaspoon salt over top

Bring to a boil 1/2 cup sugar; 1/2 cup Wesson oil; 1/2 cup vinegar. Pour over ingredients. DO NOT STIR. Seal with plastic wrap and do not open for 24 hours. Good as long as you have any. If you want to make more; just add more of everything. *Yield: 4-6 servings.*

Lucille Cudd
Chester, SC

Corn Salad

2	cans shoe peg corn, drained
1/2	cup chopped green onions
2	ripe tomatoes, diced
	Jalapeño peppers, chopped (to taste)
1	teaspoon lemon pepper seasoning
4	tablespoons mayonnaise

Mix all ingredients and refrigerate overnight. Good served with Triscuit crackers.

Southern Tailgating
Reviewed Autumn 1996
Sandlapper

Fresh Corn Salad

8   ears corn, shucked
1/2   cup olive oil
1/4   cup cider vinegar
1   small bell pepper, cut into
      strips
1/2   cup green onion, chopped
2   large tomatoes, peeled,
      seeded and chopped
      salt and freshly ground
      pepper to taste
2   tablespoons fresh basil,
      minced
1   tablespoon fresh lemon
      juice
2   teaspoons Dijon mustard
1/4   cup parsley, minced
      lettuce

Partially fill a large kettle with water and bring to boiling point. Add corn and cover. Return to boiling point, remove from heat; let stand 5-10 minutes. Drain and cool. Cut kernels off cobs. Combine oil, vinegar, lemon juice and mustard. Mix well. Add salt and pepper. Stir in parsley and basil; mix well. Add corn and toss. Add tomatoes, bell pepper and onion, toss again. Heap salad into a lettuce-lined bowl. *Yield: 6 servings.*

Stir Crazy!
Junior Welfare League of Florence
Reviewed Summer 1996
Sandlapper

Cucumber Salad

1-2   cucumbers, sliced very thin
1/4   cup water
1/4   cup vinegar (regular white)
2-3   tablespoons sugar
      pinch of salt and pepper
      pinch of celery seeds
      (optional)

Put thinly sliced cucumber into a jar. Boil the water, vinegar, sugar, salt and pepper for 20 seconds and pour over cucumber. May add some celery seed at this time. Seal jar and let sit until cooled. Refrigerate when cooled. Great for summer salad or picnic. *Yield: 4 servings.*

Ursula Monika Lain
Lexington, SC

Paella Salad

1	(7-ounce) package yellow rice, cooked
1	cup shrimp, boiled and peeled
2	tablespoons tarragon vinegar
1	bell pepper, chopped
1/3	cup oil
1/2	cup green onion, chopped
1/8	teaspoon salt
1/3	cup celery, thinly sliced
1/8	teaspoon dry mustard
1	tablespoon pimento, chopped
2	tablespoons black olives, chopped
1	teaspoon salt
2	cups chicken, cooked and diced
1	large tomato, chopped

Combine rice, vinegar, oil, salt and mustard. Cool to room temperature. Add remaining ingredients. Toss lightly and chill. *Yield: 6-8 servings.*

Stir Crazy!
Junior Welfare League of Florence
Florence, SC
Reviewed Summer 1996
Sandlapper

Tossed Green Salad
With Peggy's Roquefort Dressing

	mixed salad greens
1	teaspoon Worcestershire sauce
8	ounces Roquefort cheese, crumbled
1	tablespoon sugar
1	cup oil
1/2	cup vinegar
	salt and pepper to taste

Wash and tear salad greens. Refrigerate until ready to serve. To prepare dressing, crumble cheese by hand. Combine remaining ingredients. Stir in cheese. Do not use blender. Immediately before serving, toss salad greens with dressing. This dressing is also delicious served over chilled grapefruit.

Uptown Down South
Junior League of Greenville
Reviewed Spring 1996
Sandlapper

Fruit of the Earth Salad

3	oranges
2	pink grapefruits
1	pineapple
3/4	cup orange marmalade
1	tablespoon grated ginger root*
1/4	cup raspberry vinegar
	red and green salad greens to fill salad bowl

Wash and tear salad greens into pieces. Place in salad bowl. Cut pineapple into chunks and combine with sections of oranges and grapefruit. Add fruit to salad bowl. Melt marmalade over low heat, stirring constantly. Stir in vinegar and ginger. Drizzle marmalade mixture over greens and serve.

Nancy Rhyne
Myrtle Beach, SC

Note: You can plant ginger plants in your garden or flower bed. Ginger plants produce a white flower that fills your garden with fragrance. The root is large and crooked and may be grated and used for cooking. Otherwise, use ground ginger.

Greek Pasta Salad

1	pound box Penne Regata pasta
2	cloves garlic, diced
1	small red onion, thinly sliced
3-4	scallions, chopped
1	cup Greek style olives
1	(8-ounce) block herbed Feta cheese, crumbled
1	cup cherry tomatoes, quartered
1/4	cup olive oil
1/4	cup red wine vinegar
	juice of half a lemon
1/2	teaspoon oregano
	salt and pepper to taste

Boil pasta in salt water until tender and drain. Place pasta in large mixing bowl. Add next six ingredients and toss. Whisk oil, vinegar, lemon juice and oregano together and pour over pasta. Salt and pepper to taste and toss well to coat in dressing. *Yield: 6-8 servings.*

Dawn B. Gates
Camden, SC

My Mother's Potato Salad

6-8	potatoes, diced and cooked
3	boiled eggs, sliced
1/2	teaspoon celery seed
1	onion, chopped
3/4	cup mayonnaise
	salt and pepper

Mix all ingredients while potatoes and eggs are warm. Serve immediately or chilled. Simple and delicious!

Sally Lightsey-Jones
Greenwood, SC

7 Cup Salad

1	cup shredded coconut
1	cup mandarin orange slices
1	cup sour cream
1	can fruit cocktail
1	cup crushed pineapple
1	cup pecan halves
1	cup sugar

Mix sugar and sour cream, then add other ingredients. Keep in refrigerator overnight so flavors will blend. *Yield: 6 servings.*

Cathy Anderson
Charlotte, NC

Spaghetti Salad

1	(8-ounce) box thin spaghetti, cooked per package directions—wash in cold water and chill
1	diced bell pepper
1	cup Dukes (hearty) mayonnaise
1/2	head lettuce, shredded
3	medium diced tomatoes

Mix ingredients. Wonderful with fried chicken. Serve with any kind of crackers.

Ruth F. Polattie
Greenwood, SC

91

Sweet Potato Salad

4	medium sweet potatoes
1	cup pineapple chunks, drained
1	cup pecans, broken
1/4	cup orange juice
1	teaspoon vinegar
1	teaspoon curry powder
1	teaspoon orange rind, grated
1/4-1/2	teaspoon dried tarragon (optional)
1	cup mayonnaise
2	tablespoons half and half cream

Cook sweet potatoes until tender, but still firm. Peel and cut into chunks the size of pineapple chunks. Gently toss potatoes, pineapple, nuts and orange juice. In small bowl, combine all remaining ingredients. Pour dressing over potato mixture and gently toss. Chill several hours. To serve, arrange the salad on a bed of greens. *Yield: 6 servings.*

A. Divver Allen
Coker Classics
Hartsville, SC
Reviewed Autumn 1997
Sandlapper

Wild Rice Salad

3	cups wild rice, or wild and brown rice mixed pimento, diced (enough to give salad an interesting color) boiling water Italian salad dressing chicken stock
1/2	cup sunflower seeds, toasted
5-6	green onions, including stems, thinly sliced

Rinse rice. Place in large bowl and pour boiling water over it to cover by at least 2 inches. Cool, drain, stir and repeat. Repeat again, using a well-salted chicken stock for the last "cooking." The rice should be fluffy. If it is not, drain chicken stock and repeat. Add onions and pimento to fluffy, drained rice. Toss with Italian dressing. Refrigerate. This is best made two days ahead and should keep for one week. Just before serving, add toasted sunflower seeds. *Yield: 8 servings.*

Sharon Brinkman
Thoroughbred Fare
Aiken, SC
Reviewed Autumn 1997
Sandlapper

Sea Island Shrimp

2 pounds medium shrimp, half cooked, peeled and deveined
2 medium white onions, peeled and sliced very thin

In a non-aluminum flat casserole dish, alternately layer shrimp and onions until all are used. Cover with dressing completely.

Dressing:
3/4 cup olive oil
1/2 cup + 2 tablespoons apple cider vinegar
6 ounces capers with brine
3/4 cup sugar
2 tablespoons (or to taste) Tabasco sauce
4 tablespoons Worcestershire sauce

Combine all ingredients, mix well. Pour over shrimp and onion in casserole dish. Refrigerate overnight before serving. To serve, stir all ingredients well. Drain with slotted spoon and serve on a bed of lettuce garnished with tomato wedges and lemon wedges.

Sea Captain's House Restaurant
Myrtle Beach, SC

Shrimp and Rotini Splendor

1/2 pound Rotini (small pasta shells)
2 pounds fresh shrimp
1 small red onion
1 (10-ounce) package frozen green peas
5 stalks celery
4 ounces mayonnaise
4 ounces English mustard (a mustard such as Cherchies may be used)
1/4 teaspoon salt

Boil and devein shrimp. Cook pasta as directed. Drain and mix with 1 tablespoon mayonnaise. Cook peas al denté, chop onion and celery. Allow shrimp to cool. Mix mayonnaise and mustard together, toss all ingredients together and chill. *Yield: 8-10 servings, less when used alone as a salad.*

Mary Howard
Lexington, SC

93

Congealed Salads

Beet Salad

1   (15-ounce) can julienne
     beets (S&W brand) reserve
     liquid.
1   small package lemon gelatin
1/4 cup sugar
1/4 cup cider vinegar
1   tablespoon prepared
     horseradish (more to taste
     or use fresh-grated)

Drain beets, reserve liquid and add water to measure 1 1/2 cups. Put liquid in a medium saucepan and bring to a boil. Add gelatin and stir to dissolve *completely*. Add sugar, vinegar, horseradish. Stir in drained beets. Fills a one quart mold or clear glass serving dish. May be jelled in 8x8-inch square, cut into pieces and served on lettuce bed. Can be doubled or tripled with ease. *Yield: 6-9 servings.*

Barbara J. Manka
Salem, SC

Bing Cherry Salad

Topping:
1   (3-ounce) package lemon
     Jell-O
1   cup boiling water

Mixture:
1   (3-ounce) package black
     cherry Jell-O
1   (3-ounce) package raspberry
     Jell-O
1   No. 2 can pitted bing
     cherries
1   cup chopped pecans

Add 1 cup sour cream and dissolve. Pour in a 6-cup ring mold and congeal before adding bing cherry mixture.

Pour off juice from cherries and save. Dissolve Jell-O in 1 cup boiling water. Measure juice from cherries with 1/3 cup sherry and enough water to make 2 cups liquid. Add to Jell-O mixture. Stir in cherries and nuts; pour over congealed lemon topping. Congeal until very firm and unmold on serving plate.

Jean C. Gasque
Elloree, SC
Reprinted from January/
February 1990
Sandlapper

Blueberry Salad

2   (3-ounce) packages
    blackberry Jell-O
2   cups boiling water
1   can blueberries (can use pie
    filling)
1   (15-ounce) can crushed
    pineapple (not drained)

Topping:
1   (8-ounce) cream cheese
1   teaspoon vanilla
1/2 pint sour cream
1/2 cup sugar

Dissolve Jell-O in boiling water. Add pineapple and blueberries. Congeal. Mix and spread topping over Jell-O. Cream cheese should be very soft. Decorate with 1/2 cup chopped nuts. Note: You can use cherry or any other dark flavor of Jell-O. *Yield: 8 (1/2 cup) servings.*

Lucille Cudd
Chester, SC

Buttermilk Salad

1   (16-ounce) can crushed
    pineapple
1   (6-ounce) package gelatin
    (lime, peach or orange)
1   cup buttermilk
1   (8-ounce) container whipped
    topping
    chopped pecans

Heat crushed pineapple (with juice) in saucepan. Add gelatin to heated pineapple until it dissolves. Set aside to cool. When cool, add buttermilk and topping. Pour into container and top with chopped pecans. *Yield: 8-10 servings.*

Ann M. Huntley
Taylors, SC

Cherry Salad

1   (3-ounce) cherry Jell-O
1   cup boiling water
1   can cherry pie filling
1   large can crushed
    pineapple, drained

Combine Jell-O and boiling water. Stir until dissolved. Stir in cherry pie filling and crushed pineapple. Chill until set. Always a hit and so easy! *Yield: 6-8 servings.*

Dianne H. Cohen
Orangeburg, SC

Cranberry Salad

1   small package cherry Jell-O
       dissolved in 1 cup hot water

Add:
1/2   cup orange juice

Chill until partially thickened.

Fold in:
1   can cranberry sauce (jellied
       or whole berry)
1   small can pineapple tidbits
1   can mandarin orange
       sections
1   cup chopped pecans

Chill until ready to serve. *Yield: 6-8 servings.*

Joan Todd
Walhalla, SC

Cranberry Salad

2   (3-ounce) packages cherry
       Jell-O
2   cups boiling water
1   cup sugar
1   large can crushed pineapple
1   large orange (skin included),
       crushed in food processor
1   (10-ounce) package fresh,
       whole cranberries, crushed
       in food processor

Dissolve Jell-O in boiling water. Add sugar and cool. Add pineapple, orange and cranberries to Jell-O and refrigerate. Very good with turkey, pork and ham. *Yield: 8-12 servings.*

Maro Rogers
Lexington, SC

Coca-Cola Salad

1	(3-ounce) package cherry gelatin
1	(3-ounce) package strawberry gelatin
1	(16-ounce) can dark Bing cherries, pitted
1	(20-ounce) can crushed pineapple
8	ounces cream cheese
12	ounces Coca-Cola
1	cup chopped pecans

Drain the cherries and pineapple, reserving juice. Heat the juice and dissolve the gelatin in it. Cut the cream cheese into very small chunks and add to the gelatin mixture. Add the cherries, pineapple, Coca-Cola and pecans. Pour into a mold and chill. *Yield: 8-12 servings.*

Mary S. Gibson
Evergreen, SC
Reviewed Winter 1995/96
Sandlapper

Congealed Peach Salad

2	(3-ounce) packages peach Jell-O
1	(15 1/4-ounce) can crushed pineapple
1	(8-ounce) Cool Whip
2	cups buttermilk

Dissolve Jell-O in pineapple with juice on top of stove in saucepan. Cool. Fold in Cool Whip and buttermilk. Congeal in 2-quart oblong Pyrex dish in refrigerator. Cut in squares to serve. *Yield: 10-12 servings.*

Jean C. Gasque
Elloree, SC

"Pinkstuff" Easy Salad

Cottage Cheese
Cool Whip
Pineapple, crushed (drain well)
Large strawberry Jell-O (lime may be used also)

Put items in bowl and mix well. Cover and place in refrigerator. Do not add any water. You may prepare small containers or larger ones. *Yield: 4-6 servings.*

Linda H. Bedenbaugh
Prosperity, SC

Jell-O Surprise

1 **(24-ounce) small curd cottage cheese**
1 **(16-ounce) Cool Whip**
1 **(6-ounce) box Jell-O (any flavor - red for Christmas and Valentine's Day)**
1 **(16-ounce) can crushed pineapple, drained**

In a large bowl combine cottage cheese, Jell-O and pineapple. Fold in Cool whip and blend well. Cover bowl with Saran Wrap. Refrigerate 30 minutes or longer. *Yield: 8 servings.*

Mrs. Robert J. Tiller
Mayesville, SC

Southern Style Salad

1 **package lime Jell-O**
2 **small containers of cottage cheese**
1 **small container Cool Whip**
1 **cup chopped nuts (optional)**
1 **(16-ounce) can crushed pineapple**

Mix all ingredients together. Chill.

Nancy Rhyne
Myrtle Beach

Strawberry-Nut Salad

2 **packages strawberry gelatin**
1 **cup boiling water**
2 **(10-ounce) packages frozen, sliced strawberries (thawed and undrained)**
1 **(1-pound 4-ounce) can crushed pineapple, drained**
3 **medium bananas, mashed**
1 **cup coarsely chopped walnuts**
1 **pint sour cream**

Combine gelatin with boiling water in saucepan. Stir until dissolved. Fold in fruits and nuts. Turn 1/2 of mixture into a 12x18x2-inch baking dish. Chill until firm. Spread sour cream over firm gelatin. Spoon remaining gelatin mixture over cream; refrigerate. Slice into 12 squares. Serve on lettuce. (For buffet for crowd, leave in baking dish and let guest get serving size they wish - usually serves about 24 in this manner.

Dudley and Evelyn Williams
Columbia, SC

98

Salad Dressings

Caesar Salad Dressing

1	can anchovies
2	tablespoons red wine vinegar
6	garlic cloves
1	teaspoon Dijon mustard
1	teaspoon Worcestershire sauce
2	dashes Tabasco sauce
1/2	lemon, squeezed
1	egg
1/2	cup Parmesan cheese
1	cup olive oil
	salt and pepper to taste

Combine first nine ingredients in food processor pulsing after each ingredient. Finally add olive oil in a slow steady stream while processing. Serve over Romaine lettuce with croutons, freshly ground pepper and Parmesan cheese.

Sally Lightsey-Jones
Greenwood, SC

WARNING: There have been warnings against consuming raw or lightly cooked eggs on the grounds that the egg may be contaminated with Salmonella, a bacteria responsible for a type of food poisoning.

Jonathan's Poppy Seed Dressing

3/4 cup sugar
1 teaspoon dry mustard
1 teaspoon salt
1/2 cup white vinegar
1 1/2 tablespoons onion juice
1 cup Wesson oil
1 1/2 teaspoons poppy seeds

Mix all dry ingredients, sugar, salt and dry mustard in mixers for about 25-30 seconds or until the dry mustard has blended with the other dry ingredients. Pour in the white vinegar and blend with the dry ingredients until well blended. Add onion juice and blend thoroughly. Add the oil slowly, beating constantly until mixture thickens. Add poppy seeds and mix thoroughly. Store in refrigerator. Good on salads, especially a spinach salad with walnuts, mushrooms and strawberries or bananas.

Reverend Bernett Waitt
Summerville, SC

Salad Dressing

1 1/3 cups oil
2/3 cup sugar
1 cup catsup
1/2 cup vinegar
1/2 teaspoon black pepper
1 tablespoon salt
1/2 teaspoon celery salt
1/4 teaspoon garlic salt
1 1/3 teaspoon Worcestershire sauce
1 small onion, chopped fine or in blender

Add all other ingredients in blender after chopping onions. Blend well. Will keep for a long time in refrigerator.

Tina Beshears
Starr, SC

Fish and Seafood

Fish and Seafood

Alligator Etouffée

1	pound alligator meat
1 1/2	sticks butter
1/2	tablespoon flour
1	medium onion, chopped fine
1	tablespoon bell pepper, chopped fine
1/4	cup green onion tops, chopped
1/4	parsley, chopped
	salt and pepper to taste
	cayenne pepper to taste
2-3	cloves garlic, chopped fine
	small amount of white wine
	small amount of oil
3/4-1	cup clam juice, depending on desired thickness

Sauté vegetables in a large pot or skillet using a little bit of cooking oil. Cook only for 3-5 minutes. Remove vegetables and put aside. Next, take a small amount of white wine and deglaze the pan and pour the contents into the dish with the vegetables. Melt the butter in the pan on a medium heat then add the flour and stir until blended. Then add the dish containing the vegetables and white wine cooking until the vegetables are tender, about 10 minutes, stirring occasionally. Add the alligator and clam juice. Let this cook about 45 minutes to 1 hour on low heat, stirring occasionally. Stir in the salt, pepper and cayenne pepper to taste, green onion tops and parsley. Simmer a while, covered, until seasonings blend. Serve over rice. *Yield: 6 servings.*

Art Thomas
Greenville Technical College
Hospitality Education Department
Greenville, SC

Broiled Crab Meltaways

1	(7-ounce) can crab meat
1/4	pound margarine
1	(7-ounce) jar Old English Cheese Spread
2	tablespoons mayonnaise
1/2	teaspoon seasoned salt
1/2	teaspoon garlic salt
6	English muffins, halved and quartered

Mix first 6 ingredients, spread on muffin quarter. Freeze 30 minutes or more. Broil for 5 minutes and serve hot. Always keep some of these in the freezer for unexpected company.

Sally Lightsey-Jones
Greenwood, SC

103

Crab Mold

1	(12-ounce) package vermicelli
5	hard boiled eggs, chopped
5	stalks celery, chopped
6	sweet pickles, chopped
1/4	small yellow onion, chopped
	salt to taste
1 1/2	cups mayonnaise
2	(4 1/2-ounce) cans crab meat
	paprika

Break vermicelli in half and boil as directed on package. Drain and blanch when cooked. Add next 6 ingredients and mix well. Refrigerate after pressing into mold or Pyrex dish. Cut into squares to serve. *Yield: 8 generous servings.*

Frances Stubblefield
Columbia, SC

Hot Crab Soufflé

12	slices of good quality white sandwich bread
1/2	cup mayonnaise
1	medium onion, chopped
1	cup celery, chopped
1/4	cup green pepper, chopped
2	cups crab meat
3	cups milk
5	large eggs, slightly beaten
1	can mushroom soup
1	cup grated cheddar cheese
	paprika

Cube half of the bread and put in 9x13-inch baking dish. Mix crab, mayonnaise, onion, green pepper and celery. Spread over bread. Trim crusts from remaining bread and place over crab meat layer. Mix eggs and milk and pour over casserole. Refrigerate overnight. Bake 325° for 20 minutes. Remove from oven and spread mushroom soup over top. Sprinkle grated cheese on top. Sprinkle on paprika. Bake at 325° for one hour. Let rest 10 minutes before serving. *Yield: 8-10 servings.*

Janet Bruning
Greenville, SC

Crab Imperial Blakeley

2	pounds crab meat (check for shells)
1	stick unsalted butter (no substitution)
3	tablespoons plain flour
20	ounces (1 1/2 cups) half and half
1/2	cup sherry
1	teaspoon basil
1	tablespoon parsley (fresh if possible)
	dash of lemon pepper
1	teaspoon Worcestershire sauce
3	dashes Tabasco
	Progresso Italian bread crumbs
	Parmesan cheese (to sprinkle on top)

Melt butter over low heat. Add flour and cook for 5 minutes (very important). Add other ingredients as listed (except crab, bread crumbs and cheese). Stir. Taste and add salt if necessary. Add crab and fold into mixture. Spray individual dishes and bake in these dishes. Top with bread crumbs and sprinkle with Parmesan cheese. Bake at 350° 15-20 minutes in preheated oven or until bubbly. Very hot. *Yield: 6-8 servings.*

Betty B. Blandford
Seabrook Island, SC

Meeting Street Crab

1	pound white crab meat
4	tablespoons butter
4	tablespoons flour
1/2	pint cream
4	tablespoons sherry
1/4	cup grated sharp cheese
	salt and pepper to taste

Note: 1 1/2 pounds shrimp may be substituted for the crab.

Make a cream sauce with the butter, flour and cream. Add salt, pepper and sherry. Remove from fire and add crab meat. Pour the mixture into buttered casserole or individual baking dishes. Sprinkle with grated cheese and cook in a hot oven until cheese melts. Do not overcook. *Yield: 4 servings.*

Mary Vereen Huguenin
Charleston Receipts
Junior League of Charleston
Reviewed Autumn 1995
Sandlapper

Crab Cakes

2	pounds lump crab meat, picked of any shell
1	small onion, diced
1 1/2	cups packed fresh breadcrumbs
2	tablespoons fresh chopped parsley
3	eggs, beaten
3/4	teaspoon salt
1	teaspoon black pepper
1	teaspoon dry mustard
1/4	cup heavy cream

Lemon Dill Butter Sauce:

1	stick unsalted butter (1/4 pound), cut into 1-inch squares
2	teaspoons fresh lemon juice
2	tablespoons white wine
1	teaspoon dry dillweed or 2 teaspoons fresh dillweed, minced
	salt and pepper

To hot skillet, add 1 teaspoon cooking oil, butter or margarine and onion. Sauté until transparent (approximately 3 minutes). Remove from heat. In large mixing bowl, mix all ingredients well. Form into 3 ounce cakes (approximately 3 inches across). Roll in flour and cook in hot oil until golden brown on both sides. Serve immediately with lemon dill sauce. *Yield: 16 cakes (8 portions).*

In medium hot saucepan, put wine and butter, stirring to blend. Add lemon juice, dill and salt and pepper to taste. Serve immediately.

Sea Captain's House
Myrtle Beach, SC

106

McClellanville Crab Cakes

1	pound lump crab meat
1/2	cup mayonnaise
2	green onions, chopped fine
2	dashes Tabasco
1	dash of Worcestershire sauce
1/2	cup coarse bread crumbs
1/2	ounce fresh lemon juice
1/2	teaspoon ground thyme

Combine above ingredients thoroughly, then form into desired cake size (about 4 ounces). Make egg wash of 2 eggs and 1/4 cup half and half. Dip cakes in egg mixture, then roll in more bread crumbs. Sauté in butter or olive oil until golden brown. Serve with sweet pepper and cilantro coulis. *Yield: 4 servings.*

Sweet Pepper and Cilantro Coulis:

4	large sweet peppers (red preferred)
3	teaspoons chopped cilantro
1/2	teaspoon white pepper
1	teaspoon apple cider vinegar
3	teaspoons honey
3	large shallots
1/2	cup water

Seed and dice red pepper (medium dice). Peel and chop shallots. Sauté pepper and shallots together. Add 1/2 cup water. Simmer 20 minutes or until peppers are soft completely through. Using a high-speed blender, place peppers and shallots and all remaining ingredients (except cilantro) in a bowl, blending until smooth and then run through a medium strainer. Add cilantro and set aside at room temperature.

Chef Kish
82 Queen
Charleston, SC

Crab and Spinach Casserole

1	(10-ounce) package frozen spinach
2	tablespoons minced onion
1	cup milk
1/2	teaspoon salt
1	pound crab meat
1/4	cup plus 2 tablespoons butter
1	cup grated sharp cheddar cheese
2	tablespoons flour
1/8	teaspoon curry powder
1	tablespoon lemon juice
3/4	cup bread crumbs

Cook and drain spinach. Put in bottom of greased casserole dish. Sprinkle cheese over spinach. Melt 1/4 cup butter and sauté onion until transparent. Add remaining 2 tablespoons butter and stir in flour. Add milk. Stir constantly until thickened. Add curry and salt. Stir lemon juice and crab into sauce. Pour over spinach and cheese. Sprinkle bread crumbs on top. Preheat oven to 350°. Cook 30 minutes. Short preparation time and very nice for guests. *Yield: 4-6 servings.*

Shirley Lorick Hiller
Lexington, SC

Spinach Crab Soufflé

1	(12-ounce) package frozen spinach soufflé (I prefer Stouffer's)
2	pounds small-curd cottage cheese
6	tablespoons flour
6	eggs, beaten
1	stick butter or margarine, diced
1/2	pound sharp cheddar cheese, grated
1/2	pound fresh crab meat

Thaw frozen spinach soufflé. Mix spinach with remaining ingredients and spoon into a buttered 9-inch soufflé dish. Bake in a 350° oven for one hour. *Yield: 6-8 servings.*

Note: This is a beautiful dish to serve for a Sunday brunch or lunch.

Cari Morningstar
Greenville, SC

Baked Halibut with Orange-Chili Marinade Topped with Citrus Beurre Blanc

Fish:

1/2	cup fresh orange juice
1/2	cup fresh cilantro leaves, chopped
1	tablespoon olive oil
2	cloves garlic, peeled and minced
1	chipotle pepper, chopped
1 1/3	pounds halibut fillets (thick)
	ground black pepper to taste

Combine the orange juice, cilantro, olive oil, garlic and chipotle. Place the halibut in a glass dish and cover with the marinade. Refrigerate 1 hour. Remove the fish from the marinade and place on a rack set into a baking pan or on a broiling pan. Bake in a preheated 450° oven for 12 minutes per inch of thickness. Top with sauce. *Yield: 4 servings.*

Citrus Beurre Blanc:

1	cup lemon juice
2	shallots, peeled and chopped
	salt and white pepper to taste
1/2	cup grapefruit juice
3	sticks butter, cut into 1-inch cubes

Place lemon juice, grapefruit and shallots in a saucepan and bring to a boil. Simmer until the liquid is reduced to 2 tablespoons, about 5 minutes, depending on the size of the pan. Remove from the heat. Whisk the butter, piece by piece, into the sauce. Taste for seasoning and add salt and white pepper if necessary. Strain if needed. Makes 1-1 1/2 cups.

Jeff Daugherty
Greenville Technical College
Hospitality Education Department
Greenville, SC

Lemon Fish

Use any white fish, such as flounder, grouper, cape capensis, orange roughy, rockfish, snapper or whatever you have fresh (preferably a white-meated fish).

1	**frozen container of fresh lemonade**
2	**ounces white vinegar**
4	**tablespoons corn starch**

Mix lemonade concentrate with water. Add corn starch and vinegar along with fresh lemon and sugar. Heat in small pot long enough for mixture to bubble. Let cool. Serve over grilled, broiled or sautéed fish. Garnish with lemon wedges and parsley.

Mr. Fish
Myrtle Beach, SC

Baked Orange Roughy

1	**cup chopped green bell pepper**
1/2	**cup finely chopped onion**
1	**teaspoon olive oil**
2	**cloves garlic, minced**
1/4	**cup chablis wine**
1	**tablespoon lime juice**
1/4	**teaspoon crushed red peppers**
1	**(14 1/2-ounce) can diced tomatoes, drained**
1	**pound orange roughy fillets**
1/4	**teaspoon salt**
1/8	**teaspoon black pepper**
1/4	**cup chopped fresh parsley**

Cook green pepper and onion in olive oil over medium heat. Add garlic and cook 1 minute stirring constantly. Stir in wine, lime juice, crushed peppers and tomatoes. Bring to boil, reduce heat and simmer 5 minutes. Spoon 1/2 cup tomato mixture in bottom of 11x7-inch casserole that has been sprayed with Pam. Arrange fish over mixture. Sprinkle with salt and pepper and top with remaining tomato mixture. Bake at 350° for 25 minutes or until fish flakes. Sprinkle with fresh parsley before serving. *Yield: 2-4 servings.*

Donna Rone
West Columbia, SC

Pecan-crusted Catfish

7	ounces pecans, finely ground (about 1 cup)
1/4	cup plain dry bread crumbs
4	tablespoons chopped fresh parsley, divided
1	teaspoon salt
1/4	teaspoon pepper
1/8	teaspoon cayenne pepper
4	catfish fillets (about 1 ½ pounds)
1/4	cup all-purpose flour
2	eggs, lightly beaten
2	tablespoons olive oil
2	tablespoons margarine
2	tablespoons lemon juice lemon wedges and parsley sprigs (optional)

In a bowl combine pecans, bread crumbs, 2 tablespoons parsley, salt, pepper and cayenne; set aside. Coat both sides of fillets in flour; dip into eggs. Coat with pecan mixture; set aside on wax paper. In a nonstick skillet heat oil over medium-high heat. Add fillets, in batches if necessary. Cook, turning once, until fish flakes easily with fork, about 4 minutes per side. Transfer to serving platter; cover loosely to keep warm. In same skillet melt butter; cook until lit browns lightly, 1-2 minutes. Stir lemon juice and remaining parsley, remove from heat. Pour sauce over fillets. Serve with lemon and garnish with parsley, if desired. *Yield: 4 servings.*

Julia Derrick
Lexington, SC

Silure Secret (Secret Catfish)

1	tablespoon crushed oregano
1	tablespoon garlic powder
2	cups water

Put the above ingredients in a saucepan and set on medium heat.

1	tablespoon extra virgin olive oil
1/2	cup vinegar
1	cup raw potato, peeled and diced
1	cup onion, chopped
1	cup parsnip, peeled and diced
1	cup defatted chicken stock
1/2	teaspoon ground thyme
1	cup celery, chopped
1	cup raw carrots, chopped
1	can tomato soup
4	catfish fillets

Coat bottom of skillet with olive oil. As the water, garlic and oregano in the saucepan come to a slow boil, add the cup of vinegar. Put the potato, onion and parsnip fragments in the heated skillet and let them sauté for 3 minutes. Lay the catfish fillets atop the potato-onion-parsnip mush. Pour the chicken stock over them and immediately cover the skillet. This traps the steam in the skillet and causes the fish to get poached and also presents the dissemination of whatever smells the catfish might emit. Let the fish and vegetables cook for 10 minutes on medium heat. Add the thyme with a splash of water to the saucepan. Sprinkle the celery and carrot over the fish in the skillet and check to be sure there is still some liquid in the skillet, adding water if necessary. Try not to disturb the fillets (they will be getting fragile by now), and be sure to put the lid back on the skillet quickly. Let the skillet and saucepan quietly pursue their vocations over medium heat for another 10 minutes, during which time your house will be smelling like a Neapolitan trattoria. At the last minute stir the can of tomato soup, undiluted, into the saucepan. It will suddenly turn into a surprisingly elegant tomato sauce. You can serve the catfish fillets and vegetables straight from the skillet without the sauce if you so desire. It is delicious either way. Use the sauce later for pasta. *Yield: 4 servings.*

Robert Thomas King
Winnsboro, SC
Reprinted from Spring 1997
Sandlapper

Fillets in Coral Sauce

2	pounds fish fillets
2	tablespoons lemon juice
1	teaspoon salt
1	teaspoon onion, grated
	dash of pepper
1/4	cup butter or margarine, melted
1	teaspoon paprika

Cut fillets in serving size portions. Place in single layer, skin side down in well-greased baking pan. Combine remaining ingredients and pour over fish. Bake in 350° oven 20-25 minutes or until fish flakes easily when tested with fork. *Yield: 6 servings.*

Elizabeth Newell Whaley
Coker Classics
Hartsville, SC
Reviewed Autumn 1997
Sandlapper

Resort White Clam Sauce

4	ounces butter
4	ounces flour
1	cup white wine
4	shallots
4	cloves garlic
1	quart clam juice
1	cup chopped clams
1	cup cream

Start with white roux, butter and flour. Cook roux at least 5 minutes, do not brown. Add white wine, then shallots and garlic, finely minced. Cook in roux to release aroma about 5 minutes. Add clam juice. Cook until it coats back of spoon. Add clams and salt and pepper to taste. Toss on your favorite pasta and serve hot. *Yield: 8 servings.*

Janice S. Creasy
Palmyra, VA

Dolphin in Oyster Sauce

4	**(6-ounce) dolphin fillets (fresh)**
24	**fresh, shucked oysters with juice**
	juice of 1 lemon
1/4	**cup dry vermouth**
1	**tablespoon Balsamic vinegar**
2	**teaspoons salt**
2	**teaspoons white pepper**
1/2	**cup heavy cream**
1/2	**tablespoon Dijon mustard**

Preheat oven to 500°. Arrange dolphin fillets in a baking dish with oysters. Mix oyster juice, lemon juice, vermouth and vinegar and pour over fish and oysters. Bake for 5 minutes or until fish is just done (flakes with fork and is opaque white). DO NOT OVERCOOK. Remove the oysters to a sauté pan. Pour the juices off the fish and in the sauté pan. Bring to a furious boil. Add salt, pepper, cream and mustard to sauté pan and stir well with fork or wire whip. Remove dolphin from baking dish to dinner plates. Pour oysters and sauce over fish. *Yield: 4 servings.*

Philip Bardin
Edisto Beach, SC
Reprinted from May/June 1990
Sandlapper

Oysters Bienvielle

20	**oysters**
1	**pound shredded crab**
2	**teaspoons minced fresh garlic**
1/2	**pint fresh cream**
1/2	**cup white wine**
1	**tablespoon Pernod**
2	**teaspoons flour**

Sauté crab with garlic on low heat for 1 minute. Add Pernod, then wine, reduce liquid to about 1/4 cup. Add flour, then cream. Blend together in food processor until mixed well. Shuck approximately 20 oysters-- place on flat pan. Put oysters in oven at 375° for 4 minutes. Put mixture on top of oysters. Then broil until top is golden brown. Can also be topped with Hollandaise sauce. *Yield: 4 servings.*

Peter Ryter
1109 Restaurant
Anderson, SC

Salmon Patties

1	large can salmon
1	egg
1/3	cup minced onion
1/4	cup self-rising flour
1/4	cup self-rising or plain corn meal (any variety)

Drain salmon and set aside juice. Remove bones. In large bowl mix salmon, egg and onion until sticky. Add flour and corn meal and mix well. Form into small patties and deep fry in hot oil until golden brown. Patties will rise to top of fryer.

Judy M. Smith
Leesville, SC

Special Salmon Patties

1	can salmon, not drained
2	cups cubed old bread (dry stuffing mix may be substituted)
1/4	cup diced fresh jalapeno peppers
1/4	cup diced celery
1/4	cup diced onion
2	eggs, beaten
1/4	teaspoon soda
	sourdough starter (See Bread Machine Sourdough Bread recipe.)

Mix all ingredients adding enough sourdough starter to obtain the consistency of thick pancake batter. The amount of sourdough starter will depend on its texture. Drop in skillet with a little peanut oil and brown on both sides. Drain and serve with rice or grits. This recipe also works well baked in a casserole dish at 350° until eggs are well cooked. *Yield: 4 servings.*

E. Guy Shealy, Jr.
Batesburg-Leesville, SC

Shrimp Newburg

3	tablespoons butter
1/2	pound fresh mushrooms, sliced or 2 (4-ounce) cans sliced mushrooms, drained
3	pounds shrimp, peeled and deveined
2	cans shrimp soup
1	can mushroom soup
1/2	cup light cream
1/2	cup sherry
2	teaspoons dry mustard
1/4	teaspoon salt
1/4	teaspoon pepper
4	tablespoons grated Parmesan cheese

Melt butter in a heavy saucepan. Add mushrooms and cook about 5 minutes, until golden brown. Arrange mushrooms in the bottom of a 4 quart casserole. Add shrimp. Combine the next 7 ingredients. Pour mixture over shrimp. Sprinkle top with cheese. Bake about 30 minutes in 350° oven until sauce bubbles and shrimp are pink and firm. If a browner top is desired, place under broiler 3 inches from heat for about 2 minutes. Serve with Savory Rice. *Yield: 8-10 servings.*

Savory Rice:

6	tablespoons butter
3/4	cup finely chopped onion
2	cups raw rice
4	chicken bouillon cubes
4	cups boiling water salt and pepper
2	tablespoons chopped parsley

Heat butter in a large saucepan; add onion and cook over low heat until golden brown. Add rice and cook until lightly browned. Dissolve chicken bouillon cubes in boiling water; add to rice. Cover and cook until tender and liquid is absorbed. Season to taste with salt and pepper. Arrange in serving dish and sprinkle with chopped parsley.

Ella Calvert Bouknight
Lexington, SC

Country Shrimp Boil

1/3	cup powdered seafood boil
5	pounds medium shrimp, unpeeled
1	lemon, sliced
3	pounds smoked sausage
12	ears corn, halved
	cocktail sauce
	Dijon-style mustard

Fill a very large pot with water; add powdered seafood boil and lemon. Bring to a boil. Cut sausage into 2-inch pieces; add to boiling water and cook for 5 minutes. Add corn and continue to boil for 10 minutes. Stir in shrimp and continue cooking for 3-5 minutes. Drain. Serve with cocktail sauce and mustard. *Yield: 12 servings.*

Uptown Down South
Junior League of Greenville
Reviewed Spring 1996
Sandlapper

Shrimp and Pasta Casserole

1	(8-ounce) package orzo pasta
1	pound shrimp
1/2	stick butter
2	cans chicken broth
2	cups water
1/4	pound Feta cheese crumbled

Boil orzo in chicken broth and water until done. Boil shrimp; peel and devein. Drain pasta. Melt butter until it turns brown and mix all ingredients. Bake in a buttered casserole dish about 30 minutes at 300°. *Yield: 6 servings.*

Maro Rogers
Lexington, SC

Seafood Casserole

1/2	cup chopped onion
1/2	cup chopped green pepper
1	cup chopped celery

Sauté above in 1 tablespoon butter

1	pound crab meat ·
1	pound cooked shrimp
8	ounces fresh mushrooms, sliced and sautéd in butter
1	tablespoon pimento dash red pepper
1	cup mayonnaise
1/2	teaspoon pepper
1	teaspoon salt
1	cup half and half
1	tablespoon Worcestershire sauce
1/3	cup sherry wine
1	cup raw rice, cooked by directions

Combine all ingredients and place in a 2-quart Pyrex dish. Bake at 375° for 30 minutes. Delicious with ham. *Yield: 8-10 servings.*

Jean C. Gasque
Elloree, SC

Spicy Rock Shrimp Cakes

1	pound rock shrimp (70-90 count), cooked and rough chopped
1/2	red bell pepper, diced fine
1/2	green bell pepper, diced fine
1	small onion, diced fine
1/2	teaspoon dry red pepper flakes
1	teaspoon roasted garlic, fresh chopped
1/2	cup angel hair pasta, cooked and chopped
1	teaspoon dry Caribbean Jerk spice
1	tablespoon Lea & Perrins Worcestershire sauce
2	dashes Tabasco
1	tablespoon dry Old Bay seasoning
1	cup Hellmann's mayonnaise
1 1/2	cups crushed saltine crackers (to bind)

Mix cooked and chilled shrimp with dry ingredients, except crackers. Mix wet ingredients together and fold into shrimp. Add crackers to bind. Form into 3-ounce cakes and pan fry in 1 tablespoon olive oil 1-1 1/2 minutes each side. Serve with sauce.

Sundried Tomato Tartar Sauce:

1	ounce sundried tomatoes, rehydrated in boiling water
6	ounces Hellmann's mayonnaise
1	ounce sweet pickle relish liquid
1	tablespoon green onion, chopped
1	ounce capers
1	tablespoon fresh lemon juice
1	teaspoon dry coriander
1	pinch dry cayenne pepper

Mix all tartar sauce ingredients and refrigerate.

William Mann
Cottage Cuisine
Greenville, SC

Shrimp Casserole

2	pounds shrimp
1	tablespoon lemon juice
3	teaspoons salad oil
3/4	cup raw rice
2	tablespoons butter
1/4	cup minced onion
1/4	cup green minced pepper
1	teaspoon salt
1/8	teaspoon pepper
1/4	teaspoon mace
	dash cayenne pepper
1	can undiluted tomato soup
1	cup half and half
1/2	cup slivered almonds
1/2	cup sherry
	paprika

Shell, cook and devein shrimp. Place in 2-quart casserole and sprinkle with lemon juice and oil. Cook rice. Sauté pepper and onion in butter, add to rice and all other ingredients (reserving 1/4 cup almonds to go on top). Combine with shrimp. Top with almonds and paprika. Bake 35 minutes at 350°. *Yield: 6-8 servings.*

Margaret Adelman
S.C. Club of Nashville
Nashville, TN

Shrimp Athenian Style

2	pounds shrimp, cleaned
	juice of 1 lemon
3	tablespoons olive oil
2	Bermuda onions, finely chopped
1	clove garlic, minced
1/4	cup parsley, minced
1	teaspoon dill
1	teaspoon sugar
1/8	teaspoon dry mustard
2	cups fresh or canned tomatoes
1	cup tomato sauce
1	cup Feta cheese, crumbled

Preheat oven to 425°. Place shrimp in bowl; pour lemon juice over shrimp and set aside. Heat oil, add onions, stirring until they are tender. Add garlic, parsley, dill, sugar and stir in mustard. Add tomatoes and tomato sauce and simmer about 30 minutes. Add shrimp to tomato sauce and cook about 10 minutes. Pour mixture into casserole and sprinkle with Feta cheese. Bake 10-15 minutes or until cheese melts. Excellent served over rice. *Yield: 4-6 servings.*

Sally Lightsey-Jones
Greenwood, SC

Shrimp Delight

2	cups uncooked regular rice
1/4	cup sliced green onion
1/4	cup vegetable oil
1	quart chicken broth
2	tablespoons soy sauce, divided
1	bay leaf
2	teaspoons salt
1/2	teaspoon pepper
1	tablespoon lemon juice
2	tablespoons melted margarine
1	pound shrimp, cooked
1	(8-ounce) sour cream
1	cup shredded cheese

Sauté rice and onion in oil until rice is browned. Stir in broth, 1 tablespoon soy sauce, bay leaf, salt, pepper and lemon juice. Cover and cook 25 minutes or until liquid is absorbed. Remove bay leaf. Combine butter, shrimp and remaining soy sauce in a saucepan; cook just until thoroughly heated. Combine shrimp mixture and rice mixture; mix well. Spoon half of shrimp/rice into a greased 2 1/2-quart casserole. Spread sour cream over rice. Spoon remaining shrimp/rice mixture over sour cream; sprinkle with cheese. Bake at 450° for 10-15 minutes or until bubbly. *Yield: 6-8 servings.*

Adapted from a recipe in
Southern Living
Vera Sullivan
Chapin, SC

Southern Shrimp and Rice Casserole

1	pound cooked shrimp, shelled and deveined
3/4	cup chopped bell pepper
1/2	cup chopped onion
1	cup chopped celery
1	tablespoon Worcestershire sauce
1	tablespoon margarine or butter
1/8	teaspoon black pepper
1/2	teaspoon salt
1	can sliced mushrooms (small can)
1	cup mayonnaise
1	cup raw rice *cooked*
3/4	cup half and half or light cream
1/4	cup sherry

Sauté all vegetables in margarine or butter. Add the cooked rice, shrimp, Worcestershire, salt, pepper, mushrooms, light cream, sherry and mayonnaise. Stir well and place in a 2-quart buttered rectangular casserole dish and bake at 375° for 30 minutes. Bake covered. Yield: 8-10 servings.

Callie Wienges
St.Matthews, SC

122

Wahoo Court Seafood Casserole

Set aside:

3 1/2   cups cornbread, crumbled coarsely

3 1/2   cups white bread, crumbled

Sauté until tender:

1/2   cup butter or margarine, melted

1   cup diced celery

1/4   cup chopped green onions

1/4   cup diced green pepper

1   cup sliced mushrooms

Simmer 3 minutes:

2   cups hot chicken broth

1   pound shrimp, shelled, deveined, cut up

1   pound scallops, cut up

Combine all ingredients. (Add extra hot broth as needed for desired consistency.)

Add:

1   egg, well beaten
    dash Tabasco (to taste)

1   teaspoon herbed poultry seasoning

3   teaspoons fish seasoning (Orleans or Old Bay label)

2   teaspoons salt or to taste

1   teaspoon pepper, or to taste

Preheat oven to 400°. Spoon into greased 13x9-inch casserole dish. Bake 25 minutes or until evenly browned. *Yield: 12 servings.*

Mrs. Russell W. Sammeth, III
Edisto Island, SC

Greek Pasta with Shrimp

1   box angel hair pasta (8-ounce)

1   can quartered artichokes

1   can sliced black olives

1   can stewed tomatoes

1   bag medium frozen shrimp (60-80), cooked and de-tailed

1   bottle Kraft Greek Vinaigrette dressing (8-ounce)

Cook pasta and drain. Spread in bottom of casserole dish. Drain artichokes, olives and tomatoes and spread on top of pasta. Pour 2/3 bottle of Greek dressing on top. Cook at 325° for 30 minutes. Add shrimp and cook for 3-5 minutes longer. Top with fresh grated Parmesan cheese and serve. *Yield: 6 servings.*

Jennie Lambe
Columbia, SC

BBQ Shrimp and Grits

Low Country Grits:
1	cup heavy cream
1/4	pound butter
1	quart water
2	cups quick grits
	salt and white pepper to taste

Heat cream and water to boil. Add butter, salt and pepper. Slowly add grits and reduce heat. Cook 20 minutes, being careful not to scorch mixture.

Southern Comfort BBQ Sauce:
1/4	pound bacon, diced
1/2	cup red onion, diced fine
1/2	cup red bell pepper
1/2	cup green bell pepper
2	(14-ounce) Heinz ketchup
1/2	cup brown sugar
3-4	tablespoons Southern Comfort
	salt and pepper to taste

Cook bacon until 3/4 done. Add onions and pepper; sauté until done. Flame with Southern Comfort. Add remaining ingredients and season. Simmer for 10 minutes, then cool. Will last under refrigeration for several weeks.

Shrimp:
2	pounds

Sauté, poach or grill shrimp. Place in Southern Comfort BBQ Sauce and simmer for 1 minute. *Yield: 6 dinner portions.*

Chef Kish
82 Queen
Charleston, SC

Crab and Shrimp Au Gratin

2	cups milk
1/3	cup Kraft Cheese Whiz
4	tablespoons plain flour
1	cup grated cheese
1/3	teaspoon salt
1/3	teaspoon pepper
1/8	teaspoon Tabasco
8	ounces cooked shrimp
4	ounces crab meat

Mix flour, salt and pepper with part of the milk. Beat all lumps out. Add Cheese Whiz to rest of milk in a double boiler. When Cheese Whiz has melted, add flour mixture and Tabasco. Stir until smooth and thickened. Add shrimp and crab meat. Pour into casserole. Top with grated cheese. Bake at 350° for 20 minutes. *Yield: 4 servings.*

Frances L. Watson
Florence, SC

Tommy Condon's Shrimp and Grits

1/2	stick butter
1 1/2	pounds shrimp (60-70)
3/4	cup green peppers, chopped
3/4	cup yellow onions, chopped
1/2	cup celery, chopped
4	tablespoons Old Bay seasoning
8	dashes Worcestershire sauce
4	dashes Tabasco
8	dashes white pepper
3/4	cup black olives, sliced
3/4	cup bacon bits, chopped
1 1/2	cups Alfredo cream sauce
1	cup tomatoes, diced
3	cups white grits
1/2	cup sharp cheddar cheese, shredded

Sauté shrimp, peppers, onions and celery in butter. Add bacon bits. When shrimp is cooked, add Worcestershire, Tabasco, white pepper and Old Bay. Throw in black olives and tomatoes. Stir in Alfredo cream sauce and finish cooking in two minutes. Follow directions on grits container (use stone ground grits, if available). Grits should be slightly thick after cooking. When hot, stir in cheddar cheese. Pour sautéed shrimp sauce over cheddar grits on individual serving plates. *Yield: 4 servings.*

Tommy Condon's
Charleston's True Irish Pub &
Restaurant
Charleston, SC

Shrimp Over Grits

2	(10 3/4-ounce) cans cream of celery soup (undiluted)
1	medium size green pepper, diced
1	medium size onion, finely chopped or diced
1	tablespoon Worcestershire sauce
1	tablespoon hot sauce
1	bay leaf
1/8	teaspoon salt
1/8	teaspoon pepper
1-1 1/2	pounds peeled and deveined shrimp, uncooked
	Cooked, buttered grits

Combine the first 7 ingredients and bring to a boil. Simmer uncovered for about 20 minutes. Add shrimp and cook 3-5 minutes, stirring occasionally. Remove bay leaf and serve over buttered grits. *Yield: 8 servings.*

Given to Rev. Bernett Waitt
by Syble McInvaille
Summerville, SC

Maverick Grits

Basic Grits:
4	cups water
1/2	teaspoon salt
1	tablespoon butter
1-1 1/2	cups stone ground grits
1/4	cup cream
1	tablespoon butter

Topping:
8	sea scallops
12	shrimp, peeled and deveined
4	ounces (4 tablespoons) country ham, julienned
4	ounces smoked pork sausage cut in circles
4	tablespoons fresh tomato, seeded and diced
4	tablespoons green onion
1/8	teaspoon minced fresh garlic
	pinch of Cajun spice
1	tablespoon water
1	tablespoon butter

Bring water, salt and 1 tablespoon butter to a boil. Stir in grits. Reduce heat to low and cook, stirring occasionally, until grits are thick and creamy (approximately 40 minutes). Remove from heat and finish by stirring in cream and remaining butter. Keep warm.

Sauté ham and sausage in 1 teaspoon butter. Add shrimp and scallops and sauté for 1-2 minutes. Add garlic and Cajun spice. Sauté 30 seconds. Add green onion and tomato. Add water. Finish with remaining butter.

Spoon grits onto plates in equal portions. Place 2 scallops and 3 shrimp per person on grits and spoon equal parts of topping over each. *Yield: 4 servings.*

Chef Fran Lee
Slightly North of Broad
Charleston, SC

Mr. Fish's Killer Tuna Eggroll

1	pound cabbage, shredded
2	carrots, shredded
1	bunch green onions, shredded

Lightly steam the veggies. Sauté chopped up pieces of fresh tuna, does not have to be sushi grade, in teriyaki sauce. Mix veggies and sautéed tuna together. Press liquid out.

Seasonings:
  soy sauce
  fresh ginger (not powdered)
  sesame oil
  Chinese 5 spice powder
  white powder

Add seasonings.

Purchase eggroll skins from a supermarket. Put enough of the mixture on a skin to fill it up and roll tight. Deep fry to a golden brown. Cut the tuna roll into 4 pieces and serve with a separate bowl of dipping sauce.

Dipping Sauce:

2	ounces white vinegar
1	ounce soy sauce
6	tablespoons sugar
1	teaspoon sesame oil
1	ounce dark mushroom sauce

Chop fresh ginger and fresh garlic. Add to the entire mixture. Heat all of the ingredients and serve.

Ted Hammerman
Mr. Fish
Myrtle Beach, SC

128

Meats

Meats

Beef

Beef Brisket

1   beef brisket (up to 7
     pounds)
1   can cream of mushroom
     soup
1   package Lipton's onion
     soup

Mix the soups together. Rub both sides of meat with soup mixture. Place in flat pan, covered tightly with foil. Bake at 350° for 2-3 hours until fork tender. (Best done day before serving or freezing.) Remove from gravy, refrigerate meat. Remove grease from gravy and add water to taste. Slice next day. Pour gravy over sliced meat in Pyrex. Either heat or freeze. *Yield: 8-10 servings.*

Ann Warshaw
Walterboro, SC

Beef Tenderloin

1   whole beef tenderloin
1   cup bourbon
1   cup soy sauce
     garlic, sliced
     pepper

Generously pepper meat. Make several small incisions all over meat and insert garlic slices. Place in large zip-lock bag and pour bourbon and soy sauce over meat. Let marinate several hours. Grill over hot coals approximately 30 minutes or until desired doneness. Best if served medium-rare. *Yield: 6-8 servings, depending on size of tenderloin.*

Brenda Bowden
Camden, SC

Liberty Hall Marinated Beef Tenderloin

1/2	cup Ruby Port wine
1/4	cup olive oil
1/4	cup soy sauce
1/2	teaspoon dried thyme
1/4	teaspoon hot pepper sauce
1	bay leaf
1/2	teaspoon pepper
1/4	teaspoon salt
4	beef tenderloin steaks (6-8 ounces each)

Mix marinade ingredients together in a bowl. Place steaks in a plastic bag and pour marinade into bag. Place bag in refrigerator for 3-6 hours. Bake on rack on foil-lined pan at 450° for 8 minutes. Turn steak over and bake for an additional 8-10 minutes. Best if cooked medium-rare to medium. *Yield: 4 servings.*

Tom Jonas
Liberty Hall Inn
Pendleton, SC

Individual Beef Wellington

1	fillet of beef, 1 1/2-inch thick
2	patties Pepperidge Farm pastry shells
	liver paté
1	egg
	pepper
	garlic powder

Lightly sprinkle pepper and garlic powder over fillet. Place fillet on rack in open roasting pan. Roast 15-20 minutes at 425°. Remove from oven and let stand. In cup with fork, beat egg with 2 teaspoons water. Set aside. On lightly floured surface, roll 1 patty shell until large enough to place fillet on and have enough dough to fold up around sides. Repeat with other patty; this will be the top cover and will fold down to totally encase fillet. Place fillet on bottom piece of rolled dough. Spread top of fillet liberally with liver paté. Fold edges of dough up around fillet. Place other rolled patty on top of fillet. Gently fold edges down and press edges together gently with fork to form a solid pastry cover for the fillet. With a knife, cut design out of additional rolled patty dough (or use cookie cutter) and arrange on top of fillet. Brush top and sides with egg mixture to help seal and to glaze. On greased cookie sheet, roast fillet 30-40 minutes at 425° or until dough is well browned. May have to cover top with foil if it browns unevenly. Remove from oven and let stand about 10 minutes.

Dudley Williams
Columbia, SC

"Easy Does It" Chuck Roast

1	3-4 pound chuck roast
3/4	cup red wine
1	(10-ounce) consomme (beef), undiluted
1/2	teaspoon garlic powder
1	medium onion, sliced
1/4	cup all-purpose flour
1/4	cup Italian bread crumbs pepper, freshly ground, to taste

Mix wine, consomme, pepper, garlic and onion. (Add some of the liquid to dry ingredients to at least paste —then add rest of liquid for easier mixing.) Add flour and bread crumbs and stir in liquid. Place meat in casserole, add mixture, cover and bake at 325° about 3 hours. Makes its own gravy. *Yield: 6 servings.*

Janice S. Creasy
Palmyra, VA

Ribeye Roast

6	pounds boneless ribeye roast (preferably aged beef)
1/4	cup coarsely ground pepper
1 1/4	cups red wine vinegar
1 1/4	cups soy sauce
1 1/2	teaspoon garlic powder
3	tablespoons tomato paste

Rub pepper over roast. Blend remaining ingredients and pour over roast. Cover. Refrigerate at least 6 hours, preferably overnight. Place roast on roasting pan rack with fat side up. Bring to room temperature. Bake 2 hours for rare roast; 2 1/2 for medium-rare roast. *Yield: 14-16 servings.*

Susan R. Haile
Columbia, SC

Rob's Original London Broil

1/3	cup soy sauce
1/2	cup teriyaki marinade
1/3	cup Worcestershire sauce
1/3	cup red wine or bourbon
2	green onions, chopped
3	cloves of garlic, sliced
1	tablespoon lemon pepper seasoning
1	London broil

Bring to boil. Pour over pierced steak while still boiling. Marinate at least 8 hours. Grill over hot coals.

Rob Jones
Greenwood, SC

Peppered Ribeye Steaks

4   beef ribeye steaks (cut 1 1/2-inch thick)
1   tablespoon olive oil
1   tablespoon garlic powder
1   tablespoon paprika
2   teaspoons each thyme and oregano
1 1/2 teaspoons black pepper
1   teaspoon each salt, lemon pepper and ground red pepper

Brush steaks lightly with oil. Combine remaining ingredients; sprinkle over and press into both sides of steak. Place in glass baking dish; cover and refrigerate 1 hour. Place steaks on grid over medium-low coals. Cover. Grill 16-20 minutes for medium-rare (150°). I turn at 8 minutes. Garnish with orange slices and parsley. *Yield: 4 servings.*

Sharon W. Bickett
Chester, SC

Twin Fillets in Prosciutto Cognac Cream Sauce

2   (4-ounce) beef fillets
1   ounce prosciutto cut in thin strips
2   teaspoons butter
     salt
     cracked pepper
     pinch garlic
2   tablespoons cognac
6   tablespoons heavy cream

Grill two fillets over hot coals lightly sprinkled with cracked pepper. In a separate pan while fillets are grilling, lightly sauté prosciutto in butter with pinch of salt and garlic. Add cognac and flame away alcohol, then add cream. Reduce heat and simmer about 2 minutes. Place fillets in the center of a warm platter and top with sauce. Serve with brown mushroom rice and grilled asparagus. *Yield: 1 serving.*

George Corontzes
Clemson, SC

Oven Steak Supper

1 1/2	pounds round or chuck steak, 1-inch thick (can substitute ground chuck patties)
2	stalks celery, cut in 1-inch sticks
1	envelope onion soup mix
4	small carrots, sliced thick
3-4	medium potatoes, cut as desired
2	tablespoons margarine or butter
3	feet aluminum foil
1/2	teaspoon salt
	Black pepper as desired

Place steak in center of foil. Sprinkle with soup mix; cover with vegetables. Dot with margarine or butter and sprinkle with salt and pepper. Fold foil and seal securely to hold in juices. Place on baking sheet. Bake in hot (450°) oven 1 to 1 1/2 hours or until done. *Yield: 4 servings.*

Lucille Cudd
Chester, SC

Individual Barbequed Beef Loaves

2	pounds ground lean beef
2	eggs, slightly beaten
1/2	cup cracker crumbs
1/3	cup green bell pepper, diced
1/4	cup milk
1/4	cup ketchup
1 1/2	teaspoons salt
8	onion slices

Combine beef, eggs, crumbs, green pepper, milk, ketchup, salt and pepper. Divide into 8 portions on double thick squares of aluminum foil; shape into loaves. Top each with onion slice, 2-3 tablespoons butter barbecue sauce. Bring up sides of foil; fold down onto meat in tight double folds; fold ends over and over up close to meat. Grill 3 inches from coals 10-12 minutes; turn. Grill 10-12 minutes longer. To serve, open foil; top with tomato slice, if desired. *Yield: 8 servings.*

Butter Barbecue Sauce:

1/2	stick butter
1/2	cup chopped onion
1/2	cup ketchup
1/4	cup firmly packed brown sugar
1 1/2	teaspoons chili powder (less if desired)
3	tablespoons Worcestershire sauce
1	teaspoon salt
1/8	teaspoon pepper
	dash Tabasco sauce

Melt butter; add onion; cook until tender. Stir in remaining ingredients; simmer 5 minutes. Can store in refrigerator, warm before using. About 1 cup.

A wonderful way to grill outdoors. These can also be cooked in oven as miniature individual meat loaves. About 350°. Need to check and turn—time can vary from grilling time.

Yvonne B. McGee
Iva, SC

136

Impossible Lasagna Pie

1/2	cup cottage cheese
1	pound ground beef, cooked and drained
1	cup shredded mozzarella cheese
1/2	teaspoon salt
1/2	teaspoon oregano
1	(8-ounce) can tomato paste
1	cup milk
1/2	cup Bisquick
2	eggs

Spread cottage cheese in a 9-inch pie plate. Mix cooked ground beef, 1/2 cup of cheese, salt, oregano and tomato paste, and spoon over cottage cheese. Stir together Bisquick, milk and eggs and pour over meat mixture. Bake at 350° for 30-35 minutes until knife inserted in center comes out clean. Top with remaining cheese. Bake 1 more minute to melt. *Yield: 6 servings.*

Adapted from a Bisquick Recipe
Kay Rollings
Irmo, SC

Liver Nips

3	pounds beef roast
1/2	pound beef fat (suet) 3/4 cup
1	pound or 4 slices of liver
1	medium or large onion
2	large eggs
6	cups plain flour (enough to make batter stiff)
3	tablespoons basil
1	teaspoon black pepper
1	tablespoon salt (or salt to taste)
2	cups of pot liquor
2	tablespoons self-rising flour
5	quart pot

Put roast in oven covered with water (3/4 full) and add salt. Bake 3-4 hours. Take roast out of pot. In large bowl add; chopped or ground liver, suet, onions, eggs, basil, flour, salt and black pepper and add 2 cups of pot liquor until stiff. Put spoon in hot beef broth and drop liver batter in boiling beef stock one spoon at a time. Cover and let nips boil for 30 minutes. Let roast bake until brown and serve sliced with liver nips

Violet Porth
Lexington, SC

Mushroom Meatloaf

1 1/2	pounds ground beef
3/4	cup oatmeal (dry)
1	can cream of mushroom soup
2	eggs
1/4	cup chopped onion, fine
1/4	teaspoon pepper (preferably fresh)
1/2	teaspoon salt

Mix all ingredients together, using only 1/2 can of the mushroom soup. Bake for 1 hour at 350° in greased loaf pan. (After first 45 minutes, remove pan from oven and spread remaining 1/2 can mushroom soup over top of loaf. Return to oven to continue baking.) *Yield: 8-10 slices.*

Jocelyn Turner Ferber
Charlotte, NC

Meatloaf

1 1/2	pounds hamburger
1	cup Italian dry bread crumbs
1	tablespoon chopped onion
2	teaspoons salt
3/4	cup milk
1	egg

Topping:
1/4	cup ketchup
1/4	cup light corn syrup
1	tablespoon Worcestershire sauce

Mix loaf ingredients well. Bake at 350° for 45 minutes. (Drain, if necessary.) Mix topping ingredients and pour over loaf. Return to oven for 15 minutes.

Leah Howell
Starr, SC

138

Mama's Meat Loaf

2   pounds ground hamburger
    meat (Ground chuck makes
    a better dish.)
1   medium onion, chopped
1/2 large bell pepper, chopped
    (optional)
4   slices loaf bread
1   egg
1   teaspoon salt
1   teaspoon pepper
1   (8-ounce) can tomato sauce

Place all ingredients in a large bowl
and mix together. Place half the
mixture into two loaves. Place
aluminum foil on bottom of old iron
pan (for best results). Bake
uncovered for 1 hour at 375°. *Yield:
8-10 servings.*

Patsy Burch
Chester, SC

New Orleans Casserole

1   onion, chopped
1/2 stick margarine
1   pound ground beef
1   can tomato soup
1   can mushroom soup
    salt and pepper to taste
1   (8-ounce) package noodles,
    cooked
1/2 pound grated cheese

Cook onion in margarine for 5
minutes. Add meat and cook until
brown. Add salt and pepper and
soups. Cook about 10 minutes. Add
noodles and part of cheese. Put in
baking dish and cover with
remaining cheese. Bake 30 minutes
at 350°. Yield: 8-10 servings.

Ron Koon
Pomaria, SC

Skillet Spaghetti - One Dish Meal

1   pound ground beef
2   teaspoons chili powder
1 1/2 teaspoons oregano
1   teaspoon sugar
1   teaspoon salt
1   teaspoon garlic salt
1   (6-ounce) can tomato paste
2 1/4 cups tomato juice
2   tablespoons minced onion
1   (7-ounce) package
       uncooked spaghetti
       grated Parmesan cheese
3 1/2 cups water

Brown meat in a 12-inch skillet; drain off excess fat. Stir in chili powder, oregano, sugar, salt and garlic salt. Blend in tomato paste. Stir in tomato juice, onion and 3 1/2 cups water. Bring to boiling. Carefully add spaghetti. May be broken into smaller pieces. Cover and simmer, stirring frequently for 30 minutes. Serve with grated Parmesan cheese. *Yield: 4-6 servings.*

Ann M. Huntley
Taylors, SC

Spaghetti à la Puttanesca

6	tablespoons olive oil
4	garlic cloves
2	cans Italian-styled peeled tomatoes (2 pounds 24 ounces)
1/2	cup chopped, pitted black olives
4	teaspoons small capers, rinsed
2	teaspoons crushed, dried red pepper (or to taste)
1	teaspoon dried oregano pinch of coarsely ground black pepper
4	teaspoons chopped Italian flat-leaf parsley
1	pound pasta (We like angel hair or twist.)
3/4	can water (I rinse out the tomato cans.)

Heat oil in a large skillet. Add garlic. (Sauté onions and bell pepper with the garlic and add fresh, sliced mushrooms.) Sauté over low heat about 1 minute. Do not brown. Stir in tomatoes with their juice, water, olives, capers, mushrooms, red pepper, oregano and black pepper. Cook over medium heat, stirring to break up tomatoes, until the sauce thickens. (About 15 minutes.) Stir in parsley. Simmer 2 more minutes. Add salt to taste. While sauce is simmering, cook spaghetti in plenty of boiling water until al denté, or firm to bite. About 5 minutes. Drain well. Toss with sauce and serve in large warm pasta bowl. (We run spaghetti under cold water to chill a bit so it won't cause the sauce to evaporate. Also, don't leave in hot pot on stove hot eye. The sauce will evaporate and leave it dry.)

Dolly and Brian Patton
Columbia, SC

Good Supper

Preheat oven to 375°

1   cup chopped onion
1   tablespoon oil
1   pound ground veal or lean
         beef
1   tablespoon flour
1   cup milk
1   teaspoon salt
1/8   teaspoon white pepper
2   tablespoons chopped
         parsley
3   eggs, separated (Egg
         substitute instead of yolks.)
1   cup sour cream (Regular or
         any substitute.)
2/3   cup flour
1/2   teaspoon salt
1 1/2 cups shredded, sharp
         yellow cheddar (Not as good
         with low fat.)

In large skillet, sauté onion in oil until barely limp. Add raw meat and 1 tablespoon flour. Mix with fork. Cook until meat loses color. Drain any fat. Slowly stir in milk, salt, pepper, mix well, simmer 15 minutes. Add parsley, mix, remove from heat and set aside. Blend egg yolks and sour cream in large bowl. Mix well. Add 2/3 cup flour, 1/2 teaspoon salt, mix well. Beat egg whites to soft peaks. Fold into yolk mixture. Pam a 1 1/2-quart clear glass casserole. Pour half of egg mixture into dish, top with 3/4 cup cheese. Bake 7-10 minutes until barely set. Carefully spoon meat mixture into dish and cover with remaining egg mixture. Bake 7-10 minutes longer, sprinkle on remaining cheese. Allow to rest in turned off, open oven to melt cheese. Leftovers are divine. This does not transport well. *Yield: 6-8 servings.*

Barbara J. Manka
Salem, SC

Sandwiches

Muffuletta

1 1/2 cups chopped green olives
1 cup chopped black olives
2/3 cup olive oil
1/2 cup chopped pimentos
5 tablespoons minced fresh parsley
1 tablespoon chopped fresh oregano
2 teaspoons fresh lemon juice
1 clove garlic, minced
3/4 cup shredded lettuce
1 cup sliced tomato
4 ounces Italian salami, thinly sliced
4 ounces mozzarella cheese, thinly sliced
4 ounces pepperoni, thinly sliced
1 large round loaf Italian bread
pepper to taste

Combine the green olives, black olives, olive oil, pimentos, parsley, oregano, lemon juice, garlic and pepper in a bowl and mix well. Marinate, covered, at room temperature for 2-4 hours, stirring occasionally. Cut the bread horizontally into halves. Remove the soft bread from the bottom half carefully, leaving a 1-inch shell. Drain the olive mixture, discarding the marinade. Spoon 1/2 of the olive mixture into the bread shell, spreading to within 3/4 to 1 inch from the side. Layer with the lettuce, tomato, salami, mozzarella cheese and pepperoni. Top with the remaining olive mixture and bread top. Wrap in plastic wrap. Place the sandwich on a plate and cover with another plate. Weight the top plate down with a heavy object. This will help to compress the sandwich. Chill for 6 hours or longer. Cut into small wedges. *Yield: 15 servings.*

Down By the Water
Junior League of Columbia, Inc.
Reviewed Spring 1998
Sandlapper

143

Bubbly Hot Sandwich

1	can chicken, ham, turkey or tuna
1/4	cup mayonnaise
1/4	cup sour cream
2	tablespoons chopped onion
1/4	teaspoon garlic salt
3	tablespoons butter
1/2	long loaf French bread
6	ounces grated cheddar cheese

Combine first 6 ingredients. Slice bread lengthwise. Butter bread and spread with meat mixture. Cover with cheese. Broil until cheese is bubbly. *Yield: 3-4 servings.*

Debbie J. Nixon
Florence, SC

Shut Yo' Mouth Sandwich

	Dijon mustard
1	loaf French bread
1	large Vidalia onion
2	cups grated Swiss cheese
1/2	pound mushrooms
1	pound raw oysters or shrimp or scallops or leftover roast beef, pork or lamb

Slice bread long-ways. Smear both halves with Dijon mustard. Drain and rinse oysters, scallops or shrimp. Slice onions and mushrooms. Sauté with seafood (or substitute meat) in covered cast iron skillet. Spread on half of French bread. Cover with grated cheese. Lay other piece of bread on top. Preheat oven to 400°. Set sandwich on aluminum foil. Fold, but leave top uncovered. Bake 25-30 minutes or until bread turns brown on top and cheese melts. Slice vertically and serve. *Yield: 3-4 servings.*

Roger Pinckney
Pelican Rapids, MN

Poultry

Anne's Chicken Bog

1	**5-6 pound fat hen**
1	**small onion, chopped**
1	**small bell pepper, chopped**
6	**cups chicken broth**
4	**cups long grain white rice (do not use instant)**
1/4	**pound bacon, crumbled salt and black pepper**

This recipe was first printed in the January 1968 *Sandlapper* in an article featuring the cook who made this recipe famous, the late Anne Pearce Wallace of Florence, SC.

A 6-quart heavy aluminum pot with top will be needed. (Use top while cooking all phases except bacon.) Put chicken in pot and cover with hot water (be sure there is enough water to provide at least 6 cups broth after cooking chicken). Bring water to boil; turn heat down to simmer until chicken is very tender. While chicken is cooking, slice and chop onion and bell pepper into very small pieces. When chicken is very tender, remove from stove and let cool until it can be handled. Pull chicken from bone (leave chicken in fairly large pieces). Empty pot and return 6 cups chicken broth to pot. Add chopped onion and bell pepper. Season to taste with salt and pepper (at least a tablespoon of each, use a heavy hand since rice absorbs salt). Turn stove to high, bring broth to boil and put chicken in pot. Add rice to pot; mix well and cover. Turn stove to low and cook about an hour. Do not stir. When rice is tender and has absorbed liquids, it is done and can be removed from stove. Serve hot. Crumbled bacon can be served on top.

Rose and Bob Wilkins
Lexington, SC

Baked Chicken with Mushrooms

2	fryers, quartered
	salt, pepper and garlic
	powder
3	sliced onions
1	can chicken broth
1	pound of sliced mushrooms

In a flat pan season chicken well. Place sliced onions on top and under chicken. Bake at 350° skin side down for 30 minutes. Turn chicken and baste with juices. Add broth as needed. In 30 minutes, if not brown, broil a few minutes. Place fresh mushrooms in 1/4 cup of broth. Microwave 10 minutes. Add chicken gravy. Remove grease and pour over chicken. May be fixed early and reheated. *Yield: 4-6 servings.*

Ann Warshaw
Walterboro, SC

Chicken In Cream Sauce

8	boned, skinned chicken
	breasts
8	ounces sour cream
2	cans cream of chicken soup
1	roll Ritz crackers

Place chicken in casserole. Mix together sour cream and soup. Spread over chicken. Crumble crackers over the top. Bake at 350° for 1 hour. This is company-worthy! Serve with rice since it makes its own cream gravy. *Yield: 8 servings.*

Nancy Welch
Greer, SC

146

Chicken Breasts in Mushroom Soup

3 large chicken breasts cut in half
1 stick margarine
1 cup milk
1 can mushroom soup

Remove bones. Broil chicken in butter until well browned. Remove from skillet. Arrange side by side in flat oblong casserole dish. Pour can of mushroom soup into skillet and stir until butter and soup are mixed, thin with milk and pour over chicken. Cover casserole. Bake in slow oven for an hour or until tender. Keep covered entire time. *Yield: 6 servings.*

Sally R. Garris
Columbia, SC

Chicken and Broccoli Casserole

1 package boneless, skinless chicken breasts (4-5)
1 bunch broccoli, chopped
1 can cream of mushroom soup
1 cup mayonnaise
1 cup cheddar cheese, shredded
   salt and pepper to taste
1 cup cracker crumbs
   several pats butter

Boil chicken until done. Cube chicken and mix with broccoli, soup, mayonnaise and salt and pepper. Pour mixture into a deep casserole dish. Top with cracker crumbs and butter pats. Bake at 350° for about 45 minutes or until bubbly and cracker crumbs are slightly browned. *Yield: 6-8 servings.*

Dawn B. Gates
Camden, SC

Note: Light mayonnaise, healthy request soup and reduced fat cheese works fine in this recipe.

147

Chicken Pie

1	fryer, cooked and chopped
3	boiled eggs, chopped
1	can cream of chicken soup
1	can cream of mushroom soup
1	cup chicken broth
1	cup celery, chopped
1	onion, chopped
1	cup mushrooms, chopped (optional)
	LeSeur Peas (optional)

Sauté chopped onion, celery and mushrooms in a little margarine. Mix these with soups, peas and chicken broth. Warm in sauté pan until the mixture is bubbly. Layer large Pyrex dish with chicken and eggs; then pour mixed remaining ingredients over it.

Crust:

1	cup self-rising flour
1	cup buttermilk (can substitute 1 cup milk and 1 tablespoon lemon juice)
1	stick butter, melted
1/2	teaspoon pepper

Combine and beat with a whisk. Pour over chicken; cook 30 minutes at 425°. *Yield: 8-10 servings.*

Lib Brown
Lexington, SC
and
Lynn Snyder
Rock Hill, SC

Chicken Pie

2 cups chicken (cut up after boiling)
1 can cream of chicken soup
1 can clear chicken broth
1 cup little green peas, cooked
1 cup carrots, diced and cooked
1 stick margarine, melted
1/2 teaspoon pepper
1/2 teaspoon salt
1 cup self-rising flour
1 cup buttermilk

Place chicken in 12x9-inch casserole dish. Add peas and carrots on top. In saucepan, mix and bring to boil broth and cream of chicken soup. In another bowl, combine melted margarine, salt, pepper, flour and milk. Mix thoroughly and form batter. Pour broth and soup mixture over chicken and vegetables in casserole dish. Spoon batter mixture over the top. Bake at 425° for 25-30 minutes. *Yield: 8-10 servings.*

Kathy Cooper
Lexington, SC

Chicken and Shrimp

1 pound large shrimp (shell and devein)
1 (10-ounce) package mushrooms, sliced
1 small onion, chopped
1 pound chicken cutlets (pounded and cut into strips)
   all-purpose flour
1/2 teaspoon salt
   salad or olive oil
1/2 cup dry white wine
2 tablespoons capers
1 1/4 cups water

In large skillet over medium heat, add 1 tablespoon of oil and cook mushrooms until golden. Remove to bowl. In same skillet add 2 tablespoons oil, cook shrimp and onions until opaque. Remove to bowl with mushrooms. In same skillet add 1 tablespoon oil and cook chicken, half at a time 2-3 minutes. Remove to same bowl. In same skillet heat 1 tablespoon oil, stir in 1 tablespoon flour; cook until it begins to brown slightly, stirring constantly. Add wine slowly, salt and 1 1/4 cups water. Heat until sauce boils and thickens; boil 1 minute. Return the chicken mixture to skillet; stir in capers (or add salt to taste) and heat through. *Yield: 6 servings.*

Betty Lee Phillips Brunson
Sumter, SC

149

Chicken Spectacular

3   cups cooked chicken, diced
1   medium onion, chopped
1   small jar chopped pimentos, drained
1   can water chestnuts, sliced
1   can cream of celery soup
1   cup light mayonnaise
1   can French green beans, drained
    grated sharp cheddar to cover dish
1   package Uncle Ben's Long Grain Wild Rice

Mix all ingredients together. Spread in large, sprayed baking dish. Grate enough medium sharp cheddar cheese to cover the top of the dish. Spread over top. Bake for 30 minutes at 350°. You may omit the cheese.

Gerselda T. Scircle
Lexington, SC
1995 First Lady Cookbook
The American Cancer Society
Reviewed Summer 1995
Sandlapper

Chinese Chicken Casserole

3   cups cooked chicken, chopped
1   package white and wild rice (cooked according to package directions using 2 1/2 cups juices from beans and chestnuts)
1   can cream of celery soup
1   small jar pimento (optional)
1   medium onion, chopped
1   bell pepper, chopped
2   cans French cut green beans, drained
1/2   cup mayonnaise
1   can water chestnuts, drained
    salt and pepper
1   small can onion rings (topping)

Mix all ingredients. Crumble onion rings on top. Pour into 3-quart casserole and bake 25-30 minutes at 350°. *Yield: 8 servings.*

Joan Todd
Walhalla, SC

Hawaiian Chicken

1 (32-ounce) can pineapple juice
1 (5 1/2-ounce) bottle soy sauce
4 1/2 ounces sherry
1 1/2 cups sugar
1 1/2 teaspoons garlic powder
8 boneless, skinless chicken breasts

Combine all ingredients and marinate 36-48 hours. Brush meat with oil. Grill over medium heat. DO NOT OVERCOOK! *Yield: 6-8 servings.*

Barbara Crosby
West Columbia, SC

Jambalaya

1	cup onions, diced
4	ounces bacon fat
1	bay leaf
1/4	teaspoon cayenne pepper
1/4	teaspoon thyme
1	teaspoon chopped garlic
1	cup flour
1 1/2	quarts hot water
1	cube beef bouillon
1	cube chicken bouillon
4	ounces margarine, melted
1/2	pound bacon - cooked (rendered), chopped
2	whole diced tomatoes
1 1/2	pounds boneless chicken breast
1	pound shrimp (36-40)
1	pound sausage, Hillshire Farms smoked
1/3	pound each trinity (green peppers/onions/celery)

Place flour in oven at 350° on a sheet pan. You want to brown the flour, Keep it moving. Look for tan color. Render bacon, save fat and chop the well-cooked bacon. Place bouillon cubes in hot water and dissolve. In a saucepan, place bacon fat and margarine. Melt. Place diced onions, bay leaf, thyme, cayenne and chopped garlic in saucepan. Lightly sauté. Do not burn garlic. Place brown flour in the saucepan on medium heat. You are now making roux. Mix with a wooden spoon until it becomes a paste. At a low simmer and with a whisk, add the water/bouillon mixture slowly into the saucepan whipping constantly so that no lumps form. Skim residue on the top as it slowly forms. In a sauté pan place enough margarine to sauté the trinity until translucent. Add shrimp, chicken and sausage until a little brown. Add diced tomatoes. Add enough sauce so that it is covered to simmer. Cook until chicken is done. *Yield: 8 servings.*

Tommy Condon's
Charleston, SC

Lemon Chicken

10	chicken breasts, cooked and shredded
2	cups sour cream
2	cans cream of chicken soup
	lemon juice to taste
1	small box Ritz crackers, crumbled
	poppy seeds to taste
1	stick oleo

In flat casserole place chicken. Mix sour cream and cream of chicken soup and lemon juice. Spread over chicken. Mix Ritz crackers, poppy seeds and sprinkle over top. Drizzle melted butter over all. Heat in moderate oven (325°) until brown and bubbly. Freezes beautifully. *Yield: 10 servings.*

Marguerite Garrett
Beaufort, SC

Easy Mexican Chicken Bake

4	boneless chicken breast halves
1	can Healthy Request cream of chicken soup
1	jar salsa
1	can black beans, rinsed and drained
1	cup grated cheddar cheese
	tortilla chips, crumbled

Combine soup, salsa and black beans in large casserole dish. Arrange chicken breasts in dish so that they are covered by soup mixture. Sprinkle tortilla chips over top of the dish, top this with grated cheddar cheese. Bake uncovered at 350° for 1 hour. *Yield: 4 servings.*

Trish DuBose
Columbia, SC

153

No Peek Chicken

2   **pounds skinless chicken breasts, washed**
     medium box Uncle Ben's Wild Rice cooked as directed
1   **can celery soup**
1   **can mushroom soup**
1   **can water**
1   **package Lipton Dry Onion Soup mix**

Heat celery soup, mushroom soup and water, stirring until smooth. Add to cooked rice. Use 9x13-inch baking dish. Spray with Pam. Pour rice mixture into baking dish, lay clean raw chicken on top. Sprinkle dry onion soup mix on top of chicken and cover with foil. Bake at 350° for approximately 1 1/2-2 hours until done. *Yield: 6 servings.*

Janice Gurley Shoemaker
Georgetown, SC

Carolina Pilau

1	(3 1/2 to 4-pound) chicken
2	quarts water
1/4	pound (1 stick) unsalted butter
1	large onion, chopped (about 1 1/2 cups)
2	cups chopped celery
2-3	large tomatoes (about 1 pound), peeled and chopped
1	tablespoon fresh thyme leaves or 1 teaspoon dried
1/2	teaspoon hot red pepper flakes
	Pure salt and freshly ground black pepper to taste
2	cups long-grain white rice

Cover the chicken with the water and boil in a large pot, uncovered, for 30 minutes. Remove the chicken from the broth and reserve the broth. Skin the chicken and remove the bones, pulling the meat from the bones. Cut the meat into uniformly sized pieces. Set aside. Melt the butter in a Dutch oven on top of the stove, then add the onions and celery and cook over medium heat until the onions start to brown, about 10 minutes. Add the tomatoes and their juice and the seasonings, adding a little more salt than you might think is necessary. Add the chicken meat, rice and one quart of the reserved broth. Cover, bring to a simmer and cook slowly, without lifting the lid, for 30 minutes.. Serve with a green salad and cornbread.
Yield: 8 servings.

Hoppin' John's Lowcountry Cooking
John Martin Taylor
Charleston, SC
Reprinted from Mid-Year 1992
Sandlapper

Pilau
(choice of chicken, sausage or shrimp)

2	cups chicken broth
1	cup rice
1/4	cup oil
1	pound chopped onions
2	cans crushed tomatoes
1	teaspoon salt
1	teaspoon sugar
1/4	teaspoon thyme
1/4	teaspoon cayenne
1/4	teaspoon cumin
2	pounds cleaned shrimp OR
1	pound smoked sausage OR
1	whole chicken cut into pieces

Cook onions in oil for 10 minutes or until tender. Add tomatoes and spice. Simmer until thick. Add choice of meat. Cook for 20 minutes. Add broth and rice. (If using shrimp, add shrimp with broth and rice.) Cover and simmer for 1 hour. Stir carefully, once. *Yield: 6-8 servings.*

Barbara Crosby
West Columbia, SC

Portugese Chicken

6	large chicken breasts
	salt and pepper to taste
	paprika to taste
	garlic powder to taste
1	large onion, chopped
1	large green pepper, chopped
1/3	cup ketchup
1/3	cup orange juice
2	tablespoons soy sauce
1	teaspoon dry mustard
1	tablespoon flour
	orange slices

Place chicken in a casserole dish and sprinkle with salt, pepper, paprika and garlic powder. Top with onion and green pepper. Combine ketchup, orange juice, soy sauce, dry mustard and flour. Pour over chicken. Bake at 350° for 50 minutes. Add orange slices and cook 10 more minutes.

Sally Lightsey-Jones
Greenwood, SC

Farmers Hall Restaurant's Chicken Reuben

4   **deboned and skinned chicken breasts**
1/3   **cup all-purpose flour**
4   **tablespoons margarine**
4   **tablespoons thousand island dressing**
4   **tablespoons sauerkraut**
4   **slices Swiss cheese**

Flatten chicken with a meat mallet. Dust both sides with flour. Melt margarine in a skillet and sauté chicken on both sides until brown. Remove from skillet and spread 1 tablespoon of dressing on each chicken breast. Spread 1 tablespoon of sauerkraut evenly over each chicken breast. Top each with a slice of Swiss cheese. Place on a greased baking sheet and bake in a preheated 375° oven for 20 minutes. *Yield: 4 servings.*

Dawn O'Brien
Charlotte, NC

Ritz Cracker Chicken

1   **roll of Ritz crackers, crushed finely**
6   **chicken breasts**
    aluminum foil
    Pam

Wash and salt chicken (salt lightly). Roll in Ritz cracker crumbs. Spray aluminum foil with Pam. Lay chicken in foil and seal to keep in steam. Bake at 300° 2 hours. *Yield: 6 servings.*

Margaret Duffell
Starr, SC

B.B. Newlin's Sage Chicken

1   2 1/2 to 3 1/2 pound whole chicken, cut in half and wings cut off (wash and pat dry)
1/3-1/2 cup salt
2   tablespoons ground sage
1/2   teaspoon garlic powder (optional)
16   ounces water warm enough to dissolve the salt

Dissolve the salt and sage in the water. Light your grill, gas or charcoal, until ready to cook. Put the chicken halves on the grill with the wings away from the heat, since they cook the fastest. Cook for 15 minutes. Begin to baste with the salt mixture and turn every 10 minutes until the leg moves freely. This recipe may seem salty, but the chicken absorbs very little and the baste gives a crispy juicy taste. Can be doubled, tripled, etc. *Yield: 3-4 servings.*

Reid Morrow
Cheraw, SC

Turkey Sausage

4   pounds turkey breasts, ground raw
1   teaspoon red pepper
1   teaspoon sage
1/4   teaspoon black pepper
1/2   teaspoon oregano
1   teaspoon salt (or less)

Mix well by hand. Form 16 patties. Spray pan with Pam. Cook on medium low heat until golden brown on both sides. *Yield: 16 servings.*

Janice Gurley Shoemaker
Georgetown, SC

Barbecue Turkey Breast

1	turkey breast
1	pint cider vinegar
1	stick margarine
3	tablespoon Worcestershire
3	tablespoons ketchup
2	tablespoons salt
2	tablespoons pepper
2	tablespoons garlic powder
2	large onions, chopped
1/4-1/2	small bottle hot Texas Pete (optional)

Bring all ingredients to a boil. Put breast in and turn several times to coat. Turn heat down to simmer and cook 2 hours or until meat starts to come off bone. Let cool in liquid until you can handle breast. Shred all meat from bones. Pour all of liquid over meat.

Ella Calvert Bouknight
Lexington, SC

BBQ Turkey Breast

1	turkey breast
2	cups cider vinegar
3	tablespoons Worcestershire sauce
3	tablespoons ketchup
2	tablespoons Texas Pete
1	tablespoon mustard
1	tablespoon salt
1	tablespoon black pepper

Simmer all ingredients except turkey for 10 minutes. Place turkey in sauce pot. Cover and cook slowly for 3 hours, turning every 30 minutes. Remove skin and all bones. Shred turkey into remaining sauce and toss well. Serve on buns or rolls.

Anne Brunson Thomas
Sumter, SC

Pork

Broccoli and Ham

1	(10-ounce) package chopped frozen broccoli
12	slices loaf bread
12	slices sharp American cheese
3	cups diced, cooked ham
6	eggs, lightly beaten
3 1/2	cups milk
2	tablespoons dry minced onion
1/2	teaspoon salt
1/2	teaspoon dry mustard

Cook broccoli according to package directions, drain. Cut bread with doughnut cutter, reserving holes and doughnuts. Break remaining bread into bite size pieces and place in 13x9x2-inch pan. Arrange layers of ham, cheese, broccoli over bread pieces. Top with reserved doughnuts and holes. Combine remaining ingredients. Best to sprinkle onion, salt, mustard over the bread then pour eggs and milk mixture over all layers. Cover, refrigerate for 6 hours or overnight. Bake at 325° for 35 minutes. *Yield: 12 servings.*

Nancy Sherer
Starr, SC

Horse-Shay Grits

6	or more pieces of bacon
2	medium green peppers, chopped
2	medium onions, chopped
1 1/2	cups ground ham or turkey
6-8	tomatoes
1 1/2	cups dry grits

Fry bacon. Crumble and set aside. Add onions and peppers to bacon grease and cook until soft, stirring often. Add ham or turkey and tomatoes in a pot and simmer 30 minutes. In separate pot cook grits. Stir in cooked tomatoes and ham or turkey, then peppers and onions. Pour in square or oblong dish. Top with bacon. Serve with Rooster Spur Vinegar if desired. (Can use regular hot pepper vinegar.) *Yield: 6 servings.*

Lucille Cudd
Chester, SC

Church Ladies' Ham Loaf

2 1/4	pounds ground beef
1/2	pound ground smoked ham (not country ham)
2	large eggs
2	cups soft bread crumbs
1	cup evaporated milk
2	teaspoons salt
1/4	teaspoon ground white pepper
1	can chicken gumbo soup
1/4	teaspoon liquid smoke (optional)

Sauce:

1	cup dark brown sugar
1	cup tomato or V8 juice
1	teaspoon dry mustard
2	tablespoons cider vinegar

Combine loaf ingredients, taking care not to overwork meat. Form into a large oval loaf. Place into 9x13-inch foil-lined pan sprayed with Pam. Combine sauce ingredients, make sure sugar and mustard are dissolved. Dip 1/4 of the sauce onto meat. Bake for 1 1/2 hours, basting with sauce every 30 minutes.

Appetizers: Form into 1 1/2 inch balls, place in baking pan so they don't touch. Save 1/2 cup sauce. Bake 1 hour. Remove to heated serving receptacle, pour reserved sauce over and serve with picks. Tiny sweet pickles are good on the side. *Yield: 20 plates or 70-100 appetizers.*

Barbara J. Manka
Salem, SC

161

Pennsylvania Dutch Scrapple

2	pounds pork shoulder
1	(14-ounce) can beef broth
1/2	teaspoon salt
1/8	teaspoon black pepper
1	medium onion, chopped fine
1	teaspoon dried sage
1	tablespoon minced parsley
1	cup water
1 1/4	cups corn meal (yellow)
	flour and Crisco for frying

Simmer pork in broth along with everything from salt through parsley until meat falls apart, 2 1/2 or more hours. Remove meat with slotted spoon. Reserve broth. Discard fat, bones and gristle. Mince meat well in processor. Return to broth. Mix corn meal with water. Add some broth, stir then add all corn meal to meat and broth. Cook gently until very thick. (Can use double boiler.) Takes about 1 hour. Pour into loaf pans. Chill. When cold, unmold. Slice about 3/4-inch thick. Dredge with flour and fry in hot fat until crisp. Can serve with fried eggs. Can wrap and freeze slices. *Yield: 10-12 servings.*

Mary P. Case
Hilton Head Island, SC

Arlene's Pork and Chili

Pork in chili sauce is served at the Roadside Grille with Spanish rice, refried beans and flour tortillas.

Chili Sauce:
1   clove garlic, finely ground
4   Serrano chili peppers (2 1/2 -
     3 inches long), finely
     chopped
2   cups canned tomatoes,
     diced, in the juice
1 1/2 tablespoons oregano
     (Mexican, if available)
1/2   cup water

Spanish Rice:
Blend together and set aside:
1   clove garlic, finely ground
2/3 cup minced onion
1   cup canned tomatoes, diced
1   cup of the canned tomato
     juice
1/4 cup chili ancho (processed)
1/4 cup chili cascabel
     (processed)
6   chicken bouillon cubes

Bring chili sauce to a boil and then decrease heat to simmer. Add chunks of well trimmed pork (about 2 pounds). Simmer about 1/2 hour.

In heavy frying pan (preferably cast iron) on medium flame
1/4   cup oil - let oil get hot
2 1/2 cups Uncle Ben's long grain
     rice
Stir constantly with a wooden spoon until rice is brown.

Remove from flame, add prepared rice mixture and also add:
1   tablespoon salt
1   teaspoon pepper
2-3 celery leaves (left on the
     stalk)
7   cups hot water

Simmer uncovered until rice is cooked and water is gone. Mix a few times to see if more water is needed. If additional water is needed, be sure to add hot water. *Yield: 6 servings.*

Linda Peavy
Roadside Grille
York, SC

163

Baked Pork Chops

6   2-inch rib chops with pocket
    salt, pepper
1   (8-ounce) package herb
    stuffing
1   (3-ounce) can sliced
    mushrooms

Preheat oven to 350°. Season inside of pork chop pockets with salt and pepper. Fill pork chops with stuffing and mushrooms. Close with a pick. Arrange rest of stuffing between the pork chops and bake in covered casserole for 45 minutes. Brown without cover 15 minutes. May be cooked ahead and browned just before serving. *Yield: 6 servings.*

Dudley Williams
Columbia, SC

Pork Chops with Gravy

8   pork chops
2   tablespoons vinegar
1   can cream of chicken soup
1   soup can water
    brown sugar

Brown pork chops in butter or oil. Arrange in baking dish. Mix next 3 ingredients; pour over pork chops. Sprinkle with brown sugar. Cover with foil or lid. Bake at 350° for 1 hour. Serve with rice or dressing. *Yield: 4-6 servings.*

Barbara S. Lux
Lexington, SC

Pork Tenderloin

pork tenderloins (usually 2 come
    in one package)
1/2 cup honey
1/4 cup Dijon mustard
1/4 cup lemon juice
1/4 cup soy sauce
2   garlic cloves, crushed

Combine and pour over meat. Let marinate several hours. Grill over hot coals approximately 30 minutes or until no longer pink in center. *Yield: 6-10 servings.*

Dawn B. Gates
Camden, SC

Yella Gal

2   cans seasoned, chopped
      tomatoes
1   pound mild bulk sausage,
      ground
1   pound hot bulk sausage,
      ground
1   pepper (green),
      chopped/diced
1   onion (medium), diced
1 1/2   cups rice

Sauté pepper and onion. Brown sausage and drain. Put rice in double boiler on medium heat. Add tomatoes. Do not mix. Cook approximately 10 minutes. Place sausage, onion, pepper mixture on top (do not stir). Cover and cook on low until rice is cooked. Add additional seasoning if desired; then mix. *Yield: 8 servings.*

Charles White
Winter Haven, FL

Sausage-Stuffed Apples

4   baking apples
1/2   pound bulk pork sausage
      salt and pepper

Wash and core apples, leaving a large cavity. Lightly sprinkle inside of apples with salt and pepper. Place in an 8-inch square baking dish. Stuff apples with sausage. Bake at 350° for 30 minutes or until sausage is done. *Yield: 4 servings.*

Dudley Williams
Columbia, SC

Sausage Casserole

1   pound hot sausage (Clyde
      Cone sausage)
1   large bell pepper
1   rib of celery
1   package dry chicken noodle
      soup mix
4 1/2   cups water
1/2   cup rice

Brown meat and drain. Add pepper and celery. Cook until vegetables are tender. Set aside. Boil soup, water and rice 7 minutes. Add sausage mixture to this. Cook at 350° for 45 minutes. *Yield: 4 servings.*

Betsy Cone
Leesville, SC

Sausage Pie

Crust:

2 1/2	cups Bisquick
1/2	cup onion, chopped
5	eggs, beaten
1/2	cup milk
3	tablespoons sesame seeds

Whisk eggs and milk, add Bisquick, sesame seeds and onion. Mix until moistened.

Filling:

2 1/2	pounds sausage, cooked
16	ounces cheddar cheese, shredded
12	ounces cottage cheese
12	ounces cream cheese
5	eggs

Cook sausage and drain. Soften cream cheese, add to sausage. Add cottage cheese, cheddar cheese and eggs. Spray 3 10-inch pie plates with Pam. Pour 1/2 cup batter and spread on bottom. Divide filling between 3 pans. Pour 1/2 cup batter on top of filling and spread evenly. Cook at 350° for 35 minutes or until golden brown. *Yield: 18 servings.*

Sherri Weaver
1837 Bed & Breakfast/Tea Room
Charleston, SC

Easy and Delicious Sausage Rice

4   cups water
1   package Lipton's Chicken Noodle Soup mix
1 1/2 cups raw rice
1   pound sausage
1   medium onion, chopped
1   bell pepper, chopped
     lemon pepper and salt to taste

Bring water to boil then add soup mix, rice, lemon pepper and salt. Bring to a boil again and turn down heat to low, cover and cook 30 minutes. Stir and set aside. Brown sausage and drain. Sauté chopped onion and bell pepper in small amount of sausage grease. Mix with sausage then mix with rice. *Yield: 4 servings.*

Butler Roberson Mappus
Charleston, SC

Wild Rice and Sausage Supreme

1   pound bulk sausage (I use sage flavored.)
2   cups coarsely chopped celery
1   small whole onion, chopped
2   (4-ounce) cans mushrooms, drained (I use stems and pieces.)
1   (2-ounce) jar chopped pimento, drained
2   (10 1/2-ounce) cans condensed mushroom soup
1   clove minced garlic
2   (14 1/2-ounce) cans chicken broth
1 1/2 cups grated sharp cheddar cheese
1/2   teaspoon each marjoram, basil, thyme, sage, poultry seasoning
1 1/2 cups uncooked rinsed wild rice
     salt and pepper to taste

Crumble and brown sausage and drain. Mix all ingredients together in greased or sprayed large casserole. Bake covered about 1 1/2 hours at 325°. If too dry, add more broth and heat a little longer. May be reheated in microwave covered. May be frozen. Sometimes I divide and freeze. Wonderful for a pot luck! *Yield: 12 servings.*

Patty West
McCormick, SC

167

Venison BBQ

1	venison ham
1	small Boston butt
1	onion, quartered
	salt
	pepper
	BBQ sauce

Salt and pepper meat. Pour just enough water in crock pot to cover bottom. Place meat and onion in crock pot and cook on medium heat for 6-8 hours. Remove meat from crock pot and discard drippings. Shred meat with a fork and return to pot. Pour sauce over meat and stir. Serve over rice or as sandwiches. *Yield: 6-8 servings.*

BBQ Sauce:

1	cup ketchup
1/2	cup mustard
1/2	cup apple cider vinegar
1/4	cup honey
1/4	cup dark brown sugar
3-4	dashes Tabasco
3-4	dashes Worcestershire
1	teaspoon red pepper flakes
	pepper to taste
1/4	cup vegetable oil

Mix ingredients over low heat until ready to use.

Rob Gates
Camden, SC

Sauces

Simply Wonderful Baste for Grilling Meat

honey
kosher salt
coarse black pepper
crushed red pepper flakes

Mix ingredients to suit your taste. Baste beef, pork or chicken while grilling outdoors. Works especially well when using rotisserie. Keeps well when mixed ahead of time.

E. Guy Shealy, Jr.
Batesburg-Leesville, SC

Harry's Bar-B-Q Sauce

1	quart prepared mustard
1	tablespoon dry mustard
1	tablespoon salt
1	tablespoon sugar
1	tablespoon black pepper
1/2	teaspoon ground red pepper
1	cup vinegar
1	cup water
1	stick margarine

Melt margarine, add all other ingredients, mix well. Cook slowly for 10 minutes. Keeps well in refrigerator.

Harry Hite
Lexington Landmark Recipes
Lexington Woman's Club
Reviewed Winter 1997-98
Sandlapper

Barbeque Marinade for Chicken

1/2	cup oil
3/4	cup soy sauce
1/4	cup Worcestershire sauce
2	tablespoons dry mustard
2 1/4	teaspoons salt
1	tablespoon black pepper
1/2	cup wine vinegar
1 1/2	teaspoons parsley
1/8	teaspoon garlic
1/3	cup lemon juice

Mix well. Pour over chicken and marinate for 24 hours. *Yield: approximately 2 1/2 cups marinade.*

Thomas K. Perry
Newberry, SC

Barbeque Sauce for Turkey

1/2	cup salad oil
3/4	cup ketchup
1/3	cup lemon juice
3	tablespoons Worcestershire
1/2	teaspoon pepper
1	teaspoon paprika
2/3	cup cider vinegar
1	teaspoon cayenne pepper
3/4	cup chopped onion
3/4	cup water
3	tablespoons sugar
2	teaspoons salt

Place ingredients in blender. Blend 1-2 minutes. Makes 1 quart. Use sauce to baste 1/2 turkey on the grill or turkey breast baked in the oven. Use remainder as a dipping sauce.

Nancy W. Ragin
Surfside Beach, SC

Tanner's Seasoning with Muscle

3	cups iodized free flowing salt
2	ounces ground black pepper
2	ounces ground red pepper
1	ounce garlic powder
1	ounce MSG
1	teaspoon chili powder
1	teaspoon powdered thyme
2	teaspoons sweet basil

Place all ingredients in large bowl and mix well. You may run it through a sifter if desired. Use as you would salt when seasoning any meats or seafood. Store in shaker container in cool, dry place.

P.J. Tanner
Bluffton, SC

Vegetables and Fruits

Vegetables

Asparagus-Green Pea Casserole

2 cups Keebler Toll House
  crackers, crushed
1/2 pound cheese, grated
1 can asparagus (save juice)
1 can small green peas
1 can golden cream of
  mushroom soup
1/2 cup slivered almonds
1/2 cup margarine, melted

Grate cheese and mix well with cracker crumbs. Add liquid from asparagus to mushroom soup. Put a layer of cracker crumbs in a casserole dish that has been sprayed with Pam. Add a layer of peas and asparagus. Sprinkle with almonds. Cover with part of soup mixture. Repeat layer ending with layer of cheese and crackers on top. Pour melted butter on top and bake at 350° for about 30 minutes. *Yield: 4-6 servings.*

Joan Todd
Walhalla, SC

Asparagus Casserole

2 cans cut asparagus, drained
3 boiled eggs, sliced
1 cup (approximate) cheddar
  cheese, grated
1 small can sliced mushrooms
1 can Campbell's Cream of
  Mushroom soup
  crushed cracker crumbs
  (optional)

Place cut asparagus in small casserole/baking dish. Sprinkle grated cheddar cheese over asparagus until generously covered. Next, layer with sliced boiled eggs; then sprinkle the sliced mushrooms over eggs. Cover layers with cream of mushroom soup, smoothed over to edges of dish. Top with grated Cheese. Bake at 350° until bubbly (approximately 20 minutes). Easy and quick. Great served with brown rice and pork chops. *Yield: 8 servings.*

Fairey Belle Logan
Columbia, SC

Asparagus Casserole

1	can chopped asparagus
1	can cream of mushroom soup
1	tablespoon mayonnaise buttered Ritz crackers
2	boiled eggs, chopped
1	cup cheese, grated

Place asparagus in bottom of casserole dish. Add mushroom soup and mayonnaise over asparagus. Place chopped eggs next, then cover with grated cheese. Cover with buttered, crushed crackers. Bake at 350° until casserole bubbles (approximately 20-25 minutes). *Yield: 6 servings.*

Marie C. High
Spartanburg, SC

Asparagus Casserole

2	large cans asparagus (reserve liquid)
1/2	cup slivered almonds

Sauce:

4	tablespoons butter
4	tablespoons flour
1/2	cup milk
2/3	cup asparagus juice
1/2	cup mayonnaise
1/2	cup cracker crumbs

Make sauce with butter, flour, milk and asparagus juice. Cook until thick. Remove from heat and blend in mayonnaise. In casserole dish place layers of asparagus. Pour sauce over. Sprinkle crumbs and almonds on top. Heat 30 minutes in a 300° oven. *Yield: 6 servings.*

Annie C. Stenhouse
Simpsonville, SC

173

Sandlapper Cooks

Asparagus Casserole Soufflé

1   can asparagus; reserve
     liquid
1 1/2 cups grated cheese, medium
     Ritz crackers
2-2 1/2 cups milk
     toasted almonds

Butter casserole dish. Crush Ritz crackers to cover the bottom of the dish. Layer asparagus and cheese, then another thin layer of Ritz crackers. Heat asparagus liquid in pot; add milk to this and scald. Pour this over mixture. Add toasted almonds on top–dots of butter also. Bake at 350° about 25 minutes or until golden. Serve immediately while casserole is still puffed and bubbly. *Yield: 6-8 servings.*

Judy Lewis Wells
Columbia, SC
Reprinted from January/
February 1990
Sandlapper

Cassina Point Asparagus

Blanch fresh asparagus in chicken stock until just tender. Drain and cool.

Sherry Vinaigrette Sauce:
1   chopped shallot
1   minced garlic clove
1   cup good olive oil
1/4 cup sherry vinegar
1   teaspoon fresh-squeezed
     lemon juice
1   teaspoon salt
1   teaspoon freshly ground
     black pepper

Blend all ingredients well and ladle appropriate amount over asparagus. Garnish with fresh local tomatoes (if available) and red pepper strips.

Philip Bardin
Edisto Island, SC
Reprinted from May/June 1990
Sandlapper

Artichoke Hearts and Tomatoes

2	(1-pound) cans sliced tomatoes
2	(1-pound) cans artichoke hearts, cut up
1/3	cup onion, chopped
2	tablespoons green onions
1	stick butter or oleo
1/2	teaspoon leaf basil
2	tablespoons sugar

Preheat oven to 325°. Grease casserole dish. Drain tomatoes. Drain and rinse artichoke hearts. Sauté onions and green onions in butter. Add tomatoes, artichoke hearts, basil and sugar to onion mixture. Heat a few minutes until bubbly. Turn into casserole. Heat in oven 15-20 minutes. Elegant company vegetable, but quick and easy. *Yield: 6-8 servings.*

Bonnie Coward
Aiken, Sc

Baked Beans Supreme

1	pound cooked hamburger meat, drained
1	large can pork and beans, drained
1	cup brown sugar
1	small bottle ketchup
1	small onion, chopped
1/2	cup Karo syrup
1	tablespoon Worcestershire sauce
2	tablespoons Heinz 57 sauce
1	dash chili powder
	salt and pepper to taste
2	tablespoons mustard
	garlic salt to taste
1	small can crushed pineapple, drained

Mix together all ingredients. Cook 350° degrees for 45 minutes. *Yield: 12 servings.*

Jan Robison
Anderson, SC

175

Broccoli Casserole

2	boxes frozen, chopped broccoli, cooked as directed and drained
3/4	stick butter
1	cup mayonnaise
1	medium onion, chopped fine
2	eggs, slightly beaten
1	can cream of mushroom soup
1	cup grated sharp cheese

Mix and top with crumbled Ritz crackers. Bake 350° for 1/2 hour. *Yield: 8 servings.*

Maro Rogers
Lexington, SC

Broccoli Supreme

1	large bunch fresh broccoli, chopped and steamed
1	can English peas, drained
1	can Chinese vegetables, drained
1	can sliced water chestnuts
1	cup mayonnaise
1	can cream of mushroom soup
1	cup sharp cheddar cheese, grated
1	medium onion, chopped finely
3/4	cup bread crumbs, buttered

Drain broccoli, if necessary. Place layers of broccoli, English peas, Chinese vegetables and water chestnuts in a greased casserole dish. Mix the mayonnaise, mushroom soup, cheese and onion together. Heat this mixture until the cheese melts. Pour it over the layered items. Top with bread crumbs. Bake at 350° for 30 minutes. *Yield: 6-8 servings.*

Sarah Bowman Cooper
Spartanburg, SC

176

Baked Cabbage

4	cups shredded cabbage
1	tablespoon dill
1 1/2	teaspoons salt
1/2	teaspoon pepper
1	tablespoon sugar
1	large egg
1/2	cup flour
1	quart milk
1	tablespoon butter, melted

Preheat oven to 350°. In a large mixing bowl combine cabbage, dill, salt, pepper and sugar. Transfer to a 9x13-inch well-greased baking pan. In another bowl beat egg, then add flour and milk; mix until smooth. Pour over the cabbage; drizzle butter on top. Bake for 1 hour, uncovered, until nicely browned. If too brown at the 45 minute mark, cover with foil and continue baking. Cool for 10 minutes; cut into squares or spoon out. Its texture will be somewhat like hash browns--crisp outside and creamy inside. *Yield: 8-10 servings.*

Peggy and Jim Waller
The Inn at Merridun
Union, SC

Authentic German Red Cabbage

3 1/2 - 4 pounds red cabbage	
2	apples
1	tablespoon butter
1	medium onion
2	cups water
1/2	cup red wine vinegar
1/2	cup sugar
1/2	teaspoon salt
1/2	teaspoon pepper
2	cloves
1	bay leaf
juice of 1/2 lemon	
1 1/2	tablespoons flour

Wash cabbage. Cut up as you would for coleslaw. Peel and slice apples. Melt butter in large pot. Add apples and onions. Sauté gently for 3-5 minutes. Stir in water, vinegar, sugar, salt, pepper, cloves, bay leaf and lemon juice. Bring to a boil. Add cabbage and mix well. Cover and simmer. Should take about 45 minutes. Sprinkle flour over top. Cover and simmer 5 minutes. Mix well and cook 5 minutes longer.

Patricia W. Rawl
Lexington Landmark Recipes
Lexington Woman's Club
Reviewed Winter 1997/98
Sandlapper

177

Carrot Pudding

2	**(15-ounce) cans sliced carrots**
3/4	**cup sugar**
1/2	**stick oleo, melted**
1	**cup milk**
2	**eggs or 1/2 cup egg substitute**
2	**heaping tablespoons plain flour**
1	**teaspoon baking powder**
1/2	**teaspoon cinnamon**

Drain carrots. Mash them with a ricer. Add sugar to the carrots. Make a paste of the flour, cinnamon and some of the milk. Set aside. Add baking powder to the carrots. Beat the eggs and add to the carrots. Mix the paste and remaining milk into the carrots. Mix well. Add the melted oleo and mix well again. Pour into 8x8-inch casserole and bake at 350° for 1 hour or less if in larger, flatter dish. This casserole goes extremely well with beef, pork, chicken and turkey. *Yield: 6 servings.*

Davy-Jo Stribling Ridge
Columbia, SC

Carrots

4	**carrots**
1	**tablespoon butter**
1	**can mandarin oranges, drained**

Cut peeled carrots diagonally, 1/4-inch thick. Cook briefly in a pressure cooker. Do not over cook. Drain off cooking liquid. Add mandarin oranges, toss lightly with butter. *Yield: 2 servings.*

Juanita F. Dodds
Chester, SC

Corn Casserole

1	can whole kernel corn, drained
1	can cream corn
2	eggs, beaten
1	small onion, chopped (can be omitted)
1	cup Jiffy corn muffin mix (substitutions are not as good)
1/2	stick melted butter or margarine

Mix all ingredients and pour into a 2 quart pan. Bake at 350° for 1 hour. This is an easy dish to prepare and is delicious served with all meats. *Yield: 6 servings.*

Patricia Clark
Birmingham, AL

Corn Pudding

3	eggs
1/2	cup sugar
1/3	cup flour
1	(5-ounce) can evaporated milk
1	cup milk
1	teaspoon salt
1	(17-ounce) can whole kernel corn
1	(17-ounce) can creamed corn
1/2	stick margarine

Beat eggs. Add sugar and salt. In separate bowl, stir milks and flour together, then add to the egg mixture. Stir in the corns. Pour into a greased casserole dish and dot with margarine. Bake at 325° until golden and firming (about 1 hour). *Yield: 8 servings.*

Sarah Bowman Cooper
Spartanburg, SC

Corn Pudding

3	eggs, beaten
3	tablespoons flour
1/2	cup sugar
2	cups milk
2	cups Mexican corn, drained
1/2	teaspoon salt
1/2	stick butter

Melt butter in dish. Add other ingredients. Bake at 400° for 45-60 minutes. *Yield: 6 servings.*

Daisy Wessinger
Lexington, SC

Eggplant Casserole

1	large eggplant
1 1/2	cups saltine crackers, crumbled
1	egg
1	cup milk
1/2	cup cheese, grated
1	(7-8-ounce) can minced clams
1	tablespoon margarine

Cook eggplant until tender in small amount of water. Drain. Add margarine and a dash of salt and pepper. Add other ingredients except grated cheese. Mix well. Pour into buttered casserole dish. Sprinkle grated cheese on top. Bake 30 minutes at 400°. *Yield: 6 servings.*

Sarah Bowman Cooper
Spartanburg, SC

New Year's Day Collard Greens

2	large bunches collard greens
2	tablespoons olive oil
1	can diced tomatoes with Italian seasonings
3	cloves garlic, crushed
1	onion, chopped
4-5	slices bacon, diced
	salt and pepper

Wash greens thoroughly. Devein greens and chop. The easiest way to chop the greens is to stack several leaves, roll length-wise and slice (as you would a roll of cookie dough). In a large pot heat the olive oil over medium heat. Add bacon and onions, fry until onions are tender. Add garlic and tomatoes, let heat several minutes. Add greens, salt and pepper and toss to coat in seasonings. Reduce heat to medium-low, cover and cook until tender, stirring occasionally. These greens are great on New Year's Day with pork roast, black-eyed peas and cornbread. *Yield: 8 servings.*

Dawn B. Gates
Camden, SC

Collard Greens

1	pound fresh stuffed pork sausage, chopped in 1-inch links
2-3	pounds collard greens
1/2	cup boiling water (or sausage broth)
3	tablespoons bacon fat (or substitute vegetable oil, margarine or bouillon cubes)
1/4	teaspoon salt
1/4	teaspoon black pepper
1/2	teaspoon sugar

Cook sausage in water for about 30 minutes. Remove from broth. Use broth for water in cooking collards. Select crisp, fresh, tender collards. Strip leaves from stem. Keep outer leaves separate. Wash thoroughly in several changes of warm water. Add a small amount of salt to the last water. Chop into 2-3-inch lengths. Place outer leaves in saucepan with 1-inch water, salt and pepper. Cover and cook for 10 minutes. Add a few leaves at a time. Cook for 10-20 minutes or until tender. Do not overcook! Remove from heat; sprinkle sugar over top of collards. Serve with sausage as a side dish.

Rawl Family Recipes
Sue Rawl Wingard
Lexington, SC
Reprinted from Spring 1993
Sandlapper

Creamy Gourmet Grits

	stone ground grits
	cream
	chicken broth
	milk
	butter
	bacon grease

For example:

3	cups liquid
3/4	cup grits

Equal parts of cream, chicken broth and milk. Do not use low fat or cut back. Add butter and bacon grease for flavor. Rich and wonderful. *Yield: 8 servings.*

Janice S. Creasy
Palmyra, VA

Great Grits

1	cup grits, uncooked
1	(16-ounce) can tomatoes, chopped
6	slices bacon, cooked and crumbled
1/2	cup bell pepper, finely chopped
8	ounces sharp cheddar cheese, grated
1/2	cup onion, finely chopped
1	teaspoon chili powder
1/2	teaspoon salt

Prepare grits according to package. Mix all ingredients together, except cheese, in a greased 2 quart casserole dish. Bake at 400° for 50 minutes. Sprinkle on cheese and bake 10 more minutes.

Julia Gentles
Gates, Gaits and Golden Plates
Camden Junior Welfare League
Reviewed Summer 1997
Sandlapper
and
Mary Shaw
The Shaw House B&B
Georgetown, SC

Grits Cake with Black Bean Sauce

Cake:
left-over, cooked, whole-grain grits (enough for 4 patties)
egg wash (2 eggs and 1/4 cup milk)
1   cup flour
1   tablespoon salt
1   tablespoon pepper
        butter

Form *cold* grits into equal-sized patties. Dip carefully into the egg wash and dust lightly with a mixture of the three dry ingredients. Be careful not to break the patties. In a stick-proof sauté pan, sauté the patties in butter over medium heat. Turn once with spatula (about 1 1/2 minutes each side, until a golden color is achieved). On individual plates, coat the bottoms with warm black bean sauce (recipe follows). Place patty above. Fresh sautéed shrimp or left-over fresh boiled and peeled shrimp are a suitable garnish. *Yield: 4 servings.*

Sauce:
1/4   cup dried black beans, rinsed
4   cups strong chicken stock
1/2   cup fresh jalapeno/tomato salsa (store-bought Picante sauce can be substituted)
1   teaspoon salt
1   teaspoon pepper

Cook all ingredients over medium heat until beans are tender and sauce has thickened. (If sauce becomes too thick, dilute with heavy cream.)

Philip Bardin
Edisto Island, SC
Reprinted from May/June 1990
Sandlapper

Baked Hominy

1	quart milk
1/2	cup butter
1/3	cup butter
1	cup plain grits
1	teaspoon salt
1	teaspoon pepper
1	cup Gruyere cheese
1/3	cup grated Parmesán cheese

Combine milk, grits and 1/2 cup butter in saucepan. Cook until smooth, then add salt and pepper. Beat 5 minutes with electric mixer. Pour into 13x9-inch casserole dish and cool. Cut into rectangular pieces and arrange in buttered casserole. Sprinkle with 1/3 cup butter and cheeses. Bake 30-35 minutes at 400°.

Rachel C. MacRae
Charleston Receipts Repeats
Junior League of Charleston
Reviewed Autumn 1995
Sandlapper

Sautéed Mushroom Caps

fresh mushrooms
butter

Clean mushrooms, remove stems and discard. Melt butter over medium heat in skillet. Add mushroom caps and lightly sauté on tops and bottoms. Serve immediately.

Dudley Williams
Columbia, SC

Grilled Portabello Mushrooms

Marinate 4-6 Portabello mushrooms (5" diameter with stems removed) in the following:

2	cups oil
2	sprigs rosemary
1	teaspoon salt
1	teaspoon black pepper
1	teaspoon garlic

Vinaigrette:

3	tablespoons balsamic vinegar
1	teaspoon olive oil
1	teaspoon brown sugar
	dash salt
	dash pepper

Mix all ingredients for marinade in shallow pie pan. Place mushrooms and pour marinade over and let marinade for 1-2 hours or overnight. Mushrooms will absorb most of the marinade. Grill mushrooms 5-8 minutes per side, until tender. Remove, slice and top with balsamic vinaigrette. Garnish with goat's cheese and serve on a bed of gourmet greens.

Chef Kish
82 Queen St.
Charleston, SC

Noodle Pudding Soufflé

3	eggs, separated
1/2	cup melted butter
2	tablespoons sugar
1	pound creamed cottage cheese
1	cup sour cream
1/2	pound medium cooked noodles
1/2	cup corn flakes, crushed butter

Beat egg yolks. Add melted butter and sugar; fold in cottage cheese, sour cream and noodles. Fold in stiffly beaten egg whites. Place in 2 quart buttered casserole and sprinkle top with crushed corn flakes. Dot with butter. Bake 45 minutes in a 375° oven. *Yield: 8 servings.*

Ann Warshaw
Walterboro, SC

Cooked Green Onions

10-12	green onions
1/4	cup water
	bouillon cube (optional)
1/8	teaspoon salt
1/8	teaspoon black pepper
1	tablespoon vegetable oil (or margarine)

Select uniform onions; trim off roots and all leaves except 3 inches of green top. Slit onions; wash thoroughly; cook in water 5 minutes. Drain. Add oil, salt, bouillon and pepper. Cook 5-10 minutes. Remove from heat; pour into bowl. Serve. Variation: While onions are hot, pour 2 tablespoons vinegar over onions. Will taste like pickled onions. Delicious with vegetables.

Rawl Family Recipes
Sue Rawl Wingard
Lexington, SC
Reprinted from Spring 1993
Sandlapper

Creamed Onions

2	cups cooked, small white onions
1	(10 3/4-ounce) can cream of mushroom soup
3/4	cup sharp cheddar cheese
3/4	cup cracker crumbs
2	tablespoons melted butter

Place cooked and drained onions in 1 1/2 quart dish. Mix soup and cheese, pour over onions. Top with buttered cracker crumbs. Bake at 350° for 20 minutes or until bubbling. Goes great with Thanksgiving turkey! *Yield: 6-8 servings.*

Hint: Use a bag of these peeled, small white onions. You will find them in the frozen food section of your grocery store.

Dawn B. Gates
Camden, SC

Easy Stuffed Green Peppers

6	medium green peppers
1	teaspoon salt
1/8	teaspoon pepper
1	tablespoon Worcestershire
1/3	cup precooked rice
1	egg, beaten
1	(10-ounce) can tomato soup, divided
1/4	cup chopped onion
2	tablespoons tomato paste
1/2	cup water
1 1/2	pound ground chuck

Cut a slice from stem end of each pepper, remove seeds and membrane. Combine salt, pepper, Worcestershire, rice, egg, 3/4 cup soup, onion, tomato paste and beef. Stir. Pack each pepper with 1/2 cup of the mixture. Place filled peppers in a round microwave casserole. (Peppers should fit tightly.) Pour remaining soup and water over peppers. Cover with plastic wrap and microwave on high 15-18 minutes. Let stand covered 2-3 minutes. *Yield: 6 servings.*

Candice Kirven
Anderson, SC

Hashbrown Casserole

1	bag frozen hashbrowns, thawed
1	can cream of chicken soup
1	cup grated cheddar cheese
1	cup sour cream
1	diced onion
1	stick margarine or butter, melted
	salt and pepper to taste

Mix all ingredients. Bake at 350° for 50 minutes. *Yield: 8-10 servings.*

Sherrie Watson
Lexington, SC

Marinated Potato Wedges

8	red potatoes, leave skins on (1 1/4 pounds)
2	tablespoons Dijon mustard
1	cup olive oil
1/2	teaspoon salt
1/3	cup red wine vinegar
1/4	teaspoon ground white pepper

Cover potatoes with water and boil 8 minutes or until tender. Cool and cut into thin slices. Combine remaining ingredients and pour over potatoes. Cover and refrigerate 8 hours. Yield: 16 servings.

"Winnie" Winton Clontz Smoot
Coker Classics
Hartsville, SC
Reviewed Autumn 1997
Sandlapper

Stuffed Potatoes

4	large baking potatoes
	melted butter
	milk
	sour cream
	bacon crumbs (optional)
	chives
	cheddar cheese, medium or sharp
	finely chopped onion, sautéed

Wrap scrubbed potatoes in aluminum foil and bake or cook in microwave. Cool. With sharp knife, slice off top 1/3 of potato lengthwise. Scoop out pulp, being careful not to break potato skin. Mash pulp with melted butter. Add little milk, salt and pepper. You can now stir in such ingredients as sour cream, finely chopped and sautéed onion, bacon crumbs, chives. Consistency should be thick creamy with no lumps. Melted cheese may also be included. Return pulp mixture to the potato skin shells. Top with grated cheese and put in medium oven until cheese is melted and potato is heated through. *Yield: 4 servings.*

Dudley Williams
Columbia, SC

189

Cheesy Stuffed Potatoes

3	large baking potatoes
	vegetable oil
1	cup sharp cheddar cheese, shredded
1/2	cup cream cheese
1/2	cup milk
1/2	stick butter or margarine
3/4	cup sour cream
	Jane's Krazy Mixed-Up Salt

Variations: Any of the following may be added; crumbled bacon, 2 tablespoons prepared horseradish, 1 package frozen, chopped spinach, thawed

Wash and dry potatoes, rub with oil and coat with Jane's Krazy Mixed-Up Salt. Bake about 1 hour at 350° or until done. Cut potatoes in half length-wise and scoop pulp into a mixing bowl. Mix potato pulp with remaining ingredients, including about 1 teaspoon of Jane's Krazy Mixed-Up Salt. Fill potatoes and place in a shallow casserole dish and return to oven for about 20 minutes. *Yield: 6 servings.*

Dawn B. Gates
Camden, SC

Potato Casserole Supreme

8	medium baking potatoes
1/2	cup butter or margarine
2 1/2	teaspoons salt
1/4	teaspoon pepper
2/3	cup milk
1 1/2	cups shredded cheddar cheese
1	cup (1/2 pint) heavy cream, whipped

Peel and boil potatoes until tender. Drain and beat in a large bowl with electric mixer until fluffy, adding butter, seasonings and milk. Check seasonings and add more salt if necessary. Turn into a 9x13-inch casserole. Fold cheese into whipped cream and spread over potatoes for topping. Bake at 350° for about 25 minutes - until golden brown. Can be made ahead and topping added just before baking. *Yield: 8-10 servings.*

Margot Parrott
Charlotte, NC

190

Aunt Ruth's Brown Rice

1   cup rice (white)
1   stick oleo
1   can Campbell's Beef Bouillon soup
1   can Campbell's French Onion soup
1   small can mushrooms

Brown rice in oleo in frying pan on stove. Place soups, rice and mushrooms in greased casserole dish. Bake at 350° for 1 hour. (Stir occasionally.) *Yield: 4-6 servings.*

Carolyn G. Pumphrey
W. Columbia, SC

Red Rice

1/2   pound bacon
2   cups long-grain white rice
2   cups vine-ripened tomatoes, peeled and chopped; or one 14 1/2-ounce can peeled tomatoes, chopped, with their juice; or one 14 1/2-ounce can crushed tomatoes
1   teaspoon pure salt
1   quart chicken stock

Cut the bacon into small pieces and fry until crisp in a large skillet or saucepan that has a tight-fitting lid. Remove the bacon and reserve for garnish. Pour off some of the bacon grease, leaving about 1/4 cup of it in the pan. Add the rice and sauté over medium high heat, stirring constantly. It will begin to turn white after a few minutes; do not let it scorch or brown. Add the tomatoes and continue to sauté until most of the liquid has evaporated. Add the salt and stock (omit the salt if using canned stock). Simmer, covered, for 30 minutes or until the rice is tender. Remove from the heat and allow to sit for a few minutes before serving. Fluff the rice with a fork and garnish with the reserved bacon. *Yield: 10 servings.*

Hoppin John's Lowcountry Cooking
John Martin Taylor
Reprinted from Mid-Year 1992
Sandlapper

Rock Eagle Rice Casserole

1 cup rice, cooked
1 can mushroom soup
1 can sliced mushrooms
1/2 cup toasted almonds
1/2 cup melted butter
1/2 teaspoon nutmeg

Spread 1 layer of cooked rice in a buttered casserole. Add layer of almonds and then mushrooms. Continue layers until all is used. Sprinkle nutmeg on rice as you layer it. Spread mushroom soup over top, pour butter over top and bake at 325° for 20 minutes. You may wish to lightly stir the mushroom soup through the layers of rice prior to serving. *Yield: 6 servings.*

Evelyn Williams
Columbia, SC

Wild Rice Casserole

1 pound mushrooms, sliced
3 tablespoons chopped green onion
3 tablespoons margarine
2 packages (6 3/4 ounces each) minute long grain and wild rice
2 1/2 cups chicken broth
2 cups whipping cream
1 cup dried tart red cherries or chopped dried apricots
1 cup chopped pecans
1/2 teaspoon salt

Heat oven to 350°. Cook and stir mushrooms and onion in margarine in large saucepan 5 minutes or until golden. Stir in rice, seasoning packets, broth, whipping cream, cherries, 3/4 cup pecans and salt; mix well. Spoon into greased 3 quart casserole and cover. Bake 50 minutes or until rice is tender and most of liquid is absorbed. Uncover; sprinkle with remaining 1/4 cups pecans. Continue baking 10-15 minutes or until pecans are toasted. Let stand 10 minutes before serving. *Yield: 10-12 servings.*

Kitty Spence
Lexington, SC

Spinach Dumplings

1-2	pounds stew beef
1	bunch spring onions
1	pound fresh green spinach leaves
	salt and pepper

Batter:

1	egg
1/2	cup milk
1	cup self-rising flour

Cook beef with onions until very tender, falling apart! Leave in hot broth. Wash and stem spinach leaves. Mix leaves with spring onions. Pour batter over leaves and coat well. Drop battered leaves into meat and broth. Cover and simmer on low about 20 minutes. This will be "gooey" but good! *Yield: 10 servings.*

Pat Weathers
Lexington, SC

Squash Casserole

8-10	large summer or yellow squash (May mix in a few small zucchinis, too, for added color and flavor.)
1	large onion
1/2	stick butter
2-3	eggs
	salt and pepper to taste
	dash of Tabasco sauce (4-5 drops)
1	package of medium sharp cheese, shredded
1	package Pepperidge Farm's cornbread stuffing (small size)

Slice squash into thin rounds and dice onion. Steam or boil squash and onion in a large pot. When they are almost transparent, remove from heat and drain, pushing out as much water as possible without crushing squash completely. Let cool a moment, then add butter, salt, pepper, Tabasco sauce and eggs. (Use your judgment as to how many eggs according to how watery it is now.) Spoon half of mixture into large buttered dish. Top with stuffing crumbs. Sprinkle half of cheese over top of crumbs. Spoon remaining mixture into dish covering layers completely. Top with crumbs again. Sprinkle remaining cheese over top. Finish with more stuffing crumbs. Bake at 350° for 35 minutes. *Yield: 10-12 servings.*

Jocelyn Turner Ferber
Charlotte, NC

193

Squash Pudding

3	(or more) yellow squash
1	rounded tablespoon flour
1	cup sugar
3	eggs
1	can evaporated skim milk
1	tablespoon vanilla

Note: In place of sugar use 4 teaspoons Sweet n' Low. Can mix yellow and green squash for color.

Cut squash into slices. Steam or cook until tender. Drain and mash. Stir in rounded tablespoon of flour, sugar and eggs. Beat well. Add evaporated milk and vanilla. Pour into 8x8-inch greased casserole. Sprinkle with cinnamon and nutmeg. Bake 35 minutes at 350°. Cut into squares. Good hot or cold. *Yield: 6 servings.*

Janice S. Creasy
Palmyra, VA

Carolina Squash

1 1/2-2	pounds yellow or green squash, or some of both
1	egg
2	tablespoons onions
1/4	cup grated cheese (any kind)
1/2	cup sour cream
	salt and pepper to taste
1/4	cup Pepperidge Farm stuffing mix

Boil squash and onion until tender. Drain well and mash. Add beaten egg, cheese and fold in sour cream last. Put in 2 -quart greased casserole. Sprinkle Pepperidge Farm stuffing over all. Bake 30 minutes at 350°. *Yield: 6 servings.*

Ann Moore Webb
Charleston, SC

My Very Own Squash Casserole

6	medium squash
1	onion, diced
2	tablespoons margarine
2	tablespoons sugar
1/2	pound grated sharp cheese
2	eggs, beaten
1/2	teaspoon salt
2	tablespoons sour cream
2	tablespoons Miracle Whip
10	Ritz crackers, crushed

Cook squash (just until tender) and onion together with salt (either cook all water out or pour it off). Chop squash into little pieces. Add all ingredients; stir. Pour into buttered casserole dish. Bake at 375° for 25 minutes (or until slightly firm in middle). *Yield: 6 servings.*

Nancy Coker McFaddin
Turbeville, SC

Squash Casserole

2	pounds squash, cooked
1	teaspoon sugar
1	stick butter
1	carton sour cream
1/2	package dried onion soup
1 1/2	cups grated cheddar cheese
	saltine cracker crumbs

Cook squash until just tender and drain well. Add all other ingredients, except cracker crumbs and mix well together. Turn into a buttered casserole dish. Sprinkle with crumbs and bake in oven at 375° for 20 minutes. Shrimp may be added to this recipe if desired. *Yield: 6-8 servings.*

Lynnelle Blackwell
Summerton Diner
Summerton, SC

Granny Rawl's Squash and Onions

fresh yellow squash
fresh onions
salt, pepper and butter

Clean desired amount of squash and onions. Slice into coated frying pan. Add salt, pepper and butter to taste. Cook over medium heat and stir. Do not overcook!

Microwave version: Put squash and onions in microwavable dish. Cover; cook until tender.

Rawl Family Recipes
Sue Rawl Wingard
Lexington, SC
Reprinted from Spring 1993
Sandlapper

Grated Sweet Potato Pudding

1	stick margarine
1	cup Log Cabin syrup
1	teaspoon ground cinnamon
1	teaspoon ground allspice
1/2	teaspoon ground cloves
4	cups grated raw sweet potatoes
1	cup whole milk (not skim or 2%)
1/2-1	cup sugar
1/2	cup chopped pecans
1	cup raisins
4	eggs

Melt margarine. Mix all ingredients; add beaten eggs last. Pour mixture into greased 13x9x2-inch Pyrex baking dish. Bake in 350° oven. When crusted around edge and top, pull the edge to the middle and let crust form again. Do this two more times, allowing the last to remain. Baking time is approximately 40 minutes. I don't always add the nuts and raisins. *Yield: 10-12 servings.*

Dot Lyles
Spartanburg, SC

Sweet Potato Soufflé

6-8	medium sweet potatoes, cooked
1	cup sugar
1/3	stick margarine
1/2	cup milk
1/2	teaspoon salt
1/2	teaspoon vanilla
2	eggs, beaten

Drain and mash potatoes. Combine remaining ingredients and put into casserole sprayed with Pam. *Yield: 16 servings.*

Topping:

1	cup brown sugar
1/3	stick margarine
1/3	cup plain flour
1	cup nuts

Mix and sprinkle on casserole. Bake at 350° for 30 minutes.

Louise Pearce
Pamplico, SC

Aunt Eileen's Sweet Potato Casserole

3	cups cooked, mashed sweet potatoes
1/2 - 1	cup sugar
2	eggs, beaten
1/2	teaspoon salt
1/4	cup melted margarine
1/2	cup milk
1 1/2	teaspoons vanilla

Mix together and place in a casserole dish. Top with 1/2 cup to 1 cup brown sugar, 1/3 cup flour, 1/3 cup melted margarine, 1 cup pecans, chopped. Mix together thoroughly and spoon on top of casserole. Bake at 350° for 35 minutes. *Yield: 8-10 servings.*

Dudley and Evelyn Williams
Columbia, SC

Nana's Sweet Potato Casserole

1/2	stick margarine
2	cups sweet potatoes
1/4	cup milk
2	eggs
1	teaspoon vanilla or lemon extract
1	cup sugar
	pinch of salt

Mash potatoes and combine remaining ingredients in a 2 quart casserole dish. Spread on topping. Bake at 350° until brown. *Yield: 8-10 servings.*

Sally Lightsey-Jones
Greenwood, SC

Topping:

1	small can crushed pineapple, drained
1/2	cup sugar
1/2	stick margarine or butter
1/4	cup flour
1	egg

Candied Sweet Potatoes

3-4	medium size sweet potatoes
1/2-3/4	cup sugar
	cinnamon
3/4	stick butter or oleo
	water

Peel potatoes and slice about 1/2 inch thick. Layer in baking dish, sprinkling liberally with sugar, cinnamon and dots of butter between layers. Add about 1/2 cup water. Cover with foil and bake at 350°, basting occasionally until fork tender, about 40 minutes. Reheats well. *Yield: 6-8 servings.*

Margaret Shepard Atkinson
Fort Myers, FL

Senator Russell's Sweet Potatoes

3	cups mashed sweet potatoes
2	eggs
1/2	cup Carnation milk
1	cup sugar
1	teaspoon vanilla
1	stick margarine
	pinch of cinnamon and nutmeg

Mix ingredients. Add melted butter. Pour into greased casserole. Put topping on and bake at 350° for 30 minutes. *Yield: 6-8 servings.*

Mary B. Marsh
Florence, SC

Topping:

1	cup brown sugar
1/3	cup flour
1/3	cup melted margarine
1	cup nuts

Berry Mallow Yam Bake

1/2	cup flour
1/2	cup packed brown sugar
1/2	cup uncooked oatmeal
1	teaspoon cinnamon
1/3	cup butter
6	sweet potatoes, cooked, peeled and quartered
2	cups cranberries
1 1/2	cups mini marshmallows

Preheat oven to 350°. Mix together flour, sugar, oats and cinnamon. Cut in butter until it resembles coarse crumbs. Toss 1 cup flour mix with yams and berries. Place in 1 1/2 cup casserole dish. Bake 35 minutes. Sprinkle with marshmallows and rest of flour mix. Broil until lightly browned. *Yield: 6 servings.*

Dorothy H. Terry
Iva, SC

Tomato Pie

1	frozen pie crust
4-6	tomatoes, peeled if preferred, and sliced
1	cup chopped spring onions
1/2	cup chopped fresh basil
2	cups grated extra sharp cheddar cheese
3/4	cup mayonnaise salt and pepper to taste

Bake pie crust as directed. Mix cheese and mayonnaise. Layer tomatoes (salt and pepper to taste), basil and onions and repeat. Cover with cheese mixture and spread to cover edges. Bake at 375° for 30-35 minutes. Cool at least 15 minutes before slicing.

Donna Rone
West Columbia, SC

Tomato Dumplings

1	cup all-purpose flour
2	teaspoons baking powder
1	teaspoon salt
1	tablespoon shortening
1/2	cup buttermilk
5	cups peeled, chopped tomatoes
1	medium onion, chopped
1	tablespoon butter
2	teaspoons sugar
1/2	teaspoon basil
1	teaspoon salt
1/2	teaspoon pepper
1/2	teaspoon garlic pepper

Combine first 3 ingredients. Mix well. Cut in shortening with a pastry blender until mixture resembles coarse meal. Add milk, stirring until dry ingredients are moistened. Combine tomatoes and remaining ingredients in a Dutch oven. Bring to a boil, stirring occasionally. Drop dough by tablespoonfuls into boiling mixture. Cover, reduce heat and simmer 12 minutes without stirring. *Yield: 6 servings.*

Sharon W. Bickett
Chester, SC

Tomato Casserole

6   vine ripe tomatoes or one can of tomatoes
1   medium onion
4   slices white bread
1   tablespoon butter
1/2   cup shredded cheese

Sauté butter and onions. After onions are soft, add tomatoes, bring to a boil. Add shredded bread and stir well. Pour into casserole dish, cover with cheese. Bake at 350° for 30 minutes. Excellent! *Yield: 4 servings.*

Sandra C. Harwell
Mountville, SC

Tomato Casserole

2   (28-ounce) cans peeled tomatoes or 2 dozen fresh ones
1/3   cup dark brown sugar
     salt and pepper to taste
1   cup bread crumbs
3-4   tablespoons butter or margarine

For fresh tomatoes, peel and cut up in strips, rejecting seeds and juice. If canned, use the pulp rejecting the juice and seeds. In a buttered baking dish, make a layer of tomato strips and pulp. Sprinkle generously with brown sugar and then season with salt and pepper. Next add a layer of coarsely broken bread crumbs. Dot with butter. Repeat for a second layer. Bake for 30-35 minutes at 350°. *Yield: 8 servings.*

John H. Bennett, Jr.
Charleston, SC
Given by Great Grandmother
Eliza T. McClintock Bennett

Vegetable Lasagna

1	box lasagna noodles
1	cup fontina cheese, shredded
1	cup mozzarella cheese, shredded
1/2	cup Parmesan cheese
2	cups part skim ricotta cheese
1	egg
1	(10-ounce) package frozen chopped spinach, thawed and well drained or equivalent fresh-cooked spinach
1	cup carrot, shredded
1	cup zucchini, shredded
2-3	cloves garlic, minced or pressed
1	medium onion, chopped
2	tablespoons olive oil
1 1/2-2	jars (26 ounces each) tomato sauce or equivalent amount of homemade tomato sauce

Preheat over to 350°. Cook lasagna according to package directions, drain. Separate noodles onto waxed paper to keep them from sticking together as they cool. Sauté onion and garlic in oil until tender, set aside. Combine fontina cheese, mozzarella, ricotta cheese and egg with spinach, carrot and zucchini. Warm tomato sauce in saucepan and add onion and garlic to it. Spray bottom of 13x9-inch baking dish with oil spray. Place 1 layer of lasagna in bottom of pan. Spread with 1/3 tomato sauce mixture, then layer 1/2 of the cheese/vegetable mixture on top. Repeat layers - lasagna, tomato mixture, cheese/vegetable mixture. Put one more layer of lasagna on top then finish with tomato sauce completely covering noodles. Sprinkle with Parmesan cheese and bake at 350° for 30-40 minutes. Serve immediately. *Yield: 12 servings.*

Jocelyn Turner Ferber
Charlotte, NC

Veg-All Casserole

3	cans Veg-All, drained
1	cup grated cheese
1	cup onions
3/4	cup mayonnaise
1	can water chestnuts, drained
1	can chicken, drained (small)
1/2	can cream of chicken soup

Mix together and place in casserole dish. Top with Ritz crackers and dot with butter. Bake 20-30 minutes at 350°. *Yield: 8 servings.*

Sara G. Horne
Iva, SC

Focaccia with Grilled Vegetables and Pesto

2   **large yellow or red bell peppers**
2   **medium zucchini, sliced lengthwise**
1   **small eggplant, cut horizontally into 1/2-inch slices**
1   **medium red onion, cut into medium slices**
    basil-flavor olive oil or olive oil
    salt to taste
1   **focaccia or 1 loaf Italian bread**
    pesto or olivada to taste
2   **tomatoes, thinly sliced**
    fresh basil or arugula

Grill the bell peppers over hot coals or on a stove top grill until charred on all sides. Place the bell peppers in a nonrecycled brown paper bag immediately. Let sweat for 15 minutes. Discard the skins and seeds. Cut into large strips. Brush the zucchini, eggplant and onion with olive oil. Grill over hot coals until tender, turning and basting with olive oil frequently. Arrange the zucchini, eggplant, onion and roasted peppers in a shallow pan. Sprinkle lightly with salt. Slice the focaccia horizontally into halves. Grill the cut sides of focaccia until light brown. Spread the bottom half with the pesto. Layer the grilled vegetables, tomatoes and basil over the pesto. Top with the remaining focaccia half. Cut into slices. *Yield: 4-6 servings.*

Down by the Water
The Junior League of Columbia, Inc.
Reviewed Spring 1998
Sandlapper

Spinach Stuffed Zucchini

8	small zucchini
1/2	pound spinach
2	tablespoons olive oil
2	tablespoons chopped parsley
1/4	cup freshly grated Parmesan cheese
1/8	teaspoon freshly grated nutmeg
	salt
	freshly ground black pepper
	Parmesan cheese for topping

Steam the zucchini for 10 minutes or until they are just tender. Cool slightly. Cut lengthwise into halves and scoop out the flesh (an apple corer or melon baller works well for this), leaving a shell 1/4-inch thick. Shake well the scooped out zucchini in a colander (do not worry about losing too much liquid zucchini) and then pureé in a food processor. Wash the spinach carefully and cook in a covered saucepan over moderate heat for 5 minutes. The water clinging to the leaves is sufficient to prevent scorching. Drain well and chop coarsely. Heat the olive oil in a frying pan and cook the parsley for 1 minute. Add the chopped zucchini and cook over moderately high heat for 5 minutes, or until the zucchini are tender and turning golden. Add the chopped spinach, 1/4 cup Parmesan cheese, nutmeg, and salt and black pepper to taste. Spoon the mixture into the zucchini halves and place side by side in a well-oiled shallow baking dish. (May be prepared to this point on the morning of serving and set on the counter covered until the evening.) Sprinkle each zucchini half with a little Parmesan cheese. Bake in a preheated 400° oven for 20-25 minutes, or until the tops are golden. *Yield: 8 servings.*

Buon Appetito
Aria Girardi
Columbia, SC

Stir Fry Vegetables

2	tablespoons olive oil
1	pound asparagus spears, trimmed and cut into 1-inch pieces
4	green onions, cut diagonally (about 1 cup) or 1 Vidalia onion, sliced
2	medium carrots, diagonally sliced (about 1 cup)
1	each red and yellow pepper, chopped
1/4	teaspoon ground ginger
1	tablespoon soy sauce
1	tablespoon rice vinegar

In a skillet or wok over medium/high heat, in 1-2 tablespoons oil, stir fry vegetables about 5 minutes or until tender-crisp. Stir in seasonings, reduce heat to low. Serve over rice or angel hair pasta. Add additional soy, if desired. *Yield: 4-6 servings.*

Joan Easterling
Lexington, SC

Corn Bread Dressing

3/4	cup cooked, diced onions
3/4	cup cooked, diced celery
3/4	cup raw, diced onions
3/4	cup raw, diced celery
	sage to taste
	salt and pepper to taste
	corn bread (I use 8x12x1-inch pan)
	chicken broth

Cook 3/4 cup celery and 3/4 cup onions in small amount of water until soft; drain. Break corn bread in small pieces in a large mixing bowl. Add raw and cooked onions and celery. Add sage. Add enough broth to get desired consistency. Bake in greased pan in 350° oven about 25-35 minutes until slightly brown. *Yield: 12-15 servings.*

Lucille Cudd
Chester, SC

205

Fruits

Baked Apples

apples
butter or margarine
brown sugar
cinnamon
vanilla bean (optional)

Slice off top and bottom of apples. Core. Pack inside with brown sugar. Rub butter on outside. Optional: Stick a vanilla bean inside. Sprinkle cinnamon on outside and top. Bake 40 minutes at 350° or until sides crack.

Paula F. Paul
Orangeburg, SC

Mincemeat Glazed Apples

1   (3-ounce) package cherry gelatin
1   (3-ounce) package orange gelatin
1 1/2 cups cold water
6   baking apples
1   cup prepared mincemeat

Preheat broiler unit of range. Dissolve gelatins in boiling water. Core apples and starting at the stem end, peel each apple down about 1 inch. Place apples with peeled end up in large skillet. Fill apples with mincemeat. Pour gelatin mixture over apples and bring to boil over medium heat. Cover, reduce heat and simmer 15 minutes or until apples are tender. Remove cover and place under broiler, basting frequently, for 15 minutes. When done, apples will be glazed and lightly browned. May be prepared day ahead in covered skillet placed in refrigerator. Glaze just before serving. *Yield: 6 servings.*

Dudley Williams
Columbia, SC

Steamed Apples

6-8	medium apples
4	tablespoons margarine
1/2	cup sugar
1/2	cup water

Slice apples. Heat in large saucepan margarine, water and sugar until margarine and sugar is dissolved. Add apples. Stirring often, steam apples on high for approximately 5 minutes. Cover and continue cooking on low heat until apples are tender, approximately 10 minutes. Sprinkle with cinnamon if desired and serve hot.

Miriam Johnson
Trenton, SC

Fried Bananas

1	cup pancake batter
1/2	cup milk
1	teaspoon vanilla
2	tablespoons sugar
3	medium bananas

Mix batter and cut bananas into 2-inch lengths. Dip in batter and deep fry in hot oil quickly. Dry on paper towels. Sprinkle with powdered sugar if desired.

Kathy Miller Johnson
North Myrtle Beach, SC

Fruit Peels

3   large grapefruits
3   large navel oranges
3 1/2 cups sugar

You can make this old-time favorite up to 1 month before serving. For Christmas presents, pack into pretty glass jars.

Score peel of each fruit into quarters, cutting just through the rind and white pith. Pull peel from fruit. Cut grapefruit peel crosswise and orange peel lengthwise, into strips about 1/4-inch thick. Combine peel and enough water to cover in large saucepan. Heat over high heat to boiling. Boil 5 minutes. Drain. In large skillet, combine 2 1/2 cups sugar and 1 1/2 cups water. Cook over high heat and stir constantly until sugar dissolves and mixture boils. Continue boiling syrup 15 minutes, stirring occasionally. Add peel to syrup in skillet and stir to coat evenly. Reduce heat to medium-low and simmer, partially covered, for 1 hour or until peel has absorbed most of the syrup. Remove cover and continue simmering, stirring gently until all syrup is absorbed. Place remaining 1 cup sugar on waxed paper. With tongs, lightly roll peel, a few pieces at a time, in sugar and place in single layers on wire rack. Let peel dry at least 12 hours or overnight. Peels should be dry on the outside but still moist on the inside. Store at room temperature in tightly covered container up to 1 month. *Yield: 2 pounds.*

Nancy Rhyne
Myrtle Beach, SC

Cranberry Casserole

2 cups fresh cranberries
3 cups apples, thinly sliced, unpeeled
1/2 cup water
1 1/2 cups sugar

Topping:
1 stick margarine or butter, softened
1/2 cup chopped nuts
1/3 cup flour
1 1/2 cups oatmeal

Heat oven to 350°. Spray casserole dish with Pam. Combine cranberries, apples, water and sugar and put in casserole dish. Stir nuts, flour and oatmeal together; blend in margarine until the mixture is crumbly. Sprinkle topping over fruit mixture. Bake for 1 hour. Delicious served as a brunch item or to accompany pork or ham dishes.

Donna Rone
West Columbia, SC

Curried Fruit

3/4 stick butter or margarine
1 cup light brown sugar, firmly packed
1 1/2 teaspoons curry powder
1 large can peaches, sliced
1 large can pear halves
1 large can pineapple chunks
1 jar spiced apple rings
maraschino cherries

Combine butter, sugar and curry powder and bring to a boil. Drain the fruit and arrange in a 2-quart baking dish. Pour hot sauce over the fruit. Garnish with cherries. Bake at 325° for 35 minutes. Serve hot. *Yield: 8-10 servings.*

Sarah Bowman Cooper
Spartanburg, SC

Sherried Hot Fruit Casserole

1	large can sliced pineapple
1	large can peach halves
1	jar apple rings
1	large can pears
1	large can apricot halves
2	tablespoons flour
1/2	cup sugar
1	stick butter
1	cup sherry

Drain all fruits. Cut pineapple and peaches in halves. Arrange fruit in layers in medium shallow casserole. In double boiler, heat butter, sugar, flour and sherry over boiling water. Stir until thick as cream. Pour over fruit and let stand overnight in refrigerator. Bake at 350° for 20 minutes. Serve hot and bubbly. *Yield: 12-14 servings.*

Mrs. Joe M. Young
Anderson, SC

Baked Grapefruit

1/2	grapefruit per person
2	teaspoons butter or margarine
2	tablespoons brown sugar
1/2	teaspoon cinnamon
2	maraschino cherries with stems

Cut grapefruit in half. Loosen fruit from shell. Remove core. Dot each half with 1 teaspoon butter or margarine. Sprinkle each half with tablespoon of brown sugar. Sprinkle 1/2 teaspoon of cinnamon over brown sugar (you may also mix the brown sugar and cinnamon together and sprinkle). Place on baking sheet in preheated oven at 350° for 5 minutes, then broil until top is bubbly. Place doily in shallow serving dish. Place grapefruit on the doily and put a maraschino in the center. For a heart-healthy touch, substitute diet Coke for the butter, brown sugar and cinnamon. *Yield: 1/2 grapefruit per person.*

Annabelle Wright
Able House Inn Bed and Breakfast
Leesville, SC

Quick Fruit Compote

1 **pound mixed, dried fruit**
1 **cinnamon stick**
1 1/2 **cups lemon-lime soda**

Place fruit, cinnamon stick and soda in medium saucepan and simmer for 10 minutes. Serve warm in the winter. Chill and garnish with mint leaves in summer. This recipe is great because you can always have these ingredients on the pantry shelf, and it's good when fresh fruits aren't available. *Yield: 6-8 servings.*

Jackie Morrison
Laurel Hill Plantation B&B
McClellanville, SC

Simple Syrup for Fruits

I began using these syrups when one morning I found myself with fruit that "Mother Nature had not quite finished." I made the syrup, drizzled it on the fruit and our guests loved it.

1 **cup sugar**
1 **cup water**
  few drops of mint extract or coconut extract

Mix sugar and water in a small saucepan; bring to a boil and cook 3-5 minutes. Remove from stove and add a few drops of extract and let cool. This keeps well in the refrigerator.

Hint: Instead of extracts, steep fresh herbs (rosemary, mint, lemon, verbena, etc.) in the hot syrup, then strain and cool. Rosemary syrup is unbelievable on fresh watermelon!

Peggy Waller
Inn at Merridun
Union, SC

Desserts

Desserts

Cakes

Applesauce Cake

2	sticks margarine
2	cups sugar
2	eggs
3	cups applesauce
1	cup blackberry jam
4	cups flour
4	teaspoons soda
2	tablespoons cocoa
1	teaspoon cinnamon
1/4	teaspoon each cloves, allspice
1	tablespoon vanilla
1	cup raisins
1	cup pecans

Cream sugar and eggs, add applesauce, jam and vanilla. Mix dry ingredients and add to creamed mixture. Add raisins and nuts. Bake in greased and floured pans at 350° for 45 minutes or until top springs back. Serve iced or plain.

Carol Rogers
Magnolia House B&B
Sumter, SC

Moist and Easy Banana Cake

1	regular box yellow cake mix
2-3	bananas, mashed
1/2	cup chopped walnuts

Mix cake mix as directed on package. Add bananas and walnuts. Pour into greased loaf pans (may need two). Bake as directed on cake mix package. Cool cakes and frost with thin butter frosting. *Yield: 2 cakes.*

Frosting:

1/2	cup soft butter
2	cups confectioners sugar
2	tablespoons cream
1/2	teaspoon vanilla

Cream butter until light and fluffy. Add half of sugar and beat until smooth. Stir in cream and vanilla. Add remaining sugar, beat until smooth.

Sandra Taylor
Columbus, NC

Banana Nut Spice Cake

6	very ripe bananas
1 1/2	cups vegetable oil
1/4	pound (1 stick) butter
2	cups sugar
4	eggs (room temperature)
3	cups all-purpose flour
2	teaspoons soda
2 1/2	teaspoons ground cinnamon
1 1/2	teaspoons ground cloves
1/2	teaspoon salt
1 1/2	cups seedless raisins (white if possible)
1 1/2	cups chopped pecans

Preheat oven to 250°. Mash bananas. Pour vegetable oil over bananas and let stand while mixing cake. Cream butter and sugar. Add eggs one at a time, beating well after each addition. Stir in banana mixture and mix well. Add dry ingredients, which have been combined. Stir in raisins and pecans and mix thoroughly. Spoon mixture into three greased loaf pans and bake at 250° for 1 1/2 hours.

Rev. Bernett Waitt
Summerville, SC

215

Charleston's Lady Baltimore Cake

3/4   cup butter
1   tablespoon vanilla extract
1   cup milk
1/4   tablespoon salt
4   eggs
1 1/2 cups sugar
1/2   tablespoon almond extract
4   tablespoons baking powder
3   cups cake flour, sifted

Filling:
2   cups raisins
12   figs
2   cups pecan pieces
3   tablespoons brandy or
      sherry (optional)

Lady Baltimore Frosting (Seven-Minute White Icing):
2   egg whites
1/4   teaspoon cream of tartar
1   teaspoon vanilla extract
1 1/2 cups sugar
1/3   cup water

Cream butter until fluffy and add sugar slowly. Continue creaming at medium speed until the mixture is like whipped cream. Turn off mixer. Add flavorings to milk. Sift baking powder, salt and flour together four times. With mixer on lowest speed, add dry ingredients to cream mixture alternately with milk, ending with the dry mixture. When blended, add eggs, one at a time, beating at low speed. Mix until smooth. Pour batter into 3 greased and floured 9-inch layer cake pans. Bake at 350° for 30 minutes. Cool in pans for 15 minutes.

Cut figs and raisins finely and add to pecan pieces. Add brandy or sherry and let stand 1 hour or more. Make a double recipe of Lady Baltimore Frosting. Below is a single recipe.

In top of double boiler, combine the egg whites, sugar, cream of tartar and water. Cook over medium heat, beating with rotary beater, about 7 minutes or until stiff enough to spread. Remove pan from boiling water and stir in vanilla.
Stir 1/3 of the frosting mix into the filling. Stack bottom two layers, spreading filling on top of each. Place remaining layer on top. Spread balance of frosting generously on top and sides of cake.

Nancy Rhyne
Southern Recipes & Legends
Myrtle Beach, SC
Reviewed Winter 1996/97
Sandlapper

The Chocolate Chip Cake

1   package Duncan Hines
      yellow cake mix
      (the kind where eggs and
      oil, not butter is added)
1   bar German sweet
      chocolate, grated
4   eggs (room temperature)
1/2 cup Wesson Oil or use the
      same amount of apple sauce
      if you want to eliminate the
      fat in the recipe
1   cup cold water
1   package Jell-O French
      Vanilla instant pudding mix

Preheat oven to 350°. Beat cake mix, eggs, vanilla pudding mix, oil (or applesauce) and water until mixed well. Fold in chocolate bar which has been grated slightly fine or fine. Pour into bundt tube pan or two 9-inch layer cake pans and bake in a 350° oven for 50 minutes (or until done) in the bundt pan or 25-30 minutes in the layer cake pans. Ice with Chocolate Duncan Hines frosting that is room temperature and has been placed in microwave oven for about 15-20 seconds on high and stirred very well or use recipe for Chocolate Fudge Frosting.

Chocolate Fudge Frosting:
1/4 cup unsalted butter,
      softened
1/3 cup light corn syrup
1/2 teaspoon vanilla
1/4 teaspoon salt
1/2 cup cocoa
1   (16 ounce) package
      powdered sugar, sifted
2-4 tablespoons milk (more if
      necessary)

Cream butter, add syrup, vanilla, salt and cocoa, beating at medium speed. Add sugar and milk alternately, beating until smooth and thick enough to spread. Yields enough for one 2-layer cake. If more is needed, half or double the recipe. This frosting will keep the cake moist until the cake is all gone!

Rev. Bernett Waitt
Summerville, SC

Devil's Food Cake with Whipped Cream Filling

2 1/2 cups sifted flour
2 teaspoons baking soda
1/2 teaspoon salt
1/2 cup butter
2 1/2 cups brown sugar
3 eggs
3 (1 ounce) squares
unsweetened chocolate
1/2 cup buttermilk
1 cup boiling water

Whipped Cream Chocolate Filling and Frosting:
2 1/4 cups heavy cream
1/2 cup sugar
3 tablespoons cocoa
1 teaspoon vanilla

Sift flour, measure, sift again with soda and salt. Cream butter, then add sugar a little at a time. Add eggs one at a time. Beat well. Melt chocolate in cup over boiling water. Mix thoroughly. Stir 1/3 of the flour in the batter, stir well. Add 1/3 buttermilk. Repeat, ending with flour. Add vanilla and boiling water. Pour into three greased 8-inch cake pans. (Don't be alarmed at thinness of batter.) Bake 25-30 minutes in a 350° oven. Remove and turn cake upside down on racks to cool.

Mix (do not whip) all ingredients in a bowl. Chill in refrigerator 2 hours. Beat mixture until it holds into a peak. Will cover top, sides and between layers. Sprinkle with shaved bitter chocolate.

Maro Rogers
Lexington, SC
Adapted from *Cooking on The Ridge*

Dump Cake

1   **package Duncan Hines Deluxe yellow cake mix**
1   **(20 ounce) can crushed pineapple in syrup (undrained)**
1   **(20 ounce) can cherry pie filling**
1   **cup chopped pecans (optional)**
1   **stick margarine or butter cut into thin slices**

Preheat oven to 350°. Grease 13x9x2-inch pan. Dump undrained pineapple into pan, spread evenly. Dump pie filling on top of pineapple, spread evenly. Dump dry cake mix onto cherry layer, spread evenly. Sprinkle pecans over cake mix. Put margarine or butter over top. Bake at 350° for 48-53 minutes. Serve warm or cooled.

Lucille Cudd
Chester, SC

Fig Preserve Cake

2   **cups plain flour**
1   **teaspoon soda**
1   **teaspoon salt**
1 1/2 **cups sugar**
1   **cup oil**
3   **eggs**
1   **cup buttermilk**
1   **cup fig preserves**
1   **cup chopped nuts**
1   **teaspoon vanilla**
1   **teaspoon each ground cloves, cinnamon, nutmeg and allspice**

Sift dry ingredients. Add oil and beat well. Add eggs then buttermilk gradually. Add rest of ingredients. Pour into a greased and floured bundt pan. Bake at 325° for about 1 hour and 10 or 15 minutes. While cake is warm, pierce with tines of fork and glaze with the following:

Fig Cake Icing:
1   **cup sugar**
1   **stick margarine**
1   **teaspoon corn syrup**
1/2 **cup buttermilk**
1   **teaspoon vanilla**
1/2 **teaspoon soda**

Mix in saucepan and boil for 3 minutes. Pour over warm cake.

Swannee Reenstjerna
Lexington, SC
Lexington Landmark Recipes
Lexington Woman's Club
Reviewed Winter 1997/98
Sandlapper

Hummingbird Cake

3 cups flour
1 cup chopped pecans
2 cups sugar
1 1/2 teaspoons vanilla extract
1 teaspoon baking soda
1/2 cup butter or margarine, softened
1 teaspoon cinnamon
8 ounces cream cheese, softened
1 teaspoon salt
1 (16-ounce) package confectioners' sugar
3 eggs, beaten
1 teaspoon vanilla extract
1 1/2 cups oil
1 cup chopped pecans
1 (8-ounce) can crushed pineapple
2 cups chopped bananas

Mix flour, sugar, baking soda, cinnamon and salt in large bowl. Add eggs and oil; mix just until moistened. Stir in undrained pineapple, bananas, 1 cup pecans and 1 1/2 teaspoons vanilla. Spoon into 3 greased and floured 9-inch cake pans. Bake at 350° for 30 minutes or until layers test done. Cool in pans for 10 minutes. Remove to wire rack to cool completely. Cream butter and cream cheese in mixer bowl until smooth. Add confectioners' sugar; beat until fluffy. Mix in 1 teaspoon vanilla. Spread between layers and over top and side of cake. Sprinkle with 1 cup pecans. This is a favorite recipe of Becky Fraser, to whom the cookbook is dedicated.

Hilton Head Entertains
Hilton Head, SC
Reviewed Summer 1997
Sandlapper

Lemon Buttermilk Cake

3	cups plain flour
1/2	teaspoon salt
1/2	teaspoon soda
1/2	teaspoon baking powder
2	cups sugar
1	cup vegetable oil
4	eggs
1	cup buttermilk
2	tablespoons lemon extract

Glaze:

2 1/2	cups powdered sugar, sifted
5	tablespoons lemon juice
3	tablespoons orange juice
2	tablespoons orange marmalade
1/2	teaspoon salt

Preheat oven to 325°. Measure flour and sift, then remeasure. Re-sift flour with salt, soda and baking powder. In electric mixer on low speed, beat sugar, oil, eggs, buttermilk and extract until just blended. Add flour mixture to the egg mixture slowly while blending, then beat on medium speed for 4 minutes. Bake about 1 hour in greased and floured tube pan. Mix all glaze ingredients. When cake is done, gently loosen edges of cake while hot and in pan. Pour glaze over cake, then return cake to oven for 3 minutes. Remove and allow to cool in pan. Very moist and the pieces of fruit in marmalade look pretty on top of the cake!

Jean Suber Kell
Mountville, SC

Chocolate Chip Cheese Cake

1 1/2 cups Oreo cookie crumbs
1/3 cup sugar
1/3 cup margarine, melted
3 (8 ounce) packages cream cheese
1 (14 ounce) can sweetened condensed milk
3 eggs
2 teaspoons vanilla extract
1 1/4 cups mini chocolate chips
1/2 teaspoon flour

Preheat oven to 300°. Combine crumbs, sugar and margarine. Press firmly on bottom of 9-inch springform pan. In large mixer bowl, beat cheese until fluffy. Gradually beat in condensed milk until smooth. Add eggs and vanilla, mixing well. In small bowl, toss 1/2 chips with flour to coat; stir into cheese mixture. Pour into prepared pan. Sprinkle remaining chips evenly over top. Bake 1 hour or until center springs back when lightly touched. Chill before serving.

Kathleen Tiller
Camden, SC
Gates, Gaits, & Golden Plates
Camden Junior Welfare League
Reviewed Spring1997
Sandlapper

Pecan Cheesecake

2 (8-ounce packages) cream cheese
3 eggs
2/3 cup sugar
3/4 teaspoon almond flavoring
1/3 cup brown sugar
1/3 cup dark Karo syrup
1/4 stick butter
1 egg
1 cup pecan halves

Beat softened cream cheese until smooth. Add 3 eggs, beating well after each one. Add sugar and almond flavoring. Beat 5 minutes until smooth. Pour into 9-inch "Pammed" pan. Mix brown sugar, Karo, butter and 1 egg. Add pecan halves and stir. Fold this mixture into the cream cheese mixture. Bake at 325° for 50 minutes. Cool and serve. *Serves 6 or 8.*

Leland H. Williams
Alexandria, VA

White Chocolate Cheesecake

1	(8-ounce package) Philadelphia cream cheese, softened
2	(4-serving size) packages Jell-O White Chocolate instant pudding and pie filling
2	cups cold milk, divided
1	(8-ounce tub) Cool Whip topping, thawed
1	(6-ounce) prepared graham cracker crumb crust

Beat cream cheese and 1/2 of milk in large bowl with wire whisk until smooth. Add remaining 1 1/2 cups milk and pudding mixes. Beat with wire whisk 1 minute. Stir in whipped topping until smooth and well blended. Spoon into crust. Refrigerate 4 hours or until set. Garnish with white chocolate curls made with Baker's chocolate. Store leftovers in refrigerator. *Serves 8.*

Gail B. Smith
Cades, SC

Mom's Light Fruit Cake

1 1/2	cups butter, room temperature
1 1/2	cups sugar
1	tablespoon vanilla extract
2	tablespoons lemon extract
7	eggs, separated, room temperature
1 1/2	cups all purpose flour
1 1/2	pounds candied yellow, green and red pineapple, chopped
4	cups coarsely chopped nuts
1/2	pound golden raisins
1	pound candied red and green cherries, cut in half
1/4	pound candied citron, chopped
2	cups all purpose flour
1/4	cup brandy
1	cup additional fruit if desired, i.e. orange peel, dates, coconut

Make a brown paper liner for a 10-inch tube pan or two loaf pans. Grease both sides and fit into pan(s). Cut and grease both sides of a top for pan(s). Cream butter and sugar. Stir in flavorings. Beat egg yolks. Alternately combine fruits, nuts and raisins in large bowl; dredge with 2 cups flour and coat well. Stir into batter mixture gently. Beat egg whites until stiff, fold into batter. Spoon batter into pans and cover. Bake at 250° over pan of water for 2 1/2 - 3 hours or until tester is clean. Remove, cool, pour brandy over cake. Store in refrigerator covered tightly for 3 weeks before serving.

Lynn B. Bagnal
Walterboro, SC

223

A Pretty Fruit Cake

3	(8-ounce) packages pitted dates
1	pound candied pineapple (3 colors)
2	pounds (8 cups) whole pecans
1	pound candied cherries (2 colors)
2	cups sifted plain flour
2	teaspoons baking powder
1/2	teaspoon salt
4	eggs
1	cup sugar

Cut fruit into large pieces, leaving cherries whole. Sift dry ingredients and mix with fruit and whole nuts. Beat eggs and add sugar gradually. Combine this with fruit mixture. Bake at 275° for 1 1/2 hours in greased tube pan or in two greased loaf pans. This makes a beautiful cake. Use a sharp knife for cutting. *Can yield around 20 servings.*

Ruby T. Davis
Orangeburg, SC

Best White Fruit Cake

5	large eggs
1	cup sugar
1/2	teaspoon baking powder
3/4	pound glazed cherries, chopped
1	pound glazed pineapple, chopped
4	cups pecans, chopped
1	(1/2-ounce) bottle vanilla
1/2	pound butter, no substituting
1 3/4	cups plain flour
1/2	teaspoon salt
1	(1/2-ounce) bottle lemon extract

Cream butter and sugar until fluffy. Add well beaten eggs and blend well. Chop nuts and fruit in medium sized pieces and mix with portion of flour. Sift remaining flour, baking powder and salt together. Fold in nuts/fruit, eggs and butter mixture. Add flavorings and mix. Add fruit and nuts, mixing well. Pour into tube pan lined with wax paper or spray with Pam. Place in cold oven. Bake at 250° for 3 hours. Cool in pan on cake rack.

Alma Corley Harmon
Lexington, SC

224

Italian Creame Cake

1	stick Land of Lakes butter
1/2	cup Crisco shortening
2	cups sugar
5	eggs, divided
2	cups plain flour, divided
1	teaspoon baking soda
1	cup buttermilk, divided
1	teaspoon vanilla flavoring
1	cup coconut
1	cup chopped pecans

Cream butter and shortening. Add sugar and beat until smooth. Add egg yolks only and beat until smooth. Add 1 cup flour, baking soda, 1/2 cup buttermilk and beat until smooth. Add 1 cup flour, 1/2 cup buttermilk and beat until smooth. Add vanilla flavoring and beat until smooth. In separate bowl beat egg whites until peaks form. Fold whites into mixture and mix thoroughly until smooth. This batter requires a lot of mixing for the smoother the mixture, the better the cake. Add coconut and chopped pecans. Grease and flour cake pans (2 at a time). Mixture will make 4 thin layers. Bake at 350° for 30 minutes. Layers will pull away from the sides of the pan when done. Layers have to be completely cooled before frosting.

Frosting:

1	(8-ounce) cream cheese
1/2	stick butter
1	box powdered sugar
1	teaspoon vanilla flavoring
1/2	cup chopped nuts
1/2	cup coconut

Using a fork, mix cream cheese and butter until smooth. Add powdered sugar and mix until smooth. Add vanilla flavoring and mix until smooth. Add coconut and chopped nuts and mix until smooth. Spread between layers but do not spread thickly in order to have enough to cover the cake.

Note: This cake will become dry quickly due to the amount of pecans.

Sheril M. Rankin
Batesburg, SC

Milky Way Cake #1

8   Milky Way bars
1   cup margarine
1   cup pecans
2   cups sugar
1 1/4 cups buttermilk
3/4   teaspoon baking soda
4   eggs
2 1/2 cups flour
2   teaspoons vanilla

Over low heat, melt candy bars and margarine with pecans. Let mixture stand until cool. Mix sugar with remaining ingredients. Add candy mixture; blend. Pour into a greased 10-inch tube pan. Bake at 350° for 1 hour and 10 minutes or until cake is done.

Lynn Matthews
Camden, SC
Gates, Gaits, & Golden Plates
Camden Junior Welfare League
Reviewed Spring 1997
Sandlapper

Milky Way Cake #2

8   Milky Way candy bars
2   sticks butter
2   cups sugar
4   eggs
2 1/2 cups plain flour
1/2   teaspoon soda
1 1/4 cups buttermilk

Melt candy and 1 stick butter and set aside. Cream sugar and remaining butter; add eggs to sugar mixture. Alternate flour and soda with buttermilk; add candy bars and butter mixture. Pour into tube or bundt pan and bake at 325° for 1 hour and 10 minutes (maybe a little longer).

Milky Way Icing:
1 1/4 cups sugar
1   small can evaporated milk
       (about 3/4 cups)
1//2 stick butter
1/2   cup chocolate chips
1/2   cup marshmallow creme

Cook sugar, milk and butter until mixture forms a soft ball. Set aside and add chocolate chips and marshmallow creme. Beat with mixer and spread over cake.

Ron Koon
Pomaria, SC

Christmas Prune Cake

1	cup Wesson oil
1	cup buttermilk
2	cups flour
1	cup chopped pecans
1/2	cup sugar
3	eggs
1	cup cooked prunes, mashed
1	teaspoon vanilla
1	teaspoon nutmeg, cinnamon, allspice, soda
1/2	teaspoon salt

Sift flour with soda, salt and spices before mixing with the rest. Bake in a well greased and floured 13x9x2-inch pan for 45 minutes at 350°.

Topping:

1	cup sugar
1/2	teaspoon soda
1/2	cup buttermilk
1	stick margarine

Bring to a boil and pour over hot cake. Serve warm with a spoonful of whipped cream and a cherry on top. *Yield: 16 servings.*

Given to Maro Rogers by
Jane Blume
Trenton, SC
Reprinted from Winter 1995-96
Sandlapper

Red Velvet Cake

2 1/2   cups self-rising flour
1   cup buttermilk
1 1/2   cups vegetable oil
1   teaspoon baking soda
1   teaspoon vanilla
2   (1 ounce) bottles red food
         coloring
1 1/2   cups sugar
1   teaspoon white vinegar
1   teaspoon unsweetened
         cocoa powder
2   large eggs

Preheat over to 350°. Combine flour, baking soda, sugar and cocoa powder; set aside. In large mixing bowl, beat eggs. Add oil, vanilla, food coloring and vinegar. Alternate adding flour mixture and buttermilk to egg mixture while beating on medium speed. Pour batter equally into three greased and floured 9-inch cake pans. Bake for 20 minutes. Test for doneness with toothpick. Cool layers in pans on wire racks for 10 minutes. Carefully remove layers from pans and cool completely on cake racks. Frost. Refrigerate at least 1 hour before serving. *Serves 12.*

Frosting:
1   stick butter, softened
1   (8 ounce) package cream
         cheese, softened
1   (1 pound) box confectioners
         sugar
2   cups chopped pecans, if
         desired

Cream butter and cream cheese with mixer. Gradually add confectioners sugar. Beat until fluffy. If nuts are desired, fold in 1 1/2 cups pecans. Use to fill and frost cake. Decorate top of cake with remaining pecans.

Linda D. Matthews
Lancaster, SC

228

Snowball Cake

1   **Angel Food Cake**
1   **tablespoon lemon juice**
1/2   **teaspoon salt**
4   **tablespoons cold water**
1   **can crushed pineapple**
3   **packages Dream Whip**
1   **cup sugar**
2   **envelopes Knox gelatin**
1   **cup boiling water**

Dissolve gelatin in 4 tablespoons cold water, add 1 cup boiling water, pineapple juice, sugar, salt and lemon juice. Mix well. Place blended mixture in refrigerator until it begins to gel (approximately 45 minutes). Beat 2 packages of Dream Whip and fold into gelled mixture. Line a large mixing bowl (or whatever container you prefer) with wax paper and break the Angel Food cake into the bottom of the bowl (break into relatively small pieces). Add a portion of the mixture, repeat, patting down until all of the mixture and cake is used. Place in the refrigerator overnight. Turn the bowl over and take the cake out. Beat the remaining package of Dream Whip and use it as icing. Put the cake back into the refrigerator until ready to serve. Can be kept in the refrigerator up to two weeks. Use cherries, nuts, etc. to decorate. Food coloring in the Dream Whip can also add a festive touch. *Yield: 10-12 servings.*

Genny D. Hendrix
Kershaw, SC

Sour Cream Coconut Cake

1	package yellow cake mix
2	cups sugar
1	pint sour cream
9	ounces fresh frozen coconut

Make cake according to package directions. Make 4 layers from the 2 layers of cake by running a knife through each layer. Mix sugar, sour cream and coconut until blended. Top each layer with sour cream mixture. Cover and refrigerate for 3 days to allow the sour cream mixture to blend and soak through all four layers. Keeps up to 2 weeks.

Frosting:

1	carton whipped topping
9	ounces coconut

Fold coconut into topping and cover cake generously.

Wiggie Jones
Columbia, SC

Strawberry Kringle Cake

1 1/2	cups sugar
1 1/2	cups sour cream
1 1/2	cups mashed fresh strawberries
2	tablespoons strawberry gelatin
1/4	cup boiling water
1	(18 1/4 ounce) package yellow cake mix
1 1/2	cups frozen whipped topping, thawed

Four days before serving, combine sugar, sour cream and strawberries. Dissolve dry strawberry gelatin in boiling water, cool and add to sour cream mixture. Store in refrigerator overnight. Prepare and bake layer cake according to package directions. Cool layers, cut each in two horizontally to make a total of 4 layers. Spread sour cream mixture between layers and on top. Store cake for 3 days in refrigerator. Before serving, spread top and sides with whipped topping. *Yield: 10-12 servings.*

Kitty Spence
Lexington, SC

Plain Cake

3 cups sugar
1 cup butter or margarine
(Fleishman's)
1/2 cup Crisco
5 eggs
3 cups + 2 tablespoons flour
(White Lily) (measure after
sifting)
3/4-1 cup milk
2 teaspoons vanilla
1/2 teaspoon baking powder

Cream margarine, Crisco and sugar well; add eggs, beating after each. Add flour and milk alternately; add vanilla. Pour into greased and floured tube cake pan. Bake at 350° for 1 hour and 10 minutes.

Vivian M. Richardson
Pendleton, SC

Best Pound Cake

3 1/2 cups cake flour
3 cups sugar
8 eggs
2 sticks margarine
2 sticks butter
1 small can Carnation milk
1 teaspoon vanilla

In mixing bowl, add butter, margarine and sugar and beat. Add eggs 2 at a time and beat. Add flour one cup at a time and after every cup add 2 tablespoons cream, using all cream. Beat and add vanilla. Spray pan with Pam. Bake at 325° for 1 hour and 25 minutes.

Mary Shaw
The Shaw House B & B
Georgetown, SC

Cream Cheese Pound Cake

3   sticks butter, softened
1   (8 ounce) package cream
     cheese, softened
3   cups sugar
6   extra large eggs
3   cups sifted cake flour
2   teaspoons vanilla

Preheat oven to 325°. With heavy duty mixer, cream together butter and cream cheese. Gradually add sugar. Beat until light and fluffy (5 minutes). Add eggs one at a time. Beat well after each addition. Add flour to creamed mixture, beat well. Stir in vanilla. Pour batter into well greased tube pan. Bake at 325° for 1 1/4 to 1 1/2 hours or until cake tests done. Cool in pan 10 minutes. Remove. Cool completely. *Serves 12+.*

Janet L. Rudd
West Columbia, SC

Five Flavored Pound Cake

2   sticks butter
1/2 cup shortening
3   cups sugar
6   eggs
3   cups flour
1   teaspoon baking powder
1   teaspoon salt
1   cup milk
2   teaspoons each vanilla,
     coconut, almond, rum and
     butter flavoring

Cream butter and shortening, add sugar, blend until fluffy. Add eggs one at a time, mixing well after each. Mix together flour, salt and baking powder in separate bowl. In a measuring cup, measure milk and add flavorings to milk, alternating flour then milk into the butter mixture until mixed well (3 minutes). Bake in greased and floured tube pan at 350° for 1 hour, or test for doneness. This cake is great with cream cheese icing or fresh whipped cream and fruit.

Teresa James
The Garden Café
York, SC

Ina Jones Pound Cake

1	pound butter
2 2/3	cups sugar
3 1/2	cups sifted flour
8	eggs
8	tablespoons evaporated milk
1	teaspoon vanilla

Separate eggs. Beat whites into stiff peaks, add 6 level tablespoons of the sugar and refrigerate until rest of cake is mixed. Cream butter and remaining sugar, beating until light. Add egg yolks, beating until well blended. Add flour and milk alternately, beating until mixture is light. Add vanilla. Fold in egg whites. Pour into a greased 10-inch tube pan. Bake at 300° for 1 hour and 25 minutes or until done. Makes a large cake. *Serves 20.*

Note: I also use this as a base for my fruit cake.

Fruit Cake Using Ina Jones Pound Cake

Mix cake as directed and add as follows:

1	pound candied cherries
1	pound candied pineapple
1/2	pound citron
2	boxes raisins
1	box dates
1	pound orange candy, if desired
2	pounds pecans
2	teaspoons cake spice (add to cake mix)

Roll raisins and chopped dates in 1/2 cup additional flour. Chop fruit and candy, break pecans in pieces. Add all ingredients to the cake batter and mix well with spoon. Grease and line pans with wax paper. Bake at 250° for approximately 3 hours or until done. Makes one large 10-inch tube pan plus one 3-pound loaf pan (5X9-inch) or one large 10-inch tube pan plus 3 one-pound loaf pans. The small pans will cook quicker than the large ones.

Annie C. Stenhouse
Simpsonville, SC

Mama Lee's Cold Oven Pound Cake

2	sticks butter
1/2	cup Crisco
2 2/3	cups sugar
5	eggs
3	cups all-purpose flour
1	teaspoon baking powder
1	teaspoon vanilla flavoring
1	tablespoon lemon flavoring
1	cup milk

Cream together butter, Crisco and sugar. Add eggs and beat until smooth. Add rest of ingredients and beat 3 or 4 minutes, scraping sides of bowl several times. Pour into greased tube pan. Bump on counter to remove bubbles. Bake 1 hour and 20 minutes at 325°. DO NOT PREHEAT OVEN. *Serves 16.*

Maria Lindler-Steinlie
Sparta, NJ

No Fail Pound Cake

All ingredients MUST be room temperature.

2	sticks butter or margarine
1/2	cup Crisco
1	cup sweet milk
3 1/2	cups flour (before sifting)
6	eggs
3	cups sugar
1	teaspoon baking powder
1/2	teaspoon salt
1	tablespoon flavoring (any)

Cream together butter/margarine and Crisco. Add milk and flour alternately, starting and ending with flour. Add eggs one at a time, beating after each. Add remaining ingredients and beat. Pour into greased and lightly floured tube pan. Bake at 325° for 1 1/2 hours. Do not open oven door during the first hour. *Serves 20.*

Anita Stoddard
Spartanburg, SC

Old Fashioned Pound Cake

1	pound butter, softened (not margarine)
2 1/2	cups sugar
10	eggs
4	cups flour, sifted twice (White Lily)
2	teaspoons vanilla flavoring
1	teaspoon lemon flavoring

Cream the soft butter and sugar well until it is light and fluffy. Add unbeaten eggs one at a time, beating after each addition. When the last egg has been added, beat one minute. Add flour one cup at a time and mix well. Add flavoring. Turn into a greased and floured tube pan. Put in a cold oven and bake at 275° for 1 hour and 50 minutes. Ice with Boiled Fluffy Frosting. *Serves 20.*

Boiled Fluffy Frosting:

2 1/2	cups sugar
2/3	cup cold water
2	eggs whites with pinch salt
3	tablespoons white corn syrup
1	teaspoon vanilla

Cook sugar, syrup and water until the "soft ball" stage. Remove from heat and add gradually 3 tablespoons to the stiffly beaten whites. Return remaining syrup to the unit and boil until it spins a thread (long). Add to the egg white mixture. Beat well at high speed. Add flavoring.

Mary Hillhouse Axmann
Anderson, SC

Ruth's Pound Cake

2 sticks butter
1/2 cup Crisco
5 large eggs
3 cups plain flour
1/2 teaspoon baking powder
1/4 teaspoon salt
1 cup milk
1 teaspoon lemon flavoring
1 teaspoon vanilla flavoring
1 teaspoon orange flavoring

Sift dry ingredients; cream butter, Crisco and sugar. Cut sugar mixture into dry ingredients and add milk and flavorings. Bake for 1 1/4 to 1 1/2 hours at 325°.

Bobby Wilburn
Chester, SC

Pound Cake Squares

1 package pound cake mix
1 stick butter, melted
2 eggs
1 (16 ounce) box confectioners sugar (reserve 2 tablespoons)
2 eggs
1 (8 ounce) package cream cheese
1 teaspoon almond extract
1 cup chopped pecans

Mix together pound cake mix, melted butter and 2 eggs. Spread into greased 9x13-inch pan. Mix confectioners sugar (less 2 tablespoons), eggs, cream cheese and almond extract in food processor. Spread over first layer. Sprinkle with chopped pecans and bake at 350° for 45-55 minutes. When slightly cooled, sprinkle with reserved sugar (through strainer or sifter). Cut into 48 pieces.

Janet Bruning
Greenville, SC

Cookies

Basic Brownies

1	cup plain flour
1/2	teaspoon baking powder
1/4	teaspoon salt
1/3	cup cocoa
1/3	cup shortening, softened
1	cup sugar
1	egg
1/4	cup evaporated milk
1/2	cup chopped pecans

Sift together flour, baking powder, salt and cocoa. Cream shortening, sugar and eggs until light and fluffy. Add milk. Gradually mix in flour mixture. Stir in nuts. Spread in a greased 8-inch square pan. Bake at 350° for 25 to 30 minutes. Cut into squares while warm. Cool in pan. *Yield: 25 squares.*

Ann M. Huntley
Taylors, SC

Chocolate Fudge Brownie

2/3	stick butter
2	squares unsweetened chocolate
1	cup sugar
2	eggs, beaten
2/3	cup self rising-flour
1/2	cup chopped nuts
1	teaspoon vanilla

Melt butter and chocolate in double boiler. Mix remaining ingredients and add to butter and chocolate. Bake in greased 7 1/2x12 1/2-inch pan for 20-25 minutes at 350°. Do not overbake. *Yield: 16 squares.*

Frosting:

3	tablespoons melted butter
2	squares unsweetened chocolate
1	box 4X sugar
1/2	cup evaporated milk

Melt butter and chocolate in double boiler. Add 4X sugar gradually along with 1/2 cup evaporated milk. Alternate sugar and milk until you have used the box of sugar. It might not take quite 1/2 cup milk. Use enough to give a good spreading consistency. Mix well; add 1 teaspoon vanilla and 1/2 cup chopped nuts.

Joan C. McKissick
Summerville, SC

Chocolate Syrup Brownie

1	stick butter
1	cup sugar
4	eggs
1	cup self-rising flour
1	teaspoon vanilla

Melt 1 stick butter, add sugar, eggs, flour and vanilla. Beat at low speed until smooth. Pour into greased and floured 15x10-inch pan and bake at 350° for 20-25 minutes. (May use 13x9-inch pan for thicker brownie, baking 30-35 minutes.) *Yield: 48 squares.*

Frosting:

1	stick butter
3	tablespoons cocoa
1	pound box confectioners sugar
2	tablespoons milk
3/4	cup chopped pecans

Melt butter, add confectioners sugar, cocoa and milk. Mix until smooth. Stir in nuts, spread on hot cake.

Virginia Buckley
Easley, SC

Glorified Brownies

2   cups sugar
1 1/3   cups oil
4   eggs
2   cups + 2 tablespoons plain
        flour
4   tablespoons white Karo
        syrup
1 1/2   cups chopped pecans
6   tablespoons cocoa
        Pinch or two of salt
1   tablespoon baking powder
1   large jar Marshmallow
        Creme
10.5   ounces of miniature or cut-
        up regular size
        marshmallows
1   stick butter, softened
6   tablespoons cocoa
1/2   cup Carnation milk
1   box 4X sugar

Add lightly beaten eggs to sugar and oil. Add other ingredients, mix well and bake at 350° for 35 to 40 minutes. Put miniature or cut-up marshmallows on top of hot brownies. Spread Marshmallow Creme filling over top. While brownies are cooking, make icing. Stir all ingredients together and add immediately to the top of hot brownies and marshmallows. Wait overnight to cut into squares. *Yield: 30-50, depending on size.*

Estelle M. Mauldin
Greenwood, SC

Benne (Sesame) Seed Wafer

*History of Benne: When Africans first came to SC, they brought with them--
as their most valued possession--a little handful of benne seed (Sesamum
Indicum), which they believed to be for them the secret of health and good
luck. Planted near the slave quarters, benne became a part of the South.*

2   cups loosely packed brown sugar
1   stick butter, softened
1   egg, beaten
1   cup all-purpose flour
3/4   cup sesame (benne) seed, toasted
1/2   teaspoon baking powder
1   teaspoon vanilla extract
1/4   salt

Preheat oven to 325° degrees.
Cream together butter and sugar.
Add beaten egg. Sift together flour,
baking powder and salt and add to
butter mixture. Add vanilla and
sesame seed. Drop by teaspoonsful
on greased cookie sheet. Bake for
12-15 minutes. Allow to cool for one
minute before removing from pan.
Yield: 42.

Maison du Pre Inn
Charleston, SC
Reprinted from Winter 1996/96
Sandlapper

Best Ever Chocolate Chip Cookies #1

1   cup each brown and white sugar
1   cup sweet butter
2   eggs
2   tablespoons milk
2   teaspoons vanilla
2   cups flour
1   teaspoon salt
1   teaspoon each baking powder and soda
2 1/2 cups old fashioned oats
18   ounces semi-sweet chocolate chips
1 1/2 cups chopped walnuts

Beat sugars and butter until smooth
and fluffy. Add eggs, milk and
vanilla. Combine flour, salt, soda
and powder. Gradually add to butter.
By hand, stir in oats, chips and nuts.
Chill dough and roll into ping-pong
ball shapes. Place dough on
ungreased baking sheets. Bake at
350° about 12 minutes (chewy) or 14
minutes (crispy). Cookie puffs in
middle when done. (Watch closely.)
Yield: about 48 cookies.

Cathy Anderson
Charlotte, NC

Best Ever Chocolate Chip Cookies #2

2	cups flour
1	teaspoon soda
1/2	teaspoon salt
1/2	cup butter, softened
1/2	cup shortening
1/2	cup granulated sugar
3/4	cup packed brown sugar
1	teaspoon vanilla
1	egg
12	ounces milk chocolate chips
1/2	cup chopped nuts

Preheat oven to 375°. In small bowl combine flour, soda and salt. In large bowl combine butter, shortening, sugars and vanilla. Beat until creamy. Beat in egg. Gradually add flour mixture and mix well. Stir in chips and nuts and mix well. Drop by rounded teaspoonfuls 2 inches apart onto ungreased cookie sheet. Bake 8-10 minutes. Cool on cookie sheet 2 minutes. Remove to rack and cool completely. *Yield: 36-48 cookies.*

Dorothy H. Terry
Iva, SC

Chocolate Chip Rocks

1	cup butter
3/4	cup brown sugar
1/2	cup granulated sugar
1	egg
1	teaspoon vanilla
1 1/2	cups flour
2	cups oatmeal
1/2	teaspoon salt
1	teaspoon soda
1	teaspoon cinnamon
1/2	teaspoon cloves
1/2	teaspoon allspice
1	cup walnuts, chopped
12	ounces chocolate chips

Add sugars to butter. Cream. Add egg. Mix all dry ingredients in a bowl. Add to sugar mix. Add nuts and chocolate chips. Drop large tablespoon size balls on ungreased cookie sheet. Bake at 375° for 10-12 minutes. *Yield: 4 dozen.*

Barbara Parks
Lexington, SC

Butter Cookies

3/4   pound butter
1   cup sugar
3   cups flour
1   teaspoon soda
2   teaspoons almond flavoring

Beat thoroughly. Drop small amount on cookie sheet and flatten. Bake at 350° until delicately brown.

Kathleen Rainey
Starr, SC

Caramel Cookies

1/2   cup melted margarine
1   cup firmly packed brown sugar
18   (5-inch long) Graham crackers, halved
1/2   cup melted butter
1   cup chopped pecans

Combine margarine, butter, sugar and pecans in a saucepan. Bring to a rolling boil over low heat; boil 3 minutes, stirring constantly. Place graham crackers in a 15x10x1-inch pan; spoon butter mixture over crackers. Bake at 350° for 10-12 minutes. Watch carefully; they burn easily. Cut into squares. *Yield: 36 cookies.*

Southern Tailgating: Game Day Recipes and Traditions
Reviewed Autumn 1996
Sandlapper

Carolina Crunchy Cookies

1/2	box graham crackers (Each box has 3 packages. Use 1 1/2 packages, breaking each cracker in half.)
2	sticks butter
1/2	cup brown sugar (or white)
1/2	teaspoon vanilla
1	cup chopped pecans

Line cookie sheet with edges with aluminum foil. Place crackers on sheet as close as possible. Bring butter and sugar to a rolling boil for 3 minutes. Add vanilla. Pour evenly over crackers, sprinkle with pecans. Bake 10 minutes at 350°. Let cool and peel off foil. Break apart. Store in a tin container. *Yield: 48 @ 4 per serving; approximately 12 servings.*

Mary Ellen Chapman
Fletcher, NC

Graham Cracker Crisp

1/2	(16 ounce) package graham crackers, broken into quarters
1	cup chopped pecans
1/2	cup butter
1/2	cup margarine
1/2	cup sugar

Place cracker pieces on foil-lined baking sheet. Sprinkle pecans on crackers. Combine butter, margarine and sugar in saucepan. Bring to a boil and cook for 3 minutes or until blended and thickened. Pour sauce evenly over pecans and crackers. Bake at 325° for 7 minutes. Turn oven off; do not remove from oven for 15 minutes. Pieces will harden when cool. *Yield: 10-12 servings.*

Joan Todd
Walhalla, SC

Chocolate Caramel Bars

1	(14 ounce) bag Kraft caramels
1	(5 ounce) can evaporated milk
1	(18 1/2 ounce) package German chocolate cake mix
3/4	cup butter or margarine, melted
1	cup chopped walnuts
1	cup semi-sweet chocolate chips

Melt caramels and 1/3 cup of the evaporated milk together (microwave OK). Combine cake mix, melted butter and remaining evaporated milk. Spread half of cake mixture in Pam sprayed 9x13-inch pan. Bake for 6 minutes at 350°. Remove from oven. sprinkle with nuts and chocolate chips. Spread melted caramel over top. Spread remaining cake mixture over all. Bake 15-18 minutes more in 350° oven or until top is set. Cool and cut into 48 pieces.

Janet Bruning
Greenville, SC

Doris' Christmas Cookies

1/2	cup butter
1	cup brown sugar
3	eggs well beaten
3	cups flour
1/2	teaspoon soda
1	teaspoon cinnamon
1/2	cup sherry wine
2	tablespoons sherry flavoring
7	cups chopped nuts
6	slices candied pineapple, chopped
2	cups candied cherries, chopped
2	cups chopped dates
3/4	cup white raisins

Mix first 8 ingredients. Fold in fruits well. Drop by tablespoons on ungreased cookie sheet. Bake at 300° for 20 or 25 minutes. *Yield: 12 dozen cookies.*

Frances Stubblefield
Columbia, SC

Date Nut Balls

1/2 cup butter or margarine
3/4 cup sugar
1 (8 ounce) package whole dates, chopped (Don't use pre-chopped dates--balls won't hold together.)
2 1/2 cups Rice Krispies
1 cup chopped pecans
Flaked coconut or 10X sugar

Combine butter, sugar and dates in medium saucepan. Bring to boil, cook, stirring constantly for 3 minutes. Remove from heat. Stir in cereal and pecans. Allow to cool to touch. Shape into 1-inch balls and roll each in coconut or powdered sugar. *Yield: 4 dozen cookies.*

Cathy Anderson
Charolotte, NC

Fruit Cake Cookies

1 cup melted butter or oleo
1 cup firmly packed brown sugar
3 eggs
3 cups all purpose flour
1 teaspoon soda
1 teaspoon ground cinnamon
1/2 cup milk
2 teaspoons cream sherry (optional)
6 slices candied pineapple, finely chopped
1 cup candied red cherries, finely chopped
1 cup candied green cherries, finely chopped
2 cups dates
1 (15-ounce) package white raisins
7 cups chopped pecans

Combine butter and sugar, mixing well. Add eggs and beat well. Combine dry ingredients: add to butter mixture alternately with milk; mixing well after each addition. Stir in sherry (if desired). Stir fruits and nuts into dough, mixing well. Drop dough by heaping teaspoons onto well-greased cookie sheets. Bake at 300° for about 20 minutes. *Yield: about 16 dozen cookies.*

Adapted from a
Southern Living Recipe
Ruby T. Davis
Orangeburg, SC

No Bake Fudge Cookie

1	stick margarine
2	cups sugar
1/4	cup cocoa
1/2	cup canned milk
1	teaspoon vanilla
1/2	cup peanut butter
1 1/4	cups uncooked oats
1	cup chopped pecans

Mix margarine, sugar, cocoa and milk together. Bring to a boil. Boil for 2 minutes. Remove from heat. Add vanilla, peanut butter, oats and pecans. Drop by teaspoon onto wax paper.

Barbara S. Lux
Lexington, SC
1995 First Lady Cookbook
American Cancer Society
Reviewed Summer 1995
Sandlapper

Haystacks

1	(12-ounce) package butterscotch morsels
1	(11-ounce) can cocktail peanuts (can substitute cashews)
1	(3-ounce) can chow mein noodles
	dash of salt

Melt morsels over boiling water. Remove from heat and add peanuts, noodles and salt. Spoon onto wax paper. Cool. *Yield: about 2 1/2 dozen.*

Lynn Lyles, Spartanburg, SC
Lou Lucas Ardren, Ft. Mill, SC
Wiggie Lucas Jones, Columbia, SC
Under One Roof
Reprinted from Winter 1995/96
Sandlapper

Melting Moments

1   cup butter or margarine,
     softened
1/3 cup sifted powdered sugar
1 1/4 cups all-purpose flour
1/2 cup cornstarch

Cream butter; add sugar and beat well. Gradually add flour and cornstarch, beating until smooth. Drop mixture by level teaspoonfuls onto ungreased cookie sheets. Bake at 350° for 10-12 minutes. (Cookies do not brown on top.) Cool slightly on cookie sheets; remove cookies to wire racks to cool completely. Frost with lemon frosting. (These cookies are fragile.) *Yield: about 7 dozen.*

Lemon Frosting:
1/4 cup butter or margarine,
     softened
1 1/2 cups sifted powdered sugar
2   tablespoons lemon juice
1   tablespoon grated lemon
     rind

Cream butter; gradually add powdered sugar and lemon juice, beating until smooth Stir in lemon rind. *Yield: 2 cups.*

Louise Dickard
Anderson, SC

Miracle Peanut Butter Cookies

1   cup peanut butter (smooth
     or chunky)
1   cup sugar
1   beaten egg
1   teaspoon vanilla

Combine peanut butter and sugar; mix well. Stir in egg and vanilla. Roll dough into 3/4 inch balls. Place balls on ungreased cookie sheet and flatten with fork. Bake at 350° for 10 minutes. *Yield: 4 dozen cookies.*

Ann M Huntley
Taylors, SC

248

Peanut Butter Cookies

1	cup peanut butter (creamy or crunchy)
1	cup sugar
1	egg

Mix together and place by tablespoon onto cookie sheet at least 2" apart. Bake at 375° for 8-12 minutes. *Yield: 4 dozen cookies.*

Donna Rone
West Columbia, SC

White Chocolate Lace Oatmeal Cookies

13/4	cups cake flour
1	teaspoon baking soda
1	teaspoon cinnamon
1	teaspoon allspice
1	teaspoon salt
1	cup butter or margarine, softened
1	cup packed light brown sugar
1	cup sugar
2	eggs
1	teaspoon vanilla extract
3	cups old fashioned rolled oats
1	cup broken pecans
6	ounces white chocolate

Sift the cake flour, baking soda, cinnamon, allspice and salt into a bowl and mix well. Beat the butter, brown sugar and sugar in a mixer bowl until creamy, scraping the bowl occasionally. Add the eggs 1 at a time, beating well after each addition. Add the vanilla and mix well. Stir the flour mixture into the butter mixture. Fold in the oats and pecans. Drop by rounded tablespoonfuls onto a greased and floured cookie sheet. Bake at 350° for 9-10 minutes or until light brown. Cool on the cookie sheet for 3 minutes. Remove to a wire rack. Heat the white chocolate in a double boiler over hot water until melted, stirring frequently. Drizzle over the top of each cookie in a lacy design. *Yield: 3 dozen cookies.*

Down By the Water
The Junior League of Columbia, Inc.
Reviewed Spring 1998
Sandlapper

Orange Slice Cookies

1   **cup Crisco**
1   **cup sugar**
1   **cup packed brown sugar**
2   **eggs**
1   **teaspoon vanilla**
2   **cups plain flour**
1   **teaspoon baking powder**
1   **teaspoon baking soda**
2   **cups quick-cooking rolled oats**
2   **cups (12 ounces) candy orange slices, chopped**
1   **cup (3 1/2 ounce can) flaked coconut**

In large bowl, cream sugars and Crisco until fluffy. Add eggs and vanilla. Beat well. Stir together flour, baking powder and salt. Stir into creamed mixture. Stir in oats, candy and coconut. Using about 1 teaspoon of mixture, roll into 1-inch balls. Line cookie sheets with aluminum foil and drop mixture onto foil. Bake at 350° for 10-12 minutes.

Joan Todd
Walhalla, SC

Pecan Drops

1/2   **cup butter**
2 1/2   **cups cake flour**
1/2   **cup plus 2 tablespoons shortening**
1   **cup nuts, coarsely chopped**
1   **cup powdered sugar**
2   **teaspoons vanilla**

Cream butter and shortening. Add sugar. Gradually add flour, nuts and vanilla. Drop on ungreased cookie sheet. Bake at 325° for 10-12 minutes. (They do not turn brown.) *Yield: 4 1/2 dozen.*

Idella Bodie
Thoroughbred Fare
Aiken, SC
Reviewed Autumn 1997
Sandlapper

Seven-Layer Bars

1/2	stick real butter
1	cup graham cracker crumbs
1	(6-ounce) bag chocolate chips
1	(6-ounce) bag butterscotch chips
1	cup shredded coconut
1	cup chopped nuts
1	(14-ounce) can condensed milk

Melt butter in 13x9-inch pan. Spread in pan in the following order: crumbs, 2 chips, coconut, nuts and condensed milk. Bake at 350° for 30 minutes or until lightly browned. Cool and cut into bars. *Yield: 12 bars.*

Owen Clark
Johnston, SC

Shortbread Bars

3	sticks butter, softened
1	cup confectioners sugar
3	cups flour, sifted
1/2	teaspoon salt
1/2	teaspoon vanilla
1/4	cup sugar

Cream butter and sugar together until light, then sift flour and salt together and add to creamed mixture. Add vanilla, roll into large ball and chill for 30 minutes on 2 jelly roll pans lined with parchment paper. Spray with shortening spray. Press dough out with fingertips or roll with rolling pin floured with confectioners sugar. Dust cookies before cooking with 1/4 cup granulated sugar. Bake 20 minutes in a preheated oven at 350°. Do not let brown. Cut bars with pizza cutter when cookies are still hot. Leave in pan until cookies are completely cool. Great and buttery!

The Garden Café
Teresa James
York, SC

Shortbread Cookies

1 1/2 cups butter
1/2 teaspoon salt
1 cup powdered sugar
1/2 teaspoon vanilla extract
3 cups plain flour, sifted
1/4 cup sugar

Cream butter and powdered sugar until smooth. Sift flour and salt together; add to butter mixture. Add vanilla; blend thoroughly. Wrap dough in waxed paper and chill until firm. Roll dough to 5/8-inch thickness and cut with 3-inch cookie cutter. Place cookies on ungreased cookie sheet; sprinkle with granulated sugar. Refrigerate for 20 minutes. Bake at 325° for 20 minutes. Cookies should not be brown around edges. *Yield: 20 cookies.*

Uptown Down South Cookbook
Junior League of Greenville, SC
Reviewed Spring 1996
Sandlapper

Pies

To keep a pie crust from getting soggy, sprinkle about 3 tablespoons of sugar on bottom of pie shell before putting filling on the crust.

T. Lois King
Anderson, SC

Deep Dish Apple Pie

6-8	apples, peeled and sliced
3/4	cup sugar
1/2	teaspoon cinnamon
3	tablespoons flour
1	tablespoon lemon juice
1	unbaked pie crust

Place sliced apples in large bowl. Mix other ingredients. Pour over apples and mix well. Pour mixture into deep pie plate. Dot with margarine. Dribble over mixture lemon juice. Top with pie crust. Bake at 325° degrees for 1 hour. Pie will be juicy. *Yield: 6 servings.*

Blanche W. Floyd
Myrtle Beach

Paper Bag Apple Pie

Step #1:

1	unbaked deep-dish pie shell
1/2	cup sugar
1/2	teaspoon lemon juice
4	large, tart apples
2	tablespoons flour

Step #2:

1/2	cup flour
1/2	cup sugar
1/2	cup butter or margarine (I use less, 1/3)

Mix ingredients in Step #1 and put in pie crust. Mix ingredients in Step #2. Cut in butter and sprinkle over top. Smooth to edges. Place pie inside a brown grocery bag and set on top of a cookie sheet. Staple corners to lie flat. Bake at 425° for 1 hour and 10 minutes. (I do 2 at a time.) *Yield: 6 servings per pie.*

Idella Bodie
Aiken, SC

253

Sour Cream Apple Pie

This recipe won 13th in Red Band flour cooking contest in Charlotte, NC.

2   eggs
1   cup (8-ounce) sour cream
1   cup sugar
6   tablespoons all-purpose flour, divided
1   teaspoon vanilla extract
1/4   teaspoon salt
3   cups chopped, peeled, baking apples
1   unbaked pie shell (9-inch deep dish)
3   tablespoons butter
1/4   cup packed brown sugar

In a large bowl, beat eggs. Add sour cream. Stir in sugar and 2 tablespoons flour, vanilla and salt; mix well. Stir in apples. Pour into pie shell. Bake at 375° for 15 minutes. Meanwhile, combine butter, brown sugar and remaining flour. Sprinkle over top of pie. Return to oven for 25 minutes, or until set. Cool and refrigerate. *Yield: 8 servings.*

Sharon W. Bickett
Chester, SC

Chocolate Bar Pie

1   large or 2 small pie shells
1   jumbo Hershey bar with almonds
1   (9-ounce) container Cool Whip

Bake and cool pie shell. Melt Hershey bar in double boiler. Remove from heat and quickly stir in Cool Whip. Mix well, then turn into pie shell. Refrigerate until set.

Cathy Anderson
Charlotte, NC

Chocolate Fudge Pie

1	cup sugar
2	tablespoons flour
1	egg
	pinch salt
1	square semi-sweet chocolate
1/3	stick margarine

Mix ingredients.

Melt ingredients and pour into first mixture. Add 1/2 cup milk and 1 teaspoon vanilla. Pour into unbaked pie shell. Sprinkle with 1/2 cup chopped pecans. Bake at 325° for 30 minutes. Cool and refrigerate. Tastes best with a dollop of vanilla ice cream on top. *Yield: 6-8 servings.*

Vera Sullivan
Chapin, SC
Libby Allen
Columbia, SC

Coconut Pie

4	eggs, well beaten
1/2	cup self-rising flour
1 3/4	cup sugar
1/2	stick margarine, melted
1	teaspoon vanilla
2	cups milk
2	cups coconut, shredded

Mix the ingredients in order and pour into 2 9-inch greased pie pans. Bake at 350° for 30-40 minutes or until lightly browned on the top. *Yield: 2 thin pies, 12 servings.*

Sarah Bowman Cooper
Spartanburg, SC

255

Aunt Merrie's Coconut Pie

1 1/2 cups white sugar
3 eggs, whole
1 stick melted margarine
4 teaspoons fresh lemon juice (the secret)
1 teaspoon vanilla
1 (3-ounce) can flaked coconut

Add sugar and eggs to margarine and beat well. Add coconut. Add lemon juice and vanilla. Pour into unbaked pie shell. Bake at 350° 45 minutes. Very rich! *Yield: 8 servings.*

Janice S. Creasy
Palmyra, VA

Old Fashion Coconut Pie With Its Own Crust

6 eggs, beaten
1 3/4 cups sugar
1/2 cup flour
2 cups milk
1/2 stick melted butter
1 (7-ounce) package coconut
1 teaspoon vanilla

Combine all ingredients. Mix well. Pour into 2 pie plates. Bake at 325° for 30 minutes.

Ella Calvert Bouknight
Lexington, SC

Wynette's Coconut Pie

4 eggs
1 1/2 cups sugar
1 teaspoon vanilla
1 1/2 cups coconut
1 cup milk

Beat eggs and sugar, add vanilla, coconut and milk. Pour into 9-inch deep dish pie shell. Bake for 50 minutes at 350°. Cool. *Yield: serves 8.*

Wynette Gunter
Leesville, SC

Crust for Peach, Apple or Berry Pie

1   cup flour
1   cup sugar
1   cup milk
1   stick oleo

Mix all into bowl together, mixing well. Have fruit in pan to bake. Pour over top of fruit. It will and should all sink to the bottom. As it cooks it will come to the top to make the crust. Bake at 375° (moderate oven). Brown to your taste.

T. Lois King
Anderson, SC

Easy Cherry Pie

1   can sour pitted cherries
1   can condensed milk
     juice of two lemons
1   (14-ounce) Cool Whip
2   graham cracker crusts

Drain cherries and slice. (Keep juice.) Mix with 1 can condensed milk, juice of two lemons and carton of Cool Whip. Thin with small amount of cherry juice. Pour into 2 pie crusts. Refrigerate. (For Washington's birthday, Valentine's Day, etc. add a few drops of red coloring.) *Yield: serves 6.*

Barbara McCabe
Clemson, SC

Chocolate Chess Pie

1 1/2 cups sugar
3 1/2 tablespoons cocoa
1/2   stick melted butter
1 1/2 teaspoons vanilla
1   small can evaporated milk
2   eggs
3/4   cup chopped pecans
     (optional)

Mix all together. Put in unbaked pie shell. Bake 45 minutes at 350°.

Betty Lee Phillips Brunson
Sumter, SC

Jefferson House Delight Pie

1   (8-ounce) package cream cheese, softened
1   can Eagle Brand milk
1/3 cup lemon juice
2   graham cracker crusts
1   (8-ounce) whipped topping
1   cup strawberries or peaches or bananas

Blend cream cheese and milk together. Add lemon juice and stir well. Pour into graham cracker crusts. Place fruit on top of mixture. Sprinkle powdered sugar over fruit. Spread whipped topping over fruit. Chill 24 hours. *Yield: serves 6-8.*

(Use chocolate Eagle Brand milk with bananas for a really great treat.)

Vaughnde Morris
The Jefferson House B&B
Anderson, SC

Derby Pie

1   deep dish pie shell
1   cup sugar
1/2 cup plain flour
1   tablespoon vanilla
2   eggs
1   cup chopped pecans
1   cup (8 ounces) chocolate chips
1   stick butter, melted

In a bowl beat eggs until foamy; add sugar, melted butter and flour. Beat until well blended. Add vanilla, nuts and chocolate chips. Pour into unbaked pie shell. Bake at 350° for 45 minutes. *Yield: 6 servings.*

Sarah Weiss
Lexington, SC

Lemon Cooler Pie

2	graham cracker crusts
1	(12-ounce) frozen lemonade, thawed
1/2	gallon vanilla ice cream or ice milk, softened in refrigerator
1 1/2	teaspoons ground cinnamon

Sprinkle cinnamon in pie crusts. In a large bowl, mix ice cream and lemonade together, using a hand mixer if necessary. Divide mixture between the pie crusts. Freeze. Take out of freezer 10 minutes before serving. Garnish with cool whip or whipped cream, a lemon slice and a sprig of mint. Delicious, easy and light.

Donna Rone
West Columbia, SC

Aunt Mae's Lemon Pie

8	eggs (8 yolks + 4 whites + 4 whites)
2	lemons, grated and juiced
1 1/2	cups sugar (1 cup + 1/2 cup)
2	teaspoons plain flour
2	tablespoons water

Put yolks, grated lemon rind, lemon juice, 1 cup of sugar, flour and water into top of double boiler. Mix well and cook until mixture thickens. Beat 4 egg whites and 1/2 cup of sugar in bowl, mix well and beat until thick. Fold this into lemon mixture and mix well. Pour into prebaked pie crust. Put remaining 4 egg whites and 1/2 cup sugar into bowl and whip to soft peaks. Add to top of pie. Brown in moderate oven.

Philip Bardin
Edisto Island, SC
Reprinted from May/June 1990
Sandlapper

The Original Winthrop College Lemon Sugar Pie

1	pound or 2 cups sugar
4	ounces or 1 stick or 1/2 cup butter
3	eggs
3	lemons (juice)
2	ounces or 1/2 cup flour

Cream butter and sugar. Add eggs, lemon juice and flour. Pour into uncooked pastry shell. Bake in oven about 375° until done. *Yield: 6 ample slices.*

As given to Eleanor Foxworth by Miss Zula Threlkeld, former dietitian.
Eleanor Winn Foxworth
Kingstree, SC

Frozen Lemon Mousse

30	(about) lemon or vanilla wafers
4	egg whites
4	egg yolks
1/8	teaspoon cream of tartar
1/2	cup fresh lemon juice
1/8	teaspoon salt
1/4	cup sugar
3/4	cup sugar
2	tablespoons grated lemon rind
1/2	cup whipping cream

Line bottom and side of buttered 9-inch springform pan with wafers. Combine egg yolks, lemon juice, 1/4 cup sugar and lemon rind in bowl; mix well. Beat egg whites in mixer bowl until foamy. Add cream of tartar, salt and the remaining 3/4 cup sugar gradually, beating until stiff peaks form. Fold egg whites and whipping cream into egg yolk mixture. Spoon into prepared pan. Freeze until firm. Cover with foil. Freeze for 8 hours to 2 weeks. Soften in refrigerator for 1 hour before serving. Garnish with fresh strawberries.

Helen W. Malcolm
Hilton Head Entertains
Hilton Head, SC
Reviewed Summer 1996
Sandlapper

Old Fashioned Lemon Pie

2	cups milk
1	cup sugar
	grated rind of 2 lemons
2	heaping tablespoons plain flour
1	heaping tablespoon corn starch
5 or 6	tablespoons lemon juice
3	tablespoons butter
3	egg yolks
3	egg whites

Mix sugar, flour and cornstarch well. Mix in small amount of milk to moisten. Beat in egg yolks thoroughly. Add remaining milk, cook stirring constantly to prevent scorching or use double boiler. Cook to right consistency (thick) and remove from heat. Add butter, grated rind and juice. Pour in precooked crust. Cover with meringue made with 6 tablespoons sugar, 3 stiffly beaten egg whites and 1/8 teaspoon cream of tartar. Bake in 300° oven 30 minutes. *Yield: 6 servings.*

Annie Laurie Atkinson
Bishopville, SC

Millionaire Pie

1	can condensed milk
1/3	cup lemon juice
1	(12-ounce) Cool Whip, thawed
1	(20-ounce) can crushed pineapple, drained
1	cup chopped pecans
1	cup coconut
2	graham cracker pie shells

Mix ingredients. Pour into graham cracker shells. Refrigerate 3 hours before serving. *Yield: 2 pies.*

Sheril M. Rankin
Batesburg, SC

Pecan Pie

3	eggs
1	cup brown sugar
1	cup light corn syrup
1	cup pecans
1	teaspoon vanilla

Beat eggs thoroughly with sugar and corn syrup. Add pecans and vanilla. Pour into a 9-inch unbaked pie shell. Bake at 300° for 1 hour.

Kathy Cooper
Lexington, SC

Jocelyn's Famous Pecan Pie

Crust:

1 1/2	cups flour
1/4	teaspoon salt
1/2	cup shortening (Crisco is best)
3-4	tablespoons cold water

For best pie, you <u>must</u> make your own crust! Very easy to do. Mix flour and salt. Cut in shortening with pastry blender or two knives. Combine lightly until mixture looks like coarse meal or peas. Sprinkle water over flour mixture, 1 tablespoon at a time and mix lightly with fork. Use only enough water so that pastry will hold together when pressed gently into a ball. Don't handle any more than necessary—it will make pastry tough. Roll out with a rolling pin on a floured towel or board. Put into 9-inch pie pan and crimp edges with your fingers. Set aside.

Filling:

1	cup light corn syrup (Karo)
1	cup brown sugar
3	eggs
3	tablespoons melted butter
1	teaspoon vanilla
1 1/2	cups pecan halves

Mix together all ingredients and pour into lined pie pan. Bake at 425° for 10 minutes. Reduce heat to 350° and bake for 30-35 minutes. Cool completely. *Yield: 8 servings.*

Jocelyn Turner Ferber
Charlotte, NC

Kress's Pecan Chiffon Pie

1   cup coarsely chopped
     pecans, toasted
1   cup dark brown sugar (or
     light brown)
1 1/3 cups plus 2 tablespoons
     water
4   tablespoons cornstarch
1/4 cup water
2/3 cup egg whites (at room
     temperature)
1/4 cup sugar
2   (8- or 9-inch) baked pie
     shells
1/2 pint whipping cream

Spread pecans on a baking sheet and bake at 250-275° for 10-15 minutes or until nuts barely begin to brown. (Take out a few, let them cool and taste them. The toasted nuts will have a more pronounced nutty flavor.) Watch nuts carefully so they don't burn. Combine brown sugar and 1 1/3 cups plus 2 tablespoons water. Bring to a boil. Mix together cornstarch and 1/4 cup water and stir with a whisk into boiling brown sugar mixture. Stir constantly and cook until mixture becomes clear and is the consistency of a thick pudding. Remove mixture from heat. Whip egg whites at high speed until peaks form. Slowly add 1/4 cup sugar and beat until peaks are stiff. Reduce mixer speed to low and gently add the hot brown sugar mixture and nuts. As soon as everything is blended, cut off mixer. Do not overmix. Pile filling lightly into baked pie shells. (You will have higher, prettier pies if you use 8-inch pie shells for this recipe.) Whip cream until stiff, divide and spread over both pies. Sprinkle a few additional finely chopped nuts over top for garnish. The pie is best served the same day it is made, but it can be kept overnight in the refrigerator. (Should not let stand more than this, as it will fall.) *Yield: 2 pies - 16 servings.*

Janice Gurley Shoemaker
Georgetown, SC

Sand Pie

3 cups graham cracker crumbs
1 1/2 sticks melted margarine
8 ounces cream cheese
1 1/2 cups sugar
2 packs Dream Whip with 1 cup cold milk or 12-ounce Cool Whip
2 cans cherry pie filling

Mix cream cheese and sugar. Add to cream cheese mixture whipped Dream Whip with cold milk or Cool Whip. Mix in graham cracker crumbs, margarine and a little milk. Divide into two equal parts. Use a 9x13-inch pan. Place half the crumb mixture in the bottom, followed by half the cream cheese mixture, the cherry pie filling, remaining cream cheese mixture and the rest of the crumb mixture. *Yield: 10 servings.*

Lorine T. Linder
Fort Lawn, SC

Sweet Potato Custard Pie in Orange Crust

2   cups cooked, mashed and sieved sweet potatoes
3   large eggs, beaten
1   cup sugar
1/3   cup light cream
1/4   cup butter, melted
1   tablespoon fresh orange juice
1   teaspoon vanilla extract
1/8   teaspoon lemon extract
    Pinch freshly grated nutmeg (optional)
1/3   cup milk

Orange-Crust Pie Pastry:
(Makes 2 10-inch pie shells)
2 1/2 cups all-purpose flour
1/2   cup chilled, unsalted butter, cut in pieces
1/2   cup chilled shortening, cut in pieces
1   teaspoon grated orange rind
6-8   tablespoons chilled orange juice
1/8   teaspoon finely grated nutmeg
2   teaspoons sugar
1/2   teaspoon salt

Preheat oven to 350°. In a medium bowl, combine the eggs, sugar and sweet potato. Beat together to mix thoroughly. Add the milk and light cream and stir until combined. Add the melted butter, orange juice, vanilla and lemon extract and nutmeg and stir to mix well. Pour the mixture into the unbaked pie shell and bake in the preheated oven for 40-45 minutes or until the custard is set and a knife inserted in the middle comes out clean. Best served warm.

In a large bowl, sift together the flour and salt. Cut in the butter, shortening and orange rind with a pastry blender until the mixture has the texture of coarse crumbs. In a small bowl, combine 6 tablespoons of the orange juice with the sugar and nutmeg. Using a fork or knife, cut the orange juice mixture into the flour mixture to form a soft dough, adding additional orange juice, if necessary. Do not overmix. Refrigerate for at least 1 hour. Roll out half the chilled dough on a floured surface to form a crust about 10 inches in diameter. Firmly press the crust into a pie plate. Trim edges to 3/4 inch and flute with fingers or crimp with a fork. Repeat with second half of dough. Freeze or use immediately.

Dori Sanders
Dori Sanders Country Cooking,
Recipes and Stories from
the Family Farm Stand
York County, SC
Reviewed Winter 1996/97
Sandlapper

Sweet Tooth Pies

3	pie shells, unbaked
3	cups sugar
	pinch of salt
7	tablespoons cocoa
1	cup chopped pecans
4	eggs partially beaten
1	teaspoon vanilla
1	large can evaporated milk
1	stick melted margarine
2	cups coconut

Combine sugar, salt and cocoa. Add eggs and mix well. Add vanilla and milk, then margarine, coconut and nuts. Mix well. Pour into unbaked pie shells. Bake at 350° for 40 minutes or until firm. *Yield: 3 pies with 8 servings each.*

Louise L. Bess
Lake City, SC

Strawberry Delight

1	cup flour
1	cup sugar
1/2	cup chopped pecans
2	teaspoons fresh lemon juice
1/2	cup melted butter
2	egg whites
1/4	cup packed brown sugar
1	cup whipping cream, whipped
1	(10-ounce) container frozen strawberries, thawed
	Sliced fresh strawberries

Combine flour, pecans, butter and brown sugar in bowl; mix well. Pour into 8-inch square baking pan. Bake at 350° for 20 minutes, stirring occasionally. Cool to room temperature. Combine thawed strawberries, sugar, lemon juice and egg whites in a mixer bowl. Beat at high speed for 10-12 minutes or until stiff peaks form. Fold in whipped cream. Press 2/3 of the baked crumb mixture into a 9-inch springform pan. Spoon strawberry mixture into the pan; sprinkle with remaining crumbs. Freeze, covered, until firm. Remove sides of pan and garnish with sliced strawberries.

Mary Ann Hall
Hilton Head Entertains
Hilton Head, SC
Reviewed Summer 1996
Sandlapper

Assorted

Hot Apple Crisp

This is a very versatile and easy recipe. You may omit the sautéed apples and substitute fresh or canned fruit of your choice; top with the crisp mixture and you have a great new recipe. To make it even easier, I often make up the crisp mixture (without the nuts and butter) and keep it on hand in a zip lock bag. Our guests love this served with a baby scoop of ice cream; we promise not to tell their children they had ice cream for breakfast.

6	**cups peeled, diced apples**
1/2	**stick margarine**

Crisp:

1/3	**cup flour**
1	**cup oatmeal**
1/2	**cup brown sugar**
1/2	**teaspoon salt**
1	**teaspoon cinnamon**
	dash fresh nutmeg
1/4	**cup walnuts**
3	**tablespoons melted butter**

Sauté apples in a skillet with margarine until almost tender. Place in 8x8-inch baking dish. CRISP: Mix all ingredients together except nuts and melted butter; sprinkle crisp mixture over apples. Sprinkle nuts on top and drizzle with melted butter. Bake at 350° for 15-30 minutes until bubbly and top crust is browned. Serve warm with cream, whipped cream or ice cream.

Peggy and Jim Waller
The Inn at Merridun
Union, SC

Apricot After All Dessert

1	pound wafer-type crackers, crumbled
1/2	cup butter, softened
1/2	cup confectioners sugar
2	eggs
3/4	cup chopped pecans
1	(16 ounce) can apricot halves
2	cups whipping cream, whipped and sweetened

Spread 2/3 of the cracker crumbs in serving dish. Cream butter and confectioners sugar in a mixer bowl until light and fluffy. Add eggs; beat well. Spread over cracker crumb layer. Sprinkle with half the pecans. Mash apricots. Spread over layers. Sprinkle with remaining pecans and cracker crumbs. Chill in refrigerator overnight. Spread sweetened whipped cream over dessert.

Janie Wilkerson
Hilton Head Entertains
Hilton Head, SC
Reviewed Summer 1996
Sandlapper

Robert's Favorite Banana Pudding

1	package instant vanilla pudding
1 3/4	cups whole milk
8	ounces sour cream
8	ounces whipped topping
6	medium bananas, sliced
1	box vanilla wafers

Mix pudding and milk until well blended. Add sour cream and whipped topping until smooth. Line deep dish with wafers, top with bananas, top with pudding mixture. Continue layers ending with pudding. For decorative purposes, top with red cherries or top with beaten egg whites and brown under broiler for approximately 1 minute.

Egg White Mixture:

3	egg whites
1/4	cup sugar

Beat whites until peaks form, add sugar and beat until stiff. Add 1 teaspoon vanilla if desired.

Judy M. Smith
Leesville, SC

Blueberry Dumplings

Sauce:
2   cups fresh or frozen
     blueberries
1/2 cup sugar
1   cup water
1   tablespoon lemon juice

Dumplings:
1   cup plain flour
2   teaspoons baking powder
     dash of salt
1/2 teaspoon sugar
1/2-3/4 cup milk

Cook blueberry sauce about 20-25 minutes until berries are tender (in medium saucepan). Mix dumpling mixture and drop by tablespoon into sauce. Cook approximately 20 minutes over medium. Serve warm with whipped cream. *Yield: should make 8-10 dumplings.*

Janice Gurley Shoemaker
Georgetown, SC

Blueberry Yum Yum

2 1/2 cups graham cracker
      crumbs
1 1/2 sticks margarine, melted
1 1/2 cups sugar
2   cans blueberry pie filling
2   boxes dessert topping mix
1   large package cream cheese
1   cup milk

Combine cracker crumbs, ½ cup sugar and margarine; mix well. Blend cream cheese, 1 cup sugar, dessert topping mix and cold milk. Spread half of crumb mixture in oblong baking dish; add half of cream cheese mixture. Spread on blueberry pie filling; add remaining cream cheese mixture. Top with remaining crumbs. Refrigerate several hours before serving.

Recipe of Vermelle Porth
Lexington, SC
Submitted by David Arnold
Ridgeland, SC

Southern Blackberry Cobbler

1   box Pillsbury refrigerated
       pie Crusts (2 to a box)
2 1/2 cups fresh blackberries
2   tablespoons flour
1   cup sugar
       several pats butter

Grease bottom of deep casserole dish. Place 1 pie crust in bottom of dish, press to fit in bottom and up sides. Toss berries in flour and sugar and pour into dish. Put 4-5 pats butter on top of berries. Place second pie crust on top and crimp edges of the two crusts together. Slice several vent holes in top crust. Top with several pats of butter and sprinkle with a few pinches of sugar. Bake at 350° for 30-45 minutes or until crust slightly browns. Serve warm with vanilla ice cream. *Yield: 6 servings.*

Dawn B. Gates
Camden, SC

Chocolate Bread Pudding

1 1/2 cups sugar
1/3   cup melted butter
4   tablespoons cocoa
1/4   teaspoon salt
3   eggs, beaten
1   teaspoon vanilla
3   cups sweet milk
3   cups bread crumbs

Blend sugar and cocoa. Add eggs, butter, vanilla, salt and milk. Mix good. Add bread crumbs and mix well. Pour into a buttered casserole dish and bake at 350° for 35-45 minutes or until pudding is set. *Yield: 12 servings.*

Aileen M. Alexander
Iva, SC

Chocolate Delight

1	stick butter
1	cup cake flour (Swans Down)
1	cup chopped pecans
1	(8-ounce) cream cheese
1	(12-ounce) container Cool Whip
1	cup powdered sugar
2	packages chocolate pudding (instant)
3	cups milk
1	Hershey candy bar with almonds
	toasted almonds

1st layer: Mix butter, flour and pecans. Press in 9x13-inch dish. Bake 25-30 minutes at 300°. Cool completely. 2nd layer: Mix cream cheese, powdered sugar and 1 cup of Cool Whip and spread over 1st layer. 3rd layer: Mix pudding and 3 cups milk together for 2 minutes and let set 2 minutes. Pour slowly over 2nd layer. 4th layer: Add remaining Cool Whip and 1 Hershey bar grated over the 3rd layer. Top with toasted almonds. *Yield: about 15 servings.*

Carolyn Hellams
Lexington, SC

Chocolate Layer Dessert

1	large package instant chocolate pudding
3	cups cold milk
	chocolate graham crackers (about 1 1/2 stacks)
1	large Cool Whip
1	(8-ounce) cream cheese
1	stick margarine
1	tablespoon milk
1	tablespoon sugar

Mix pudding with milk. Let stand until thick. Add 1 1/2 cups Cool Whip and set aside. Crush chocolate graham crackers. Add margarine. Place in bottom of 9x13-inch dish. Combine cream cheese, tablespoon milk, tablespoon sugar and 1 1/2 cups Cool Whip. Spread over cracker crumb layer. Spread chocolate pudding over top of cream cheese. Top with Cool Whip. Sprinkle a few cracker crumbs over top. *Yield: 10 servings.*

Betty Dean
Anderson, SC

Coffee Charlotte with Cold Chocolate Sauce

Ladyfingers (amount depends on type of mold used)
1/4   cup dark rum, separated
2   sticks unsalted butter, room temperature
1   cup sugar
2   tablespoons instant coffee dissolved in 1 1/2 teaspoon water
1 1/2 cup heavy cream, whipped to soft peaks
1/2   cup heavy cream, stiffly whipped (for decoration)

Line the base of a 1 1/2 quart Charlotte mold or soufflé dish with wax paper. Line the sides as well, fringing the overhanging paper. Stand up ladyfingers all around side, fitting them as snugly as possible. Set aside. With mixer, combine unsalted butter, sugar, dissolved coffee and 1/2 the rum. Fold in whipped cream. Spoon 1/2 mixture into prepared mold. Add a layer of ladyfingers, closely fitting them together. Sprinkle with remaining rum. Spoon in remaining mixture. Cover and chill until well set - at least 3 hours. Unmold Charlotte onto a platter. Remove waxed paper and decorate with stiffly whipped cream, using a star tip with a pastry bag. Serve with cold chocolate sauce, if desired.

Cold Chocolate Sauce:
3 1/2 ounces semi-sweet chocolate
6 1/2 tablespoons milk
2   teaspoons heavy cream (or substitute 1/2 cup half and half for milk and cream)
5   teaspoons sugar
2 1/2 teaspoons unsalted butter, softened

Melt chocolate with gentle heat in double boiler or in microwave. Stir. In a saucepan, bring milk and cream (or half and half) to a boil. Remove from heat. Stir in the sugar, then the chocolate and finally the butter. Allow to cool. Serve separately with the Charlotte.

Dudley Williams
Columbia, SC

Cranberry Cobbler

4 or 5 apples
6 tablespoons butter, room
temperature
1 1/2 cup sugar
1 1/2 cup flour
cranberries

Slice apples thinly (1/8- to 1/16-inch) and arrange in a greased casserole. Sprinkle plenty of fresh cranberries over the arranged apples. Combine butter, sugar and flour and crumble together evenly over fruit. Bake at 375° for 45 minutes. This can be a dessert or it goes very well with your Thanksgiving turkey. *Yield: 4-6 servings.*

Barbara Darden
Lexington, SC

Cranberry/Raspberry Dessert

1 package frozen raspberries,
thawed
2 cups cranberries*
1/2 cup sugar
3 tablespoons port or sweet
sherry
1 cup vanilla yogurt (or plain
yogurt with 1 tablespoon
vanilla extract stirred in)
1/2 cup heavy cream, whipped
pound cake

*Canned whole berry cranberry sauce can be substituted for fresh cranberries.

Pureé raspberries in food processor or blender. Sieve raspberries in order to remove seeds. Simmer raspberry pureé with cranberries (covered) for 5 minutes or until berries are just tender. Gently stir in sugar, then port or sherry. Chill. Stir yogurt to soften. Fold in whipped cream and chill. Serve cranberry/raspberry mixture on top of yogurt cream on slices of pound cake.

Combine a 1-pound can of cranberry sauce with the pureéd and seeded raspberries. Omit sugar. Add wine and chill. *Yield: 6 servings.*

Dudley Williams
Columbia, SC

273

Date Delight

12	packaged cream-filled chocolate cookies, crushed
1	(8-ounce) package (1 cup) pitted dates, cut up
3/4	cup water
1/4	teaspoon salt
2	cups tiny marshmallows or 16 marshmallows
1/2	cup chopped California walnuts (pecans can be used)
1	cup heavy cream
1/2	teaspoon vanilla walnut halves

Reserve 1/4 cup cookie crumbs; spread remainder in 10x6x1 1/2-inch baking dish. In saucepan, combine dates, water and salt; bring to boiling, reduce heat and simmer 3 minutes. Remove from heat, add marshmallows and stir until melted. Cool to room temperature. Stir in chopped nuts. Spread date mixture over crumbs in dish. Combine cream and vanilla; whip, swirl over dates. Sprinkle with reserved crumbs; top with walnuts. Chill overnight. Cut into squares. *Yield: 8 servings.*

Varina Simpson
Iva, SC

5-Minute Fudge

1	small can evaporated milk
1 2/3	cups sugar
1/2	teaspoon salt
1 1/2	cups semi-sweet chocolate pieces
1	teaspoon vanilla
1 1/2	cups (16 medium) diced marshmallows
1/2	cup chopped nuts

Mix 2/3 cup (1 small can) evaporated milk, sugar and salt in saucepan over medium heat. Bring to boil; cook 5 minutes, stirring constantly. (Time when mixture starts to "bubble" around edges of pan.) Remove from heat. Add semi-sweet chocolate pieces, vanilla and marshmallows. Stir vigorously for 1 minute or until marshmallows melt. Pour into 8-inch square buttered pan. Garnish with nuts. Cool. Cut into squares. Optional: add 1/2 cup chopped nuts to fudge mixture before pouring into pan. *Yield: 20 pieces.*

Dudley and Evelyn Williams
Columbia, SC

Grape Cooler

	white seedless grapes
2-3	tablespoons sour cream
1-2	tablespoons dark brown sugar

Arrange grapes in separate bowls (as many as you need). Top with sour cream and sprinkle with sugar.

Ann Moore Webb
Charleston, SC

Graham Cracker Torte

3	eggs beaten
1	cup sugar
1	cup graham crackers, rolled fine

Add in order given. Put in an ungreased pie pan and bake at 350° for 45 minutes. Serve with whipped cream or ice cream.

Maro Rogers
Lexington, SC

Add to crackers:

1	teaspoon baking powder
1/4	teaspoon salt
1	cup ground nuts
1	teaspoon vanilla

Lemon Torte

8	eggs
1 1/2	cups sugar
3	teaspoons vinegar
1	teaspoon vanilla

Beat 1 cup egg whites until very stiff. Add sugar slowly until it gets chewy. Add vinegar and vanilla. Bake at 250° for 1 hour and 20 minutes in greased torte (springform) pan.

Lemon Jelly Filling:

4	egg yolks
1	cup sugar
	grated juice and rind of 2 lemons
1 1/2	tablespoons cornstarch
	lump of butter (generous tablespoon)

Put mixture in double boiler until thickened. Chill. Put on top of torte and top with whipped cream. *Yield: Approximately 10 servings, depending on size of portions.*

Gwen Howell
Spartanburg, SC
Reprinted from January/
February 1990
Sandlapper

Fruit Filled Meringues

Meringue Shells:
2   egg whites
3   drops vinegar
1/2 teaspoon water
     pinch of salt
1/2 cup sugar
1/2 teaspoon vanilla

Beat egg whites until stiff enough to form peaks. Fold in vinegar, water and salt. Gradually add sugar, beating after each addition. Add vanilla. Beat until stiff but not dry. Drop by spoonful onto a greased cookie sheet. Form a hollow for filling in each meringue with back of spoon. Bake 1 hour at 250°. Cool slowly. Top with desired filling. *Yield: serves 8. Do not prepare meringues on a rainy day.*

Berry Filling:
1   (10-ounce) package frozen raspberries or strawberries
1   cup heavy cream, whipped

Thaw berries, reserving juice. Spoon berries and juice over meringues. Top with whipped cream. I tried this recipe with fresh raspberries, strawberries and blackberries, which I sugared before serving. After filling meringue, you may want to add whipped topping.

Stir Crazy!
Junior Welfare League of Florence
Reviewed Summer 1996
Sandlapper

Peach Tarts

Pastry:
3 ounces cream cheese, room temperature
1 stick butter, room temperature
3 tablespoons sugar
1 teaspoon fresh lemon juice
1 1/2 cups unbleached all-purpose flour

Make the pastry: In a medium-size bowl cream together the cream cheese, butter, sugar and lemon juice until fluffy. Gradually add the flour, stirring after each addition, to make a soft dough. Refrigerate 30 minutes. Preheat the oven to 375°. Pinch off pieces of dough to make 24 1-inch balls and press the balls into miniature muffin tins. Bake 10 minutes; lightly press down the center of each pastry cup and continue baking until light brown, about 10 minutes. Cool.

Filling:
4 tablespoons plus 3 tablespoons sugar
4 tablespoons cornstarch
2 cups pureéd fresh peaches
3/4 cup chopped pecans
1 tablespoon butter

In a medium-size saucepan combine the 4 tablespoons of sugar and the cornstarch. Add the 3 tablespoons of sugar to the pureéd peaches and gradually add the peaches to the sugar and cornstarch. Bring the mixture to a boil over medium heat, stirring constantly. Add the pecans and cook until the mixture has thickened, about 5 minutes. Remove from the heat and stir in the butter. Cool slightly and spoon into the tarts.

Kara Anderson Berly
Party Receipts Cookbook
Junior League of Charleston
Reviewed Autumn 1995
Sandlapper

277

Home Churned Peach Ice Cream

7   cups fresh peaches
1   (12-ounce) can evaporated
     milk
3   cups milk, divided
2 1/2 cups sugar
3   large eggs, beaten
1   (12-ounce) can peach nectar

Combine half of peaches (peeled and sliced) and 1/2 cup milk in blender. Process until smooth. Transfer to a medium bowl, and repeat procedure with remaining peaches and 1/4 cup milk. Set aside. Combine remaining 2 1/2 cups milk and next 3 ingredients. Cook over medium heat 8 minutes, stirring occasionally. Remove from heat; stir in peach mixture and nectar. Pour into container of 4-quart electric freezer churn. Freeze according to manufacturer's instructions. Yields 1 gallon.

Louise H. Ott
A Taste of the South
Santee, SC
Reviewed Summer 1997
Sandlapper

Banana Split Ice Cream

2   (3-ounce) packages vanilla
     instant pudding
1   (14-ounce) can sweetened
     condensed milk
1   envelope dry whipped
     topping mix
     pinch of salt
1   teaspoon vanilla
1/2   cup chopped nuts
3-4   bananas, mashed
1   small jar maraschino
     cherries, drained and cut up
     milk

Mix together pudding with sweetened condensed milk, topping mix and salt. Add a small amount of regular milk. Mix all ingredients well. Add vanilla, nuts, bananas and cherries. Add enough milk to bring mixture to fill line of freezer container. Stir well. Freeze according to manufacturer's directions. *Yield: 1 gallon.*

Lucille Cudd
Chester, SC

Butter Pecan Ice Cream

2 quarts half and half
1 large container of Cool Whip
1 box light brown sugar
1 can condensed milk
2 teaspoons vanilla
1 1/2 cups pecans sautéed in ½ stick butter

Mix well in above order in 4 quart churn. Freeze according to manufacturer's instructions. *Yield: 1 gallon.*

George Boozer
Lexington, SC

Milky Way Ice Cream

12 (1 3/4-ounce) Milky Way bars
1 (15.5-ounce) can chocolate syrup
1 (14-ounce) can condensed milk
3 quarts milk

Break up candy bars. Melt over low heat and add condensed milk; stir constantly. Let cool and stir occasionally. Add 1 quart milk and beat until well blended. Pour mixture into container of electric ice cream churn. Stir in chocolate syrup and enough of remaining milk until mixture is 4 inches from top. Freeze according to manufacturer's instructions. *Yield: 1 1/2 gallons.*

Uptown Down South
Junior League of Greenville
Reviewed Spring 96
Sandlapper

Mom's Chocolate Sauce

1 1/2 ounces chocolate
1/2 teaspoon vanilla
1 1/3 cups evaporated milk
few grains salt
1 cup sugar

Melt chocolate with sugar and salt, stirring as chocolate melts. Add evaporated milk gradually and cook for approximately five minutes. Add vanilla flavoring stirring well to blend all ingredients. Store in the refrigerator until ready to serve. May be reheated as often as needed. *Yield: approximately 1 1/2 cups topping for ice cream or brownies.*

Genny D. Hendrix
Kershaw, SC

Strawberry Delight

1 cup all-purpose flour
1/2 cup chopped pecans
1/2 cup butter or margarine, melted
1/4 cup firmly packed brown sugar
1 (10-ounce) package frozen strawberries, thawed
1 cup sugar
2 teaspoons fresh lemon juice
2 egg whites
1 cup whipping cream, whipped

Combine first 4 ingredients in 8-inch square baking pan, stir well. Bake at 350° for 20 minutes, stirring occasionally; cool. Combine strawberries, sugar, lemon juice and egg whites in large mixing bowl. Beat at high speed until stiff peaks form. Fold in whipped cream. Press 2/3 of crumb mixture into 9-inch springform pan; spoon in strawberry mixture. Sprinkle remaining crumbs on top. Freeze until firm. Garnish with fresh berries if desired. *Yield: 8-10 servings.*

Janice S. Creasy
Palmyra, VA

Summer Strawberry Dessert

1	(12-ounce) carton low-fat Cool Whip
2	(6-ounce) cartons low-fat strawberry yogurt
1	teaspoon vanilla extract
1/2	commercial angel food cake, torn into bitesize pieces
3	cups fresh strawberries, sliced
2	tablespoons sliced almonds, toasted

Fold Cool Whip, yogurt and vanilla together. Layer half each of cake, yogurt mix, strawberries in a trifle dish. Repeat layers and sprinkle with almonds on top. Cover and chill at least 2 hours.

Mary Howard
Lexington, SC

Strawberries Romanoff

1	(14-ounce) Eagle Brand milk (not evaporated milk)
3/4	cup cold water
4	tablespoons orange flavored liqueur (triple sec)
1	(4-serving size) package instant vanilla flavor pudding mix
2	cups (1 pint) whipping cream, stiffly whipped
1	quart fresh strawberries, sliced

In a large bowl combine milk, water and liqueur. Add pudding mix. Beat well. Chill 15 minutes. Fold in whipped cream. Cover and chill. Just before serving, fold in strawberries. Spoon into custard dishes. Garnish. *Yield: 10-12 servings.*

Sharon W. Bickett
Chester, SC

Annie Jenkins' Stickies
(A La Cathy Fairey)

2　cups white flour
3　teaspoons baking soda
4　tablespoons Crisco
2/3　cup milk
2　teaspoons baking powder
1　teaspoon salt

Filling:
1　cup butter, room
　　temperature
1 1/3 cups sugar

Sift together flour, salt, baking powder and baking soda. Mix in Crisco until dough is crumbly. Add milk to dough and mix together.

Cream butter and sugar together well. Divide dough into four sections. Roll each section onto floured surface. Make squares by cutting dough horizontally and then vertically, using a 3-inch wide piece of legal paper as your guide. Melt 3 tablespoons of butter in a 9x13-inch pan. Set aside. Put about a heaping teaspoon of filling in the middle of each square. Bring corners of dough up diagonally so they meet. Pinch together the ends to close at the top. Place each square into the baking pan so they are touching. Bake at 400° until light brown.

Miss Effie's Stickies

3	cups plain flour
1	cup Crisco
1	teaspoon salt
1	egg
2	cups sugar
1	cup butter
1	cup whole milk
2	teaspoons vanilla

Blend flour, salt and shortening until crumbly. Beat egg and add water to make 3/4 cup. Mix with flour mixture to form a soft, pliable dough. Divide into two parts and chill at least 1-2 hours. Mix butter and sugar; let stand at room temperature until easy to spread. Roll out one section of the dough at a time, thin as possible, spreading half of the sugar mixture on each, out to the edges. Roll up like a jelly roll and refrigerate several hours or overnight. Slice into 1/2-inch pinwheels and place close together in a well greased and floured 10x15x2-inch heavy pan. Bake at 375° until brown, about 50 minutes. Heat milk, but do not boil, and add the flavoring. Pour this over the stickies and return to over for drying off, about 5-10 minutes. Remove from pan while hot.

Stickie recipes taken from
Winter 1996/97
Sandlapper
from an article written by
Jayne Scarborough

Cream Mints

1	box 10X sugar (3 1/2 cups)
1/2	stick oleo or butter
3	tablespoons boiling water
13	drops peppermint oil
	few drops food coloring (your choice)

Combine ingredients. Cream well with hands until smooth. Make small balls and dip in granulated sugar. Press ball into candy mold and pop out on wax paper. Let dry. *Yield: 10 dozen.*

Iris W. Polattie
Greenwood, SC

Miscellaneous

Miscellaneous

Alabama Tomato Sauce

2	cans tomatoes
1	large onion
1	cup vinegar
3/4	cup sugar
1/2	teaspoon black pepper

Use potato masher to macerate tomatoes. Cut onion into small pieces. Mix all ingredients and cook slowly until thick. Our family uses it on most vegetables and it is delicious with pork.

Mimi Rattray
Columbia, SC

Chutney

1	cup white vinegar
1	cup white sugar
2	cups peeled, chopped pears
1/4	cup golden raisins
1 1/2	tablespoons minced fresh ginger
1/2	cup lemon juice
2	cloves garlic, minced
1	medium onion, chopped
1	rib celery, chopped
1/2	teaspoon coriander
	Tabasco sauce, 2-3 dashes

Combine vinegar and sugar in saucepan. Bring to a boil; add pears, raisins, garlic, onions, celery, ginger, coriander, Tabasco. Cook over low heat, uncovered, stirring occasionally for 45 minutes. Add lemon juice to taste. Salt to taste. Can be refrigerated in a sealed jar several weeks.

Chef Francois Fiscera
Fleur de Lys Culinary Institute
Columbia, SC

Pear Chutney

20	cups pears, peeled and sliced
2	limes, seeded and chopped
4	cloves garlic, chopped
3	large onions, chopped
5	cups raisins
3	ounces crystalized ginger, chopped or 1 small ginger root, chopped
2	small hot peppers, chopped
2	cups lime juice
3	cups cider vinegar
8	cups brown sugar
1	cup Worcestershire sauce

Cut pears in 1 inch by 1/4 inch slices and soak in cold salt water while assembling other ingredients. Place other ingredients in a big kettle and cook for half an hour. Drain pear slices and put with other ingredients and cook for 1 hour. Pack in sterilized jars and keep for at least 2 weeks before using. You may find that there is more juice than you need for the amount of pears. The extra juice is a great glaze for baked ham. Yield: 5 bottles.

Susan Smythe Bennett
Charleston, SC

Note: Great on cold or hot brie cheese. Also, perfect with ham and fowl.

Pear Marmalade

7	pounds pears
2	cups crushed pineapple, drained
1	orange
1	lemon
1	lime
1	2-ounce bottle maraschino cherries, drained
5	pounds sugar

Peel and cut pears into quarters. Weigh pears. Cut and squeeze out juice from fruit. Juice will not be used. Grind fruit rinds. Combine pears, rinds, pineapple and sugar. Cook 45 minutes over medium heat, stirring frequently. Grind and add cherries about half way through cooking time. Pour into sterilized pint jars. Seal and process by submerging in water. Boil 10 minutes after water comes to boil.

Lucille Cudd
Chester, SC

287

Green Tomato Pickle

7	pounds green tomatoes
3	cups lime
5	pounds sugar
4	pints vinegar
5	teaspoons pickling spice

Slice 7 pounds green tomatoes very thin. Soak in 2 gallons water with lime for 24 hours. Drain and soak in fresh water for 4 hours, changing water every hour. Make a syrup of sugar, vinegar and pickling spice. Bring to a boil and pour over tomatoes and let stand overnight. Next morning, boil gently one hour, pack in hot jars. Handle carefully taking from lime water. They break easily. Will seal themselves. Hot jars, hot tops and rings! *Yield: 10 pints.*

Janice S. Creasy
Palmyra, VA

Pickled Vidalia Onions

8	cups (approximately) Vidalia onions, sliced
1	cup vinegar
2	cups sugar
1	tablespoon salt

Combine vinegar, sugar and salt. Heat to boiling. Pour over sliced onions. Cool and refrigerate overnight. Put in 1 cup containers and keep in freezer until you are ready to eat them.

Lucille Cudd
Chester, SC

Beet Relish

1	teaspoon salt
3/4	cup sugar
2	cups chopped celery
1/2	teaspoon flour
4	cups diced beets
1/2	cup vinegar
1	cup chopped onions

Mix beets, celery and onions. Add to dry ingredients. Mix all well. Cook in double boiler until thick. Let set at least 2 days. Yield: 8 servings.

Ethiel L. McGee
Starr, SC

Sunshine Relish

16	medium carrots
2	large green peppers, seeded
2	sweet red peppers (medium)
6	onions (medium)
1	tablespoon celery seed
8	medium cucumbers
2	cups white vinegar
3 1/2	cups sugar
1	tablespoon mustard seed

Grind all vegetables. Combine other ingredients with ground vegetables. Heat to a boil and simmer 15 minutes. Put in sterile pint jars and seal. Cover with water in a large pot and process 10 minutes. If you like relish spicy, add a few seeded and chopped hot peppers.

Lucille Cudd
Chester, SC

Salsa

4	cups chopped tomatoes
4	cups chopped bell peppers (red or green)
1	cup chopped onions
3/4	cup vinegar
2	garlic cloves
1	tablespoon salt and sugar
1	teaspoon paprika
1	teaspoon oregano
	Jalapeño peppers to taste
6	ounces tomato paste
1/4	cup parsley flakes

Combine first 9 ingredients. Bring to boil then simmer uncovered for 1 hour. Add tomato paste and parsley flakes; mix thoroughly then simmer for 10 minutes. Pour into sterilized jars then seal or place in bath (boil for 10 minutes).

Betty Quarles Padgett
Johnston, SC

Wild Plum Jelly and Jam

6   **pounds wild plums**
1   **box prepared fruit pectin (1
    3/4 dry ounces) for every 6
    cups cooked plum juice**
7 1/2 **cups sugar**

Wash plums and place in a pan with 2 cups of water, cover with lid and heat on high until mixture boils. Reduce heat and stir the mush while the fruit is softening. This process takes no longer than 30 minutes. Once "mushified," leave the plum residue to cool, then pour into a jelly bag draped over a colander inserted into another pot. Drip until all juice has been collected. May take several hours. Don't squeeze plums to get juice out or you'll cloud the jelly. Bring 6 cups collected juice to a boil, add pectin. Add sugar and stir to avoid scorching. Bring to boil again for 1 minute. Remove from heat. Skim the foam off top and pour the remaining hot juice into jars and seal. You can use paraffin or seal with domed lids according to package directions. *Yield: 4-5 pints.*

Bill Weekes
Spartanburg, SC

Doggie Biscuits for Man's Best Friend

4   **cups whole wheat flour**
4   **tablespoons shortening or
    oil**
1   **cup cooked oatmeal**
1 1/2 **cups hot water**
2   **bouillon cubes (chicken)**

Dissolve bouillon cubes in water. Add other ingredients. Roll to 1/2-inch thickness. Cut into 1x2-inch strips or use cookie cutter. Bake at 325° until crisp. Cover when cool.

Lynn B. Bagnal
Walterboro, SC

Doggie Biscotti

3	eggs, well beaten or use egg replacer
1/2	cup unsweetened applesauce
1	cup chicken stock
2	cloves garlic, pressed
2	cups kamut flour
1	cup millet flour
1	cup ground sunflower seeds
2	teaspoons baking powder
1	teaspoon kelp

Mix the wet ingredients together. Mix dry ingredients together, separately, combining well to ensure the baking powder is well blended. Combine wet and dry ingredients, adding flour or more liquid to make the dough stiff enough to handle, yet still slightly sticky. Preheat the oven to 350°. Form the dough into three rolls approximately 14 inches long each and lay them on one baking sheet. To keep the dough from sticking to your hands, slightly oil your hands with olive oil. Bake for about 25 minutes. Remove from the oven and let cool for about 10 minutes. Reduce the oven temperature to 325°. Slice biscotti on a slant, about 1/2 inch per cookie. Lay the biscotti flat and bake for about 30 additional minutes or until dry. Turn off the oven and let the cookies cool in the oven for a harder biscotti. Freeze to retain freshness. Yield: About 6 dozen biscuits.

Jan Pollack
Lexington, SC

Drying Flowers

1	cup yellow self-rising cornmeal
1	cup Borox detergent
3	tablespoons salt

Mix thoroughly and sift over flowers, covering completely. Leave for 1 week in dry area. Can reuse mixture.

Kathy Cagle
North Myrtle Beach, SC

For Children

Bubbles

1	cup Joy liquid dish washing detergent
2	cups warm water
3-4	tablespoons glycerine (found at drugstores)
1	teaspoon sugar

Gently stir all of the ingredients together in a big plastic container.

Season'd With Fun
Junior Woman's Club of Lexington
Lexington, SC

Finger Paints

3	tablespoons sugar
1/2	cup cornstarch
2	cups cold water
	food coloring
	soap flakes or liquid dish washing detergent

Mix sugar and cornstarch together in a medium saucepan over low heat. Add the water and continue stirring until mixture is thick. Remove from heat. Divide the mixture into 4 or 5 portions. Add a drop or two of different food coloring to each portion and pinch of soap flakes or a drop of detergent to each. Stir and let cool. Use the shiny side of freezer paper to paint on.

Season'd with Fun
Junior Woman's Club of Lexington
Lexington, SC

Play Dough

1	cup flour
1	cup water
1/2	cup salt
1	tablespoon oil
1	teaspoon cream of tartar
	food coloring

Mix flour, water, salt, oil and cream of tartar in a small pan. Add food coloring slowly until you get the color you want. Cook over medium heat until mixture pulls away from the side of the pan. Knead until it becomes soft play dough texture. Store in airtight container.

Season'd with Fun
Junior Woman's Club of Lexington

Contributors

Name	Town/City	Page Number
Adelman, Margaret	Nashville, TN	120
Alexander, Aileen M.	Iva	270
Allen, A. Divver	Hartsville	92
Allen, Debra C.	St. Matthews	4,29,35
Allen, Libby	Columbia	255
Anderson, Cathy	Charlotte, NC	20,65,91,241,246,254
Ardren, Lou Lucas	Fort Mill	247
Atkinson, Annie Laurie	Bishopville	261
Atkinson, Margaret S.	Ft. Myers, FL	198
Axmann, Mary H.	Anderson	235
Bagnal, Lynn B.	Walterboro	66,223,290
Bardin, Philip	Edisto Island	114,174,184,259
Beasley, Gov. & Mrs.	Columbia	81
Bedenbaugh, Linda H.	Prosperity	97
Bennett, Susan Smythe	Charleston	287
Bennett, John H., Jr.	Charleston	19,201
Berly, Kara A.	Charleston	277
Beshears, Tina	Starr	100
Bess, Louise L.	Lake City	266
Best, Emily	Bethune	66
Bickett, Sharon W.	Chester	44,134,200,254,281
Bischoff, Kathleen	Darlington	20
Blackwell, Lynnelle	Summerton	195
Blandford, Betty B.	Seabrook Island	105
Bodie, Idella	Aiken	250,253
Bolchoz, Mike Calder	Charleston	85
Boozer, George	Lexington	67,279
Bouknight, Ella Calvert	Lexington	80,116,159,256
Bowden, Brenda	Camden	130
Bozard, Jan	Lexington	13
Brinkman, Sharon	Aiken	92
Brooks, Anne W.	Lexington	3
Brown, Lib	Lexington	148
Bruning, Janet	Greenville	46,54,104,236,245
Brunson, Betty L.P.	Sumter	149,257
Buckley, Virginia	Easley	40,239
Burch, Patsy	Chester	139
Cagle, Kathy	N. Myrtle Beach	13, 291
Carter, Jeff	Greenville	62

Sandlapper Cooks

Sandlapper Cooks

Contributors

Sandlapper Cooks

Name	Town/City	Page Number
Sharpe, Ella	W. Columbia	82
Shaw, Mary	Georgetown	28,50,59,183,231
Shealy, E. Guy, Jr.	Batesburg-Leesville	31,115,169
Sherer, Nancy	Starr	160
Shoemaker, Janice G.	Georgetown	5,85,86,154,158, 263,269
Shreve, Jay	W. Columbia	42
Simpson, Varina	Iva	274
Smith, Judy M.	Leesville	115,268
Smith, Gail B.	Cades	223
Smoot, Winnie	Hartsville	189
Snyder, Lynn	Rock Hill	148
Spears, Guest House	Cheraw	54
Spence, Kitty	Lexington	14,80,192,230
Stenhouse, Annie C.	Simpsonville	173,233
Stoddard, Anita	Spartanburg	234
Stokes, Diane D.	Myrtle Beach	8
Stubblefield, Frances	Columbia	104,245
Suber, Ethel	Columbia	78
Sullivan, Vera	Chapin	121,255
Surrett, Buck	Easley	58
Sutton, Betty	Greensboro, NC	36
Tanner, P. J.	Bluffton	170
Tapp, Cheryse	Irmo	36
Taylor, Sandra	Columbus, NC	86,215
Taylor, John Martin	Charleston	155,191
Terry, Dorothy H.	Iva	199,242
Thomas, Anne Brunson	Sumter	159
Thomas, Art	Greenville	102
Tiller, Kathleen	Camden	222
Tiller, Mrs. Robert J.	Mayesville	98
Todd, Joan	Walhalla	29,30,41,96,150,172, 244,250
Truesdale, Louis L.,Jr.	Lexington	67
Uhrig, Jay	Union	10
Waitt, Bernett	Summerville	100,126,215,217
Wakefield, Marian	Iva	65
Waller, Jim and Peggy	Union	21,24,26,36,71,177, 211,267
Warshaw, Ann	Walterboro	5,130,146,186
Watson, Sherrie	Lexington	188
Watson, Frances L.	Florence	125
Weathers, Pat	Lexington	193

Contributors

Reviewed Cookbook Names and Addresses

Southern Recipes and Legends
Sandlapper Publishing Co., Inc.
P. O. Box 730
Orangeburg, SC 29116
(803) 531-1658

A Taste of the South
Marilyn Ott Thompson
P. O. Box 1122
Santee, SC 29412

Gates, Gaits and Golden Plates
Camden Junior Welfare League
P. O. Box 578
Camden, SC 29020

Charleston Receipts
Charleston Receipts Repeats
Charleston Party Receipts
The Junior League of Charleston
51 Folly Road
Charleston, SC 29407
(843) 763-5284

Down By the Water
Junior League of Columbia
2926 Devine St.
Columbia, SC 29205
(803) 252-4552

Hilton Head Entertains
8 Fox Grape Rd.
Hilton Head Island, SC 29928
(843) 671-2286

Lexington Landmark Recipes
Lexington Woman's Club
P. O. Box 745
Lexington, SC 29071

Carolina Fare - A Taste of Home
American Cancer Society 1995 First
Lady Cookbook
128 Stonemark Lane
Columbia, SC 29210
(800) 227-2345

Uptown Down South
Junior League of Greenville
17 W. North St.
Greenville, SC 29601
(864) 232-1286

Stir Crazy!
Junior Welfare League of Florence
P. O. Box 3715
Florence, SC 29502-0715

Southern Tailgating: Game Day
Recipes and Traditions
Vision Press
P. O. Box 1106
Northport, AL 35476

Coker Classics
Coker College
Hartsville, SC 29550
(803) 383-8016

Thoroughbred Fare
Aiken Office Supply
2560 Whiskey Road
Aiken, SC 29803
(803) 648-8339

Tested By Time
Porter-Gaud Parents Guild
P. O. Box 30431
Charleston, SC 29417
(843) 723-0015

Culinary Memories of Merridun
The Inn at Merridun
100 Merridun Place
Union, SC 29379
(864) 427-7052

Bed and Breakfast and Restaurant
.Contributors

Jay Uhrig
Juxa Plantation
Union, SC
Page 10

Jim and Peggy Waller
The Inn at Merridun
Union, SC
Page 21,24,26,36,71,177,211,267

Kyle Segars
Missouri Inn
Hartsville, SC
Page 11

Walnut Lane
Lyman, SC
Page 14

Mary Shaw
The Shaw House
Georgetown, SC
Page 28,50,59,183,231

Wesley and Bonnie Park
The Breeden Inn & Carriage House
Bennettsville, SC
Page 33,43

Naomi Perryman
Richland Street B & B
Columbia, SC
Page 33,44,53

Jackie Morrison
Laurel Hill Plantion
McClellanville, SC
Page 39,51,211

Emmagene Rhodes
Bed & Breakfast in Summerville
Summerville, SC
Page 40

Pat Clark
Anderson's River Inn
Anderson, SC
Page 46,52

Craig Riley
195 East Main Bed & Breakfast
Pendleton, SC
Page 53

Spears Guest House
Cheraw, SC
Page 54

Carroll and Ron Kay
TwoSuns Inn
Beaufort, SC
Page 55

Gloria Kiriakides
Pettigru Place
Greenville, SC
Page 56

Sandlapper Cooks

Marshall Wile
DuPre House
Georgetown, SC
Page 57

Jo Ann Celaine
Candlelight Inn
Camden, SC
Page 58

Tom Jonas
Liberty Hall Inn
Pendleton, SC
Page 131

Sherri Weaver
1837 B&B/Tea Room
Charleston, SC
Page 166

Annabelle Wright
Able House Inn
Leesville, SC
Page 210

Carol Rogers
Magnolia House
Sumter, SC
Page 214

Vaughnde Morris
The Jefferson House
Anderson, SC
Page 258

Patty Griffey
Abingdon Manor B&B
Latta, SC
Page 45

Alan Kemp
Magnolia Inn B&B
Dillon, SC
Page 47

Teresa James
The Garden Cafe
York, SC
Page 232,251

Chef Francios Fiscera
Fleur de Lys Culinary Institute
Columbia, SC
Page 286

Chef Jeff Carter
Cottage Cuisine
Greenville, SC
Page 62

Chef Kish
82 Queen
Charleston, SC
Page 68,107,124,186

Tommy Condon's
Charleston, SC
Page 72,125,152

Virginia P. Huckabee
#10 Downing Street
Aiken, SC
Page 74

Mike Calder Bolchoz
Mike Calder's Pub
Charleston, SC
Page 85

Sea Captain's House Restaurant
Myrtle Beach, SC
Page 93,106

Ted Hammerman
Mr. Fish
Myrtle Beach, SC
Page 110,128

302

Contributors

Peter Ryter
1109 Restaurant
Anderson, SC
Page 114

William Mann
Cottage Cuisine
Greenville, SC
Page 119

Chef Fran Lee
Slightly North of Broad
Charleston, SC
Page 127

Linda Peavy
Roadside Grille
York, SC
Page 163

Tom Jonas
Liberty Hall Inn
Pendleton, SC
Page 131

Buck Surrett
Buck's Drive-in Restaurant
Easley, SC
Page 58

Sylvia Woods
Sylvia's Soul Food
New York, NY
Page 38

Jay Shreve
Courtyard Coffeehouse
West Columbia, SC
Page 42

Libby Wiersema
Buddy's Bagelry
Florence, SC
Page 15

Chef Philip Bardin
Edisto Island, SC
Page 114,174,184,259

Lynnelle Blackwell
Summerton Diner
Summerton, SC
Page 195

Membership Order Form

Name:_____

Address:_____

City/State/Zip_____

Send $20 each for an individual or gift membership to: Sandlapper Society, Inc., P. O. Box 1108, Lexington, SC 29071; (803) 359-9954; FAX (803) 359-0629. We accept checks, Visa and Master Card. For other categories of membership, see page vi.

For gift memberships, please list names and addresses of recipients for membership.

Gift Recipients:

Name:_____

Address:_____

City/State/Zip_____

Name:_____

Address:_____

City/State/Zip_____

_____ Check enclosed for $_____

_____ Visa # _____ Expiration:_____

_____ MasterCard # _____ Expiration:_____

Signature: _____

Sandlapper Society, Inc. is a tax exempt organization under IRC Section 501(c)(3). Consult your tax advisor regarding how this may apply to you.

Cookbook Order Form

SANDLAPPER COOKS

Sandlapper Society, Inc.
P. O. Box 1108
Lexington, SC 29071-1108

Please send _____ copy(ies) of *Sandlapper Cooks* @ $16.95 each
(Sandlapper Society members deduct 10% discount and pay $15.25)

$_____

Shipping and Handling $3.00 for one and $1 for $_____
each additional book

Total $_____

ShipTo:

Name: _____

Address:_____

City/State/Zip_____

Method of Payment _____Check _____Credit Card

Please make checks payable to Sandlapper Society, Inc.

Visa/Master Card Number:_____

Expiration Date:_____

Signature:_____

Credit card orders may be placed by calling (803) 359-9954 or FAX:
(803) 359-3609

Index

Sandlapper Cooks

Index

Sandlapper Cooks

Dear God,

So far today,
I've done all right
I haven't gossiped.
I haven't lost my temper.
I haven't been greedy, grumpy,
nasty, selfish or overindulgent.

I'm very thankful for that.

But in a few minutes, God,
I'm going to get out of bed;
and from then on I'm probably
going to need a lot more help.

Barbara Anderson
Florence, SC